THE SPIRITUAL POWER OF MASKS

"This book is a gem! As always, Nigel Pennick explores his intriguing subject with ferocious intensity, beautifully balancing his lenses from telescopic to macroscopic. He writes with a density of detail and archival attention, galloping through centuries in single sentences, crisscrossing countries and even continents in single bounds. His prodigious knowledge, gathered and retained over a lifetime, pours forth—a cornucopia of richness—and sometimes may seem like simple lists but which transcend as categorical abundance of evidence that lead up to his anecdotal expansions. Well done, Mr. Pennick!"

LINDA KELSEY-JONES, PRESIDENT OF SAN MARCOS AREA
ARTS COUNCIL AND DIRECTOR/CURATOR OF
THE WALKERS' GALLERY, SAN MARCOS

Praise for
Previous Works by Nigel Pennick

"Nigel Pennick is a true initiate who can demonstrate to the reader how nature and cosmos correlate to each other. He explains medieval traditions and Celtic magic in a way that helps us understand how these topics are universal, gives us knowledge about ourselves, and is of highest relevance for humankind today. I regularly return to Nigel Pennick's books."

THOMAS KARLSSON, PH.D., AUTHOR OF *NIGHTSIDE OF THE RUNES*

"Written by one of the great wisdom keepers of British lore, *The Ancestral Power of Amulets, Talismans, and Mascots* [contains] . . . folklore by which people have kept themselves safe against plagues . . . and evils of many kinds. Very highly recommended as an authentic sourcebook of protective wisdom."

CAITLÍN MATTHEWS, COAUTHOR OF *THE LOST BOOK OF THE GRAIL*

"Richly researched! *Magic in the Landscape* is a fascinating insight into a practice in need of returning, one that will go a long way in healing and reclaiming a magical relationship with the sacred landscape."

PHILIP CARR-GOMM, AUTHOR OF
DRUID MYSTERIES AND *LESSONS IN MAGIC*

"[*Elemental Magic* is] one of Nigel Pennick's best! Thorough, practical, and informed by a profound grasp of traditional European lore, this classic book on the art and practice of natural magic belongs on the bookshelf of any working mage."

JOHN MICHAEL GREER, AUTHOR OF
THE DRUID MAGIC HANDBOOK AND *THE DRUIDRY HANDBOOK*

"Nigel Pennick is one of the greatest living runic experts, bringing meticulous research and a profound magical understanding to his subject. This important book [*Runic Lore and Legend*] examines the distinctive Anglo-Saxon Futhark of Northumbria, essentially setting the thirty-three runes in the context of both time and place."

ANNA FRANKLIN, AUTHOR OF *PAGAN WAYS TAROT*

"Well-researched and wonderfully illustrated, Pennick's telling of local history and mythology is written in an accessible, interesting, and enthralling way and kept me engrossed from beginning to end. *Witchcraft and Secret Societies of Rural England* is very highly recommended!"

JUNE KENT, EDITOR OF *INDIE SHAMAN* MAGAZINE

"Whether we call it magic or folklore (or even superstition), the traditional, often pre-Christian knowledge described in *Pagan Magic of the Northern Tradition* is fascinating. I've been referring to Pennick's books for years when I need a fact or an example of some interesting early magic to cite in my books and blogs. I learned something new on every page!"

BARBARA ARDINGER, PH.D., AUTHOR OF
PAGAN EVERY DAY AND *SECRET LIVES*

"*Operative Witchcraft* is an unromanticized 'warts and all' survey of the real history and lore of witchcraft in the author's native England and elsewhere. One could not ask for a more knowledgeable and sympathetic guide through these shadow-filled realms than Nigel Pennick."

MICHAEL MOYNIHAN, COAUTHOR OF *LORDS OF CHAOS* AND
COEDITOR OF THE JOURNAL *TYR: MYTH—CULTURE—TRADITION*

"Solidly referenced and carefully illustrated, *The Book of Primal Signs* seems to travel everywhere and touch everything."

RICHARD HEATH, AUTHOR OF *SACRED NUMBER AND THE ORIGINS OF CIVILIZATION* AND *SACRED NUMBER AND THE LORDS OF TIME*

THE
SPIRITUAL POWER
OF MASKS

Doorways to
Realms Unseen

NIGEL PENNICK

Destiny Books
Rochester, Vermont

One Park Street
Rochester, Vermont 05767
www.DestinyBooks.com

Text stock is SFI certified

Destiny Books is a division of Inner Traditions International

Cataloging-in-Publication Data for this title is available from the Library of Congress

ISBN 978-1-64411-404-9 (print)
ISBN 978-1-64411-405-6 (ebook)

Printed and bound in the United States by Lake Book Manufacturing, Inc.
The text stock is SFI certified. The Sustainable Forestry Initiative® program
promotes sustainable forest management.

10 9 8 7 6 5 4 3 2 1

Text design and layout by Priscilla Harris Baker
This book was typeset in Garamond Premier Pro with Belwe, Amber Taste, and
Gill Sans used as display typefaces

To send correspondence to the author of this book, mail a first-class letter to the
author c/o Inner Traditions • Bear & Company, One Park Street, Rochester, VT
05767, and we will forward the communication.

Contents

PREFACE

The Meaning and Function of Masks

his book is about the many variants of disguise that people have created and worn from early times until the present day. Focusing on the European tradition, it describes and discusses the meaning and function of masks, rituals, and ceremonial disguises with detailed historical and contemporary examples, mainly from Britain, where the

Fig. P.1. Demon or guiser? Medieval stone carving fragment, Wisbech Cambridgeshire, England (See also color plate 1.)

author has been a participant. The themes dealt with here all inter-
penetrate one another, from religious and rural ritual to theatrical performance, carnival, and riot. Nothing of it has ever been fixed rigidly;
all was and is in continuous flux, and new forms have emerged as conditions changed, while retaining the continuity of their underlying eternal reality. All examples presented here are generic and have occurred
over hundreds of years and recur in many places in Europe. There are
no borderlines, only transformation.

Incarnating the Spirit Depicted by the Mask

There is a spiritual power in masks, hints of other things that remain unspoken, stylized yet ideal images of ideal qualities, otherworldly substances, ritually activated. For the mask's wearer is representing the archetype, whether it be the ancestral or the dead, a divinity or a power, a being of the eldritch world or a character in a formalized play. The boundary line between human guisers, lifeless effigies, ensouled images of deities, and uncanny beings is always fluid and uncertain. The masker is located at the intersection point between the present and the past, the personal and the collective, the living and the dead, this world and the Otherworld—for the mask enacts the dialogue between the container and the contained, the exterior and the interior, the seen and the unseen. The mimesis of masked mumming means that the masker personates the mask's character for the duration of the masquerade. The person inside is subordinated to the power signified by the mask. Whatever the being so personated, the performance takes place in the here and now and is operative by its present effects. For these are the masks of anonymity, worn by nameless guisers enacting ritual roles, incarnating the spirit depicted by the mask. In so doing, they partake of something of the eternal, the archetypal, that is present in the transience of keeping up the day. This book does not intend to be a comprehensive listing of every masked and disguised performance that has ever been documented over the centuries in Europe. It is not a literalistic catalogue of "here they did this" and "here they did that," a work of numerical taxonomy, full of percentages and distribution maps that, however interesting, are artifacts of fragmentary historical documentation that often demonstrate little but drive the spirit away from an existence that is preeminently capable of infinite and joyful variation.

Tradition constructs the present out of the past, recognizing and celebrating those themes that have empowered the customs and practices of bygone days. History is not the past, and the future is not inevitable, only conditioned by what has gone before. History is a story that people tell about events of the past, and the future has no existence except in the imagination. History appropriates particular things that remain from the past and constructs a narrative from them. It is only of value if it resonates with and is useful to somebody now. Inevitably selective, tellers of history speak of things that are useful to their particular theme. They help to explain the present by recalling past happenings that preceded the present condition of things, events that explain, justify, and reinforce the present and indicate its potential.

Our experience of place is fundamental to our sense of being. Traditional society in each locality has a particular local way of looking at the world that is not reproducible or transferable. History is site specific; placeless events are impossible. In traditional societies, place-names are all descriptive. Features in the land such as the shape of mountains and hills, bends in rivers, ravines, isolated rocks, fertile meadows, types of trees and animals, and the abodes of eldritch beings all appear as elements in traditional place-names. Older languages have words that express the subtle gradations of slope, water flow, the shape of hills, the color of rocks, places where deer graze, the local names of plants and where they grow, places where snow remains longest after the winter, and the *locus terribilis* where humans ought not to trespass. The individual's being in his or her "home ground" is grounded in the local culture as the repository of local knowledge. Place, language, and everyday life are enmeshed in landwisdom, a spiritual linkage that must be nurtured or lost. To recognize this is to acknowledge the *genius loci*, the spirit of the place. This is spirit in either sense of the word, both physical and intangible, emergent from the dark world of the indeterminate.

Ancient sacred places always had their human guardians, usually a hereditary role. The divinely enthused *derilans* who kept the holy wells of Scotland and the *harrowwardens* who dwelt in tumbledown cottages among the stones of power ministered to any passing pilgrim seeking an oracle or healing. These unpaid keepers assured that the hallowed wood, well, or stone would not be profaned, misused, or destroyed. There are those today who, unobserved, tend these ancient places of the land, where they still exist. They may not be hereditary guardians in the traditional sense, but they, too, are true *dewars,* spiritual gardeners who commune with the eldritch world. Theirs is the sacred stewardship of their spiritual forebears, bearing authentic testimony to their history, assuring the continuance of positive traditional values.

All places are meaningful, but places where something human happened—or is believed to have happened—are uniquely specific. They are landmarks associated with particular stories, with mythological and historical events. Whatever the event and whoever the personage, the place is made notable and special by the interweaving of topography, history, religion, myth, and institutions that carry on and commemorate the event in observances, rituals, and performances. But without institutions to carry them on, customs and traditions must die. Institutions in the form of guilds, whether officially sanctioned, unofficial, or even prohibited, have carried on traditional observances and guarded both intangible traditions and physical artifacts. From the religious guilds of ancient Greece and Rome to the craft guilds and rural fraternities of later times, the keeping places of sacred objects, masks, costumes, dragons, hobby horses, and giants have been maintained, often in secret.

1

Ensouled Artifacts and Death Masks

The Spiritual Arts and Crafts

In contrast with the materialistic worldview that is the commonplace, there is another sort of relationship that exists among people, places, and artifacts. When we engage physically in the spiritual current, then we develop another kind of consciousness of our place within existence. An artifact made by hand according to true principles gains an inner consistency, for the act of making is a spiritual path in its own right. For example, carving a religious image or a mask according to true principles produces an ensouled artifact. The materials used come from specific places and are chosen because of their innate qualities. They are not the products of anonymous factories, made by machines in vast repeatable quantities. The spiritual arts and crafts seek to realize spiritual ideals materially through a process that itself is the craftsperson's spiritual journey. The initiation of the newcomer into a guild sets him or her on a path toward the hard-won mastery of the craft.

Ensouled artifacts emerge from the principles of traditional craftsmanship, in which, as the medieval German mystic Meister Eckhart taught, "working and becoming are the same." Traditional spirituality is

4

not just an inward thing: it also must manifest materially. "Those who lead the contemplative life and do no outward works are most mistaken, and on the wrong tack," said Eckhart, for "no person can in this life reach the point where he is excused from outward works." It is a spirituality independent of religious denominations—the world of the worker, the artisan whose function is to deal with physical reality firsthand. The realities of doing necessitate a practical approach in which the unquestionable presence of the materials always overrides abstract human theories and dogmas. This is not the dialectical materialism preached by modernity: the vision is that of the poet, the artist, the visionary, not of the professional cleric, the accountant, or the politician.

Death and Funerary Masks

The death mask is an ensouled artifact. It is a means of preserving the exact appearance of a dead person's face, an image taken directly after the last breath has flown. Death masks are made by molding and casting. A flexible material such as plaster is put on the face of the deceased and allowed to dry. Then it is removed, and the mold of the face is now the matrix, a void in the form of the face into which material is put to make a copy of the original matrix, the solid form of the face. The mold is then broken, and the material object released. The solid of the matrix becomes void in the mold, then solid again when the material fills it. The death mask makes manifest materially the mysterious interconnection between presence and absence, here and not here, positive and negative. Depressions in the mold become raised areas, and the raised areas of the mold become depressions. What was hollow is now solid, and what was solid is now hollow. The death mask and the image made from it link it with the crafts of pottery and metal casting.

Frank Byron Jevons wrote that in ancient Rome, "one mask was buried with the deceased whilst another was carefully preserved, and the masks or *imagines* . . . were worn on the occasion of a funeral of a member of the household by persons who in the funeral procession represented the deceased ancestors whose *imagines* they wore" (italics in original) (Jevons 1916, 179). Funerary masks, with an image of the deceased person's face, are well known from ancient Egypt, where they were part of the mummy case. Many Egyptian ones were made from cartonnage, a forerunner of papier mâché using linen strips with a binding material, which was then painted. Metal funerary masks were also used, the most famous of which is the solid gold mask of Tutankhamen. In 1876, a splendid gold funerary mask was discovered by archaeologist Heinrich Schliemann at Mycenae, Greece. He called it "the mask of Agamemnon," though he had no evidence that it was. Several comparable Thracian gold funerary masks have been discovered in Bulgaria; the Sventitsata mound at Kran in the Stara Zagora region contained the remains of a body dismembered according to Orphic custom. It was identified as the mask of the Odrysian king Teres, who reigned from 460 to 445 BCE. Etruscan funerary masks were made in sheet bronze and attached to urns containing the ashes of the dead. The Romans made death masks that they used as molds to make the *imagines majorum,* masks that were deposited in the family *lararium,* the family shrine of the ancestors. They were worn at funerals, where they literally represented the dead.

In medieval Europe, effigies with lifelike masks, cast from death masks in the Roman manner, appeared at state funerals of magnates and royalty. "State funerals of the fourteenth and subsequent centuries," Reginald Cocks wrote disapprovingly in Britain in 1902, "were robbed of much solemnity in this country by carrying in the procession a life-like effigy of the deceased" (Cocks 1902, 431). In the medieval period, the effigies had lifelike painted and carved wooden faces, but by the seventeenth century, they were lifelike waxworks. The faces were cast from death masks. Westminster Abbey contained the effigies of several seventeenth- and eighteenth-century British monarchs: King Charles II, William III and Mary II, and Queen Anne. The last effigy carried in a procession was that of Edmund Sheffield, the last Duke of Buckinghamshire, who died in 1735 at age nineteen (Cocks 1902, 433). It remained customary until quite recently to make a death mask of a famous person who had just died. The death mask of William Shakespeare is illustrated in figure 1.1.

Fig.1.1. Death mask of
William Shakespeare (archive)

Marks around the eyes have been claimed by medical experts to indicate the disease reputed to have killed a person. The death mask of the visionary poet William Blake still exists, and that of the Soviet dictator Josef Stalin, who died in 1953, is preserved in the Stalin Museum at Gori in Georgia.

2

Masks and Representation

Religious, Theatrical, Guising, and Carnival Masks

We live in a visual culture in which photography in its many versions is the main form of image we are presented with. This is appearance without context, separated from the living character in a fixed image that is seen from the sole angle from which it was photographed. When it is a photograph of a person with a painted face or a mask, it is divorced from the performance, which is its true place of appearance, and it becomes a separated object in its own right, which is liable to be misinterpreted or mistaken for something it is not. When seen in the proper, living context, the performer, playing the character he or she portrays, is acting within a complex of text, voice, accent, gesture, and movement within the particular costume that itself interacts with that of other performers in the parade, play, or dance and contributes to a complete scene, which takes place at a particular moment at a particular place. A photograph, even a video, is an impoverished record of the actuality of the event, and an individual artifact from it can give little understanding of the performance of which it was an integral part. Even the photographs reproduced in this book are only illustrative of any particular fragmentary moment during the performance of which their subjects were part. As illustrations of general principles or characters, they serve as examples of events, which are not definitive, but individual particular instances of them.

Ancient representations of Greek masks usually show them as part of performance. When separate, they are images in mosaics, frescos, and lamps, in jewelry and as miniature replicas, perhaps made as votive offerings to Dionysus. A series of terra-cotta miniature masks was found on the Mediterranean island of Lipari, dateable before 252 BCE because the city was destroyed in that year by the Roman army. These existing pottery masks can only be seen in isolation, away from the specific costumes that were invariably worn with particular masks and certainly not in the performances they were designed for. When they were made, their owners knew exactly what characters they represented. Funerary games in ancient Italy involved mask wearing. An Etruscan painting in the Tomba degli Auguri (Tomb of the Augurs) at Tarquinia depicts a *phersu* wearing a bearded mask and holding a rope attached around the leg of another figure, who is wielding a club and being bitten by a dog. *Phersu,* a word related to *person,* meant the director of the funeral performance (Napier 1986, 20–21). Devotees of the cult of Dionysus at Athens portrayed the god as a mask, and actors in plays in honor of the god wore masks. According to tradition, Thespis was the first playwright who used masks, stylized to express various emotions. The familiar theatrical emblem of two masks, one of comedy, the other of tragedy, originated in ancient Greek theater and was taken up as a Roman theme.

In Italy, the two Dionysiac masks appear in mosaic form in the second-century-BCE House of the Faun at Pompeii and in the second-century-CE mosaic made for the Baths of Decius on the Aventine Hill in Rome. The Greek word for a mask is *prosopon,* "a face." Masks appear on painted pottery from the fifth century BCE onward. Masks are shown hanging from trees, and the Pronomos Vase depicts actors preparing for a masked satyr play in honor of the god Dionysus.

Some fifth-century CE images show helmetlike masks that covered the whole head. The costumes that go with masks and facial disguise are equally significant, for masks were never seen without the costumes or outside the performance, except when deposited in a shrine, never to be used again. Masks were deposited at the altar of Dionysus when no longer used. This was a common ritual for disposing of ceremonial clothing, tools, and weapons at temples of deities who ruled over the trade or craft.

In the bygone era when most people had seen relatively few things, many must have had no idea what a mask was and how it worked. The effect of seeing a Gorgon mask for the first time or an actor in a mask must have been terrifying and puzzling. This is almost unimaginable now, in our era of uninterrupted viewing of vast arrays of ever-changing images. Maurice Sand describes how, in ancient Greece, "Aristophanes in his comedy of the Clouds gave one of his actors a mask which so perfectly resembled Socrates that the spectators thought to behold the man himself upon the stage" (Sand 1915, 16). Aulus Gellius, who lived in the time of the Roman emperor Hadrian, explained, "The entire head and face of the actor being enclosed within the mask, so that the voice could issue by only one restricted opening, it follows that the voice thus confined must be greatly increased in volume and distinction. This is why the Latins have given the name of *persona* to these masks, because they cause the voices of those who wear them to resound and reverberate" (Sand 1915, 16).

Despite the odd instance of a personal mask, as with Socrates, the majority of ancient masks expressed generic characters, each of which signified a particular emotional state or complex. In his *Onomastikon,* an encyclopedia of Greek words, the second-century-CE academic Julius Pollux listed forty-four different masks of the New Comedy and the costumes that went with them. Because masks, rather than costumes, have survived from antiquity and more recent masks have been preserved and collected away from the context in which they were made and used, there has been an asymmetrical emphasis on masks alone rather than on the ensembles of which they were part and the aspects of performance that they facilitated. Pollux's list records the subtlety of differences among ancient masks; each represents a different human type and the psychology inherent in that type. The forty-four different kinds of mask are a catalog of human variability, expressed and explored in the plays in which the actors wore them.

Attempts to compare the masks with any perceived ethnic characteristics must take into account the ethnicities of the time, not those current at the present day, for there have been two and a half thousand years of extensive genetic changes in the human population since they were first designed. As with ancient breeds of animals compared with present ones, humans have changed significantly in the intervening period. New Comedy masks fell into five categories: young men, old men, male slaves, old women, and young women.

Young Men: The mask of the Accomplished Youth had a lightly tanned and ruddy coloring, raised eyebrows, forehead wrinkles, and a crown of hair. The Dark Youth mask looked younger than that of the Accomplished Youth, with lowered brows. The Curly-Haired Youth mask looked even younger, with curly hair, a ruddy coloring, one wrinkle on his forehead, and lowered brows. The Delicate Youth was the youngest of all, with a pale mask with hair like that of the Accomplished Youth. The Wavy-Haired Youth is a boastful soldier

Fig. 2.1. Ancient Greek mask (See also color plate 2.)

whose mask has a dark coloration and wavy hair. Another mask, of the Fair Wavy-Haired Youth, has fair hair but an otherwise similar mask. The Boor has a darker mask, with a short nose and thicker lips and a wreath of hair. The Parasite has a dark, hooked-nosed mask, the Toady is similar but with maliciously raised eyebrows, and the Sicilian Parasite has other subtle variations.

Old Men: The First Grandfather is the oldest, with a pale mask with a downcast look, a full beard, and very short hair. The Second Grandfather has a pale, gloomy-looking mask that is taut around the eyes, with crushed ears, a beard, and red hair. The Principal Old Man is pale and flat-faced with a hooked nose, the right eyebrow raised, and a wreath of hair. The Old Man with a Long Beard has a lethargic look, neutral eyebrows, a long streaming beard, and a wreath of hair. The Wedge-Beard mask has a pointed beard with brows raised in an annoyed expression. Hermon's first mask has a big beard, raised eyebrows, the forehead extended into baldness, raised brows, and fierce eyes. His second mask has a pointed beard and a bald pate. (Hermon was either a mask maker or an actor who gave his name to these masks.) The mask of Lycomedes (wolf-cunning) has a long beard, curly hair, and a raised brow. The Pimp is a similar mask, slightly grinning, with a bald pate.

Slaves: The Grandfather is gray haired and represents a slave who has been freed. The Principal Slave's mask has raised eyebrows with the tips drawn together and a coil of red hair. The Low-Hair mask has puffy brows and a bald forehead, while the Curly Slave's mask has a brownish-red coloring, an oblique gaze, and curly hair. The mask of the slave named Maison is also brownish red and has a bald pate. Cicada's mask has an oblique gaze. It is dark brown, with a beard and curls on a bald pate. The Shorn Poppet mask signifies a slave girl with hair cut short, and the Smooth-Haired Slave Girl mask is snub-nosed, representing a courtesan's slave.

Young Women: The Talker mask is white with straight brows and hair around its face that is smoothed down. The Talker with Gray Strands signifies a former prostitute. The Curly Woman has the same facial characteristics as the Talker but has curly hair. The Virgin is a light-ochre mask with hair parted in the middle and combed down.

The Pseudo-Virgin is a lighter mask with parted hair bound around the top of the head, and the Second Pseudo-Virgin is the same, only lacking the parting. The Mature Courtesan mask is redder than those of the Pseudo-Virgins, with curls around the ears. The Nubile Courtesan is similar but with hair tied up with a band, and the Golden Courtesan has gold in the hair. The Mitered Courtesan mask is topped by a multicolored turban. The Concubine is a white mask with hair around the face, while the Little Torch has hair brought up to a point, like flames.

Old Women: The She-Wolf is an elongated pale-ochre mask with numerous wrinkles and squinting eyes. The Housekeeper is a snub-nosed mask with two teeth protruding from each jaw, and the Plump Old Woman mask depicts ample flesh, and a headband surrounds the hair (Wiles 1991, 75–77).

The Carnival Mask Tradition

The masked theater collapsed when theater in general was suppressed in the Roman Empire after the emperor Constantine abolished the old religions, closed and robbed the temples of their treasures, and imposed the Christian Church. But out in the country, it was more difficult to suppress pagan tradition. Various churchmen condemned mumming and the guising of those who clothed themselves with skins of cattle and wore the heads of animals at the New Year (Strutt 1845, 250). The guisers' masks called *Talamasca* were condemned as demonic larvae, for they were a continuation of ancient funeral masking. The church imposed the fast of Lent before Easter, but soon the compulsory fasting was mitigated by a final day before it, Shrove Tuesday, when foodstuffs banned for the next weeks had to be consumed or thrown away. Of course, this led to Shrove Tuesday becoming a day of feasting and merriment before the compulsory gloom, hunger, and penances of Lent. From this day of final consumption emerged the Carnival, literally "farewell to meat," which grew to involve masking, disguise, misrule, and the inversion of norms. In the church itself, the Feast of Fools emerged, in which young clergy would impersonate the hierarchy with parodic songs and activities. Secular Sociétes Joyeuses took over the Feast of Fools when it was abandoned by the church (Chambers 1933, 228).

Weird, eccentric behavior and disobedience that would not be tolerated at other times is normal during the Carnival. The Carnival embodies a general atmosphere of laughter, satire, and mockery mixed with potential threat. Throngs of unidentified costumed and masked people and people guising as animals or grotesque and monstrous evil spirits fill the town. Things are out of control, the world is turned upside down, and "*der Bär ist los.*" The emergence of otherworldly entities amid the Carnival throng is an ever-present possibility. Straw men might be real beings, the Butzemann might be the real Bogey Man, and one might be beaten by people in animal skins who are carrying horses' tails or clubs. Even the Wild Huntsman might appear with his throng to carry away the unwary. Processions taking place at night, such as the Perchtenlauf, Twelfth Night, and Plough Monday, with nameless disguised people running through poorly lit village streets, resemble the Wild Hunt in their threatening rout of misrule. Disguise permits license; when unrecognizable, one is enabled to do what one likes or what one must. The charivari of riotous assembly emerges as the violent, vengeful, retributional end of the carnivalesque.

Masks were used in private courtly theatrical performances that often featured members of the court as well as professional actors. The most lavish of all was the *Intermedi* staged in Florence in 1589 to celebrate the wedding of the grand duke of Tuscany, Ferdinando de'Medici, and Christine of Lorraine. The Venice Carnival, taking place as early as 1268, has been of immense influence on masking in the whole of Europe.

In Venice, the guild of the mascherari (mask makers) was given a charter in 1436, and a number of characteristic masks are traditional in the Carnival there. Masked Commedia dell'Arte characters are always present (see chapter 15), but there are a number of other masks of local origin. The Volto (countenance) or Larva (ghost) was originally a white half-mask worn by the common people that was attached to a three-cornered hat. The Bauta is a disturbing blank white mask worn with a

Fig. 2.2. Italian Carnival masks

hat and dark clothing. The Moretta is an unusual black oval mask worn by women. Just too small to cover the face, it is held on by a stud held in the mouth, which prevents the wearer from talking unless she takes off the mask. Masks with long noses are connected with the theater and opera. The longer the nose, the more stupid the character, which was probably Carlo Collodi's inspiration for Pinocchio. Related to the long-nosed mask is the beaked mask of the Medico Della Pesta (plague doctor). This originated with the French physician to royalty Charles de Lorne (1584–1678), who designed it to protect himself when dealing with people suffering from the plague. It has the terrifying appearance of a long hollow beak and round eyeholes covered with crystal or glass. It is worn with a close-fitting black hat and a long black cloak. Early gas masks worn by the German army in World War I were based on the mask of the Medico Della Pesta.

The masks of the Carnival in southern Germany are numerous. Many are old, having been passed down through the generations, and some still in use are reputed to date from the 1790s. In the Schwarzwald in springtime, keepers of tradition perform the rite of Awakening the Masks when they take them out from their hibernating places in preparation of their annual outing. Now is the masks' moment, when they will awake again and be worn to personate their particular characters in public. These masks, carved from particular woods by hereditary masters of the art, are ensouled in their own right, and those who wear them are aware of it. The German Maschkera rules stipulate

Fig. 2.3. Gas masks in trench warfare during World War I, 1916. British "bomber" (grenade thrower) attacks three German soldiers.

Fig. 2.4. Fastnacht (Shrovetide Carnival) mask costume, Donaueschingen, Germany (See also color plate 3.)

that no one must touch a guiser wearing a mask. The mask must never be worn except at the Carnival, and one must not speak when wearing a mask, but one can growl or make a murmuring sound. One must not be recognized. The rule of keeping "mum"—that is, not speaking when masked—applies in British mumming outside the mummers' play, when, of course, one must deliver one's lines. Those guising as a horse, a tup (that is, a ram), or another animal must never speak when in costume. All who have worn masks or guised as an animal know how the persona will take over and one will become the character or animal.

3

Gods, Images, and Ostenta

Images

Traditional masks, costumes, puppets, and effigies often portrayed a local ancestral hero or founder of the town where the performance took place. In reality, there are no authentic images of archaic ancestral people, the prophets and founders of most ancient religions, cities, and crafts. Aniconic religions forbade any representations, but it is impossible, anyway, to make one, for only the imagination, and not actual historical imagery, must drive the artist. Such people cannot be literally represented, and their attributes cannot change. Only an artist's impression can be made. Religions that do depict prophets and founders have traditional iconic imagery that in some cases is subject to strict artistic and doctrinal rules. How close these icons are to the individuals portrayed, it is impossible to tell. This is not the case with Greek and Roman sculptures that used the person's death mask image; or for royalty, whose images appeared on coins and as statues; or individuals who had excelled in some way, such as soldiers, orators, playwrights, and sportsmen who had their portraits made when they were alive.

When Christianity emerged as a doctrine, the problem of whether it had one or three gods was hotly debated. Because it followed on from the strictly monotheistic Judaism but had two new divine beings in addition to the original Ancient of Days, there had to be some adaptation of the Jewish understanding of God. It was suggested by the theologian Marcellus, taking the analogy of masks in the pagan tradition, that God is a *hypostasis triprosopos,* "one object with three faces." The god Janus was always depicted with two faces, one looking back and the other forward, symbolizing his function as the god of the New Year, among other things. The Christian God was visualized as if he wore three different masks at different times, and so was played as three different characters, functioning successively in the roles of creator, redeemer, and sanctifier (Prestige 1964, 161).

In abstract, it was just a semantic question, but the problem of representation was particularly difficult. The trinity could be represented by a sigil, but as a literal depiction, it required something else. Conventionally, it emerged that God the Father was portrayed as an old man (the Ancient of Days), God the Son as the familiar Jesus figure, and the Holy Spirit as a flying dove. Clearly, this was a departure from the original concept of a single individual acting through three different masks. Several pagan gods of northeastern Europe were depicted with multiple heads or faces. These images existed until the twelfth and thirteenth centuries, when they were destroyed by German Christian colonizers.

These images of Slavic pagan gods appear to have been transferred to the Dreigesicht image of the Trinity, which was a compound face with three noses, three beards, and four eyes in one head. Oskar von Zaborsky illustrated a Dreigesicht painting from Basel, Switzerland (von Zaborsky 1936, 76–78, fig. 161). He also noted an illustration of the Dreigesicht by Albrecht Dürer and a stone carving at Plau in Mecklenburg, Germany (Zaborsky 1936, 349). Mecklenburg is a land where the old gods were worshipped until 1147. At that time, Pope Eugenius III called a German crusade against the Slavic people there to conquer the land and destroy their religious culture. An alternative reading of the Dreigesicht is that it represents the three phases of the moon, which in German has the male gender. But as the Basel image has an orb for God the Father and a flaming sword for the Holy Spirit,

Fig. 3.1. A carving of masks in the church at Saint-Pierre, Alsace, France, circa 1100

this interpretation is unlikely. The image of God wearing three separate masks was not pursued in artistic representation.

Mythical and Historical Founders

In ancient traditional society, the ancestors were venerated or apotheosized into gods. Each has a particular attribute by which he or she is identified, a system of emblems and symbols—which appear in representations and performances—that present the ancestor. Death masks of family ancestors were used as molds to make masks worn by participants in Roman funerary processions and commemorations of the ancestors. Thus, the actual appearance of the dead took place in ceremonies where the masks were worn. Ancestral founders were and are commemorated in various ways, and many ancient cities celebrate their founders, mythical or historical. Each has one or more attributes, such as an animal, a weapon, or a plant that serves as an emblem. Some are associated with omens and ostenta that led to the foundation. Rome is named for Romulus, and the ancient bronze Capitoline Wolf depicts Romulus and his brother, Remus, being suckled by a wolf. According to Tacitus in his *Germania* (published in 96 CE), Tuisto or Tuisco was the ancestor of the Teutonic peoples. Like Romulus's wolf, Tuisto is associated with the ram. An engraved medallion in the book *Promptuarii Iconum Insigniorum* (published in Lyon, France, in 1553) by Guillaume Rouillé (ca. 1518–1589) shows an artist's impression of the ancestor with a small ram's head and a ram's skin as a head covering.

In his book *Mutual Aid,* Petr Kropotkin (1842–1921) wrote in 1914:

> In most cities of Western and Southern Europe, the tendency was to take for *defensor* a bishop whom the city had elected itself; and so many bishops took the lead in protecting the "immunities" of the towns and in defending their liberties, that numbers of them were considered, after their death, as saints and special patrons of different cities. . . . St. Ulrik of Augsburg, St. Wolfgang of Ratisbon [Regensburg], St. Heribert of Cologne, St. Adalbert of Prague . . . became so many cities' saints for having acted in defence of popular rights. (Kropotkin 1955, 167)

In fact, many of these saints are no longer remembered, nor are their days observed. Among the almost forgotten ones are Saint Rhadegund, patron saint of Cambridge, and Saint Erkenwald, patron of London. But in English cathedral cities, founders' days are still kept up, such as Saint Edmund's Day at Bury St Edmunds and Saint Swithun's Day at Winchester.

Fig. 3.2. Tuisto medallion

Fig. 3.3. Eighteenth-century mask of Saint Edmund. Stone carving, Bury St Edmunds, Suffolk, England (See also color plate 4.)

In former times, commemorations of the founders' days involved guild parades, with effigies or actors representing the founding characters, along with the usual carnivalesque plays that reenacted the mythical history of the city, church, or guild. The giants that are paraded in Belgian cities are effigies of heroic founders or patron saints of guilds, as was the giant Saint Christopher at Salisbury in England.

Augsburg in Bavaria was in pre-Roman times the Swabian holy city of Zizarim, locus of the goddess's shrine. After the Roman conquest, it became Augusta Vindelicorum. The church of Saint Peter-am-Perlach stands on the site of the temple of the goddess Zisa. Her emblem was the pinecone, the *stadtpyr*, which remains the emblem of the city to this day. The Hercules Fountain there has a gilded plaque at its base showing Zisa in a triumphal chariot (Pennick 2002, 107–9). In the area around Augsburg, the Christian authorities renamed Zisa's holy day, Zîstag (Tuesday), to Aftermontag to remove associations with the Swabian goddess. But she was not forgotten.

Saint Adalbert was the patron of the German inhabitants of Prague, while Libuše (Libussa) was the Czech patron. After the expulsion of ethnic Germans in 1945, Adalbert was no longer commemorated. Libuše is the legendary ancestress of the Czech people and is celebrated as having founded the city in the eighth century. The youngest of three daughters, legend tells us, she married a ploughman named Přemysi, and they were progenitors of the Přemyslid dynasty. Libuše was a seeress with the power of prophecy, and she resolved to found a city at a place where at noon a man was making the best use of his teeth. Her agents went out, and at one place at midday, they found a man sawing wood while others ate their lunch. This was the sign, as the saw's teeth were doing productive work. They asked the carpenter what he was making, and he told them it was a threshold, *prah* in the Czech language. So they founded the city there and named it Praha (Prague). There are images of Libuše at several places in the city today. Countless other ancient towns and cities have comparable founders' legends.

Guilds and Fraternities

In traditional society, crafts and trades have their own place within towns, just as they do within contemporary society. In medieval London, the guildsmen of the pepperers (grocers) were at Soper's Lane, the clothiers worked in Cornhill, the smiths and tanners in Holborn, and the braziers in Lothbury. Lawyers and scribes occupied Chancery Lane, tailors worked on Coleman Street, the drapers in Candlewick Street, and the goldsmiths in Westcheap. The district of the Vintners was called the Vintry. As in all towns, the location of the butchers was the Shambles, in London dedicated to Saint Nicholas. The great cattle market was at Smithfield, and the fishmongers worked along the north bank of the River Thames. Every town and city in Europe had similar localities where specific guilds operated. The Irish traditional song "The Dublin Jack of All Trades" is a list of all the trades of Dublin and the streets and districts where they were conducted, sung as though the singer had worked in each one of them. Many trades are enumerated, and it is a very difficult song to sing.

Guilds emerged as men's mutual support groups in the years after the collapse of the Roman Empire in the West. In northern Europe, *frith-gilds* (peace guilds) existed for mutual protection in a lawless age, providing support and aid to their members. They held regular feasts, and the word *guild,* or *gild,* meaning an association, comes from its ancient meaning as a "feast," "merrymaking," or, as Joshua Toulmin Smith put it, "the feasts of the German tribes from Scandinavia which were first called Gilds" (Smith 1870, lxvii).

So from the earliest times, guilds were not only associations for

Fig. 3.4. Woodcut of a feast of the shoemakers' guild of Paris, early seventeenth century

mutual aid but also for keeping up their location's festival days. As urban institutions evolved, the guilds played a fundamental role in civic life. From the early middle ages, craft and trade guilds were organizations that recruited, taught, and regulated their various areas of expertise. They had their own rules and statutes that were recognized by civic and royal authorities, as with the Statutes of the London Guilds, which date from the reign of King Athelstan (924–927 CE) (Smith 1870, lxxv).

The guilds were custodians of the closely guarded "mysteries" of each craft. Membership was gained through initiations with elaborate emblematic rituals that involved a symbolic death of the candidate from his old life and a resurrection to his new one. As Smith observed, "The customs of the gilds of that age were to such an extent those of the old sacred banquets, that, for centuries, prohibitions and menaces of punishment were expressly needed in order to destroy their pagan character" (Smith 1870, lxvii). Initiation included an "oath of fealty to the fraternity, swearing to observe its laws, to uphold its privileges, not to divulge its counsels, to obey its officials and not to aid any non-gildsman under cover of the newly-acquired 'freedom'" (Gross 1890, 1, 29).

Guild initiations included a lecture that explained the originator of the craft as a great master of the past, whether a mythical or historical figure. In Christian times, this was usually a biblical character or a saint. In the oath of a medieval guild in Cambridge, "which every member had to take on the relics of the patron saint of the gild, they swore faithful brotherhood to each other, not only in religious, but in secular matters" (Smith 1870, lxvi). So by the medieval period, the brewers had Saint Amand, the blacksmiths Clement, huntsmen Saint Hubertus, firemen Saint Florian, and musicians Saint Cecilia. Fraternities of fighting men revered Saint George, Saint Sebastian, and the archangel Michael, and the artillerymen's patron saint was Barbara. Pilgrims called on Saint Christopher to protect them on their sacred journeys. Many of these saints were Christianizations of earlier deities, demigods, and apotheosized heroes who had presided over the crafts and trades in pagan times. Each guild and fraternity had its own foundation myth, which was reenacted in rituals and guild ceremonies.

Craft and trade guilds were the mainstays of society. Their members participated in the replenishment of the world, keeping human culture alive and ensuring the continuity of all necessary skills as the generations came and went. Almost every man belonged to one. Guilds were responsible for the continuity of celebrating significant days in the year. They maintained funds for commemorations on their patron saints' days, supporting special chapels or even churches with candles burning, perpetually renewed. The "plough light" of the ploughmen's guild is the best known of these. Funds were also available to support sick members who could not work, as well as their widows and orphans, and to conduct decent ceremonial funerals when they died.

Each year, on the great Christian festivals, such as Corpus Christi, the trade guilds of the town or city would parade through the streets, often on horse-drawn vehicles bedecked with the emblems of the guild and with costumed people playing the parts of the appropriate saint and perhaps incidents from his or her life. In addition, the individual guilds would keep up their own saints' days with parades, ceremonial dances, and mystery plays. Costumes and theatrical properties were kept in churches sponsored by the guild. Making costumes, masks, and properties was the business of specialist guilds. In Venice, for example, the guild of

Fig. 3.5. Shrine of the coopers' (barrel makers) guild,
Antwerp Cathedral, Belgium

the mascherari (mask makers) received its charter in 1436. Religious fraternities composed of special devotees of particular saints also maintained their own chapels and performed mystery plays on appropriate days.

The destruction of the Catholic Church in Great Britain and much of northern Europe in the mid-1500s caused the suppression of all the religious guilds and the observances of religious festival days, which formerly had provided the opportunity for ritual and playful performance. After this, craft and trade guilds, rural fraternities, and sometimes secret societies were instrumental in keeping up special days, organizing the traditional festivities and performances. Each of these institutions had their own internal rituals, including initiations and signs of recognition. Over many centuries, there have been innumerable organizations, most of which left no records but during their existence maintained local traditions.

Fig. 3.6. Roman Catholic practice in Britain, having been illegal, was finally tolerated in the eighteenth century, and Catholics were emancipated during the reign of Queen Victoria in the next. Catholic devotees processing the image of Our Lady of Walsingham at Walsingham, Norfolk, England.

4

Animals as Ostenta

Guising as animals is ancient. Traditional hunters all over the world put on animal-skin disguises to camouflage themselves and empower their hunt. Stories and experiences of people entering otherworldly realms merge with accounts of Christian kings and holy men and women encountering meaningful beasts that enable them to locate the graves of saints, found churches, and determine favorable burial places. Deer encountered during hunting expeditions are significant animals in this tradition. The patron saint of hunters, Saint Hubertus (otherwise Hubert or Humber, who lived from 656 to 727 CE), is still venerated in German-speaking countries. His legend tells how, when he was out hunting, he was confronted by a stag with a shining cross between its antlers. The stag spoke to him, and he was converted to believe in Jesus. He was given an ethical code of hunting: to regard animals with compassion as God's creatures, to kill only in a quick and humane way, to take only old stags past breeding age, and to never kill a mother with her young. Subsequently, he became the bishop of Liège (now in Belgium) and is connected with miraculous *cornets de fer*, tapering iron nails consecrated in Saint Hubertus's shrine, which were claimed to be proof against rabies.

Fig. 4.1. Late medieval pilgrim's talisman of Saint Humber from Bury St Edmunds

All events must take place at a specific location that is either meaningful beforehand or defined afterward by the event. In Brittany, Count Conmore of Poher was hunting deer near Carhaix when the stag he was pursuing stopped suddenly at the lost tomb of Saint Hoiernin. His hounds then declined to attack and kill it. Seeing it as a sign, Conmore ordered a church to be built there to commemorate the event. The two main churches of Zürich in Switzerland, the cathedrals Grossmünster and Fraumünster, were both founded as the result of animal ostenta. The eighth-century emperor Charlemagne founded Grossmünster after an incident during a hunt. His horse suddenly stopped and knelt down. Seeing this as an ostentum, the ground was dug up and the tombs of the martyrs Felix and Regula were unearthed. The emperor ordered the church to be built there. Charlemagne's grandson, Louis the German, founded Fraumünster (women's monastery) in 853 CE. His daughters Bertha and Hildegard worshipped every day at Grossmünster. One day, in the woodland nearby, they noticed a stag with glowing antlers. It appeared again the next day, and the following day after that. The sisters saw it as a sign that they must found a church there. Their father was not convinced, but when he visited the site, a rope "fell from heaven," and that was enough evidence for him to give the order for its construction. An image of a stag exists over a Fraumünster door in commemoration.

According to legend, the Abbey of Andlau in Alsace, France, was founded by the empress Richardis (or Richgard) of Swabia, consort of Emperor Charles the Fat (839–888 CE). Legend tells how, falsely accused by her husband of adultery, she passed a trial by ordeal of fire. Dressed in a wax-impregnated gown, she walked through the flames unscathed. But this impressive vindication of her innocence did not convince the emperor, and so, to avoid execution, she fled to hide in the forest. There, in the Val d'Eleon, she had a vision of an angel who told her to found an abbey whose location would be revealed by a bear. She traveled around until she saw a she-bear standing on a rock. There she founded her abbey. The rock is still beneath the abbey, accessed via a trap door in the floor of the crypt. For centuries afterward, the nuns kept a bear and gave free board and lodging and free passage to all bear keepers who passed that way. Richardis's emblems are a bear and a ploughshare (Wiegand 1889, 420–21). Richardis and the bear are commemorated in a carving on the abbey, and the Fontaine de Sainte-Richardis in the town has another statue of the empress and the bear, carved by Philippe Grass (1801–1876) in 1871.

The city of Bern in Switzerland also has a tutelary bear. In 1191, supervising his men who were felling trees to construct the first buildings, Duke Berthold V of the House of Zähringen determined

Fig. 4.2. Richardis and the bear. Carving on an arch of the Abb᳐ʻAndlau, Alsace, France.

that the settlement should be named after the first animal caught at the site. It was a bear, and in acknowledgment of this, a bear pit, the Bärengraben, was made, and after that bears were always kept there as the luck of the city. In Russia, the city of Jaroslavl on the upper Volga was founded in 1010 by Prince Jaroslavl of Kiev at the place where he killed a she-bear single handed with his battle-ax. The city's coat of arms, dating from 1778, shows a black bear holding the prince's golden battle-ax. At a similar period, the lion, exterminated in southern Europe in early Roman times, was adopted as a heraldic emblem in early medieval Denmark. During the 1100s, western European warrior kings were nicknamed "the Lion" to express their strength and courage on the battlefield. They were German King Heinrich der Löwe (ca. 1130–1195), King William the Lion of Scotland (ca. 1142–1214), King Richard I Coeur de Lion (Lionheart, a.k.a. Richard le Lion, 1157–1199), and King Louis VIII le Lion of France (1187–1226). Their heraldic coats of arms bore representations of lions.

Fig. 4.3. Sixteenth-century woodcut depicting a symbolic image of King Richard I of England with his three lions shield.

Oxen were the heavy haulage animals until the invention of powered vehicles in the nineteenth century. In Celtic lands, they featured in divination rituals to determine the location of churches and the burial places of saints and kings. Ox divination was employed in church foundings by a father and his son on different occasions. The sixth-century Welsh king Gwynllyw the Warrior sought an ostentum to locate his future church. When he saw, standing on a hill, a white ox with a black spot on its forehead, he knew that was the place. The ox was called Dutelich, and the church of Saint Wooloo was built there (Baring-Gould and Fisher 1911, vol. 3, 238). The Celtic priest Cadoc, son of King Gwynllyw, with his companions Dunwyd and Tathan, also decided to build a church and to use oxen to determine its location. They loaded up the building materials on a wagon and yoked up the oxen to pull it. Then they did not lead or drive the oxen but allowed them to go where they wanted. When finally they stopped at Pen y ddau lwyn (Pendoylan)—a hill between two groves of trees—that was the place to build the church (Baring-Gould and Fisher 1908, vol. 2, 386–87).

When King Clydog of Ewyas was assassinated, his body was set on a cart to which were yoked two oxen. They were started off, being driven toward the River Momnnow. The cart came close to the riverbank when the yoke snapped and it could go no farther. This was the place, and the chapel of Clodock was founded there to contain the body of Clydog (Evans and Rhys 1893, 193–95). In Cornwall, the holy woman Saint Endelienta was a protector of cattle, for she lived only on cows' milk. Nicholas Roscarrock in his *The Lives of the Saints* tells how her burial place was found by animal divination: "When she perceived the day of her death drew nigh, she entreated her friends after her death to lay her dead body on a bed and to bury her there where certain young stots, bullocks, and calves of a day old should draw her, which being done they brought her to a place which at that time was a mirey waste ground, and a great quagmire on top of a hill, where in time after there was a church built dedicated to her" (Baring-Gould and Fisher 1908, vol. 2, 366).

In March 687 in northern England, Saint Cuthbert, bishop of Lindisfarne, died. He was buried in the monastery on the island of

Lindisfarne. But in 875, an incursion by the Danish army from their base at Repton in the midlands forced the monks to flee. Along with their valuables, they took the remains of Cuthbert. Bishop Eardulph and his monks carried the bones around northern Northumbria for seven years, stopping at various churches for varying periods. Dug up again, Cuthbert's bones were brought to a place called Wardenlawe, where a sign was revealed to "a virtuous man" called Eadmer that the remains should be buried at Dunholme. The monks, searching for the place, overheard two women talking. One was telling the other that her lost cow was at Dunholme. The monks went with her to find the cow, and on the place where the cow was, they there built a church and buried Cuthbert. So the Dun Cow of Durham was commemorated later by a carving on the cathedral.

5

Eldritch Beings

The Dark World of the Indeterminate

The Spirit World

That the world teems with sentient spirits that activate events is an ancient belief. These spirits were individual actors in their own right, with their own motivations that might be benevolent, neutral, or malevolent toward humans. Seen as in some way to be like human beings, they knew what they were doing. They could be rewarded for good deeds, placated against their anger, or warded off by apotropaic means. The historic list of supernatural beings by Michael Aislabie Denham shows the vast range of named entities perceived by people in Britain in former times. Numerous similar beings exist in folklore from all over Europe and beyond.

To the ancient Greeks, the winds were individual beings under the control of the god Aeolus in a mountain on the island of Lipari. The Gauls ascribed the winds to Vintios, who resided on the holy mountain of the winds, Mont Ventoux in Provence. When the Christian religion came into being, belief in the animated nature of the world was not questioned but was reinterpreted. Destructive storm winds were deemed to be evil

Fig. 5.1. Gustave Doré's engraving of an incident in Orlando Furioso *where the knight Ruggiero encounters a wide variety of demons and monsters, all attempting to force him to enter Alcina's city.*

spirits by the early Christian Church. "Whenever the bell sounds, let the power of enemies retire, so also the shadow of phantoms, the assault of whirlwinds, the stroke of lightnings, the harm of thunders, the injuries of tempests and every spirit of the storm winds" is a formula ascribed to an eighth-century archbishop of York, Egbert. All earthly spirits were deemed to be invariably harmful and destructive demonic beings that should be suppressed. Eight hundred years later, in 1597, in his polemic against magic, *Christliche Bedencken und Erinnerung von Zauberei*, Hermann Wilken expressed this doctrine: "The earth, the water and the air are filled with devils and invisible evil spirits, which envy the human race, are filled with hatred toward it, and see it as their enemy."

The trial of Isobel Gowdie for witchcraft in Morayshire, Scotland, in 1662 is typical of the taxonomic detail demanded of the inquisitors. "Each witch has a 'sprite' to wait upon her, some appearing in 'sad dun, some in grass green, some in sea green, some in yellow.'" Those alleged to be of Gowdie's coven were named "Robert the Jakes, Sanders the Reed-Reever, Thomas the Fairy, Swein the Roaring Lion, Thief-of-Hell-Wait-upon-Herself and MacHector," among others (Anonymous 1852, 82). This set of characters resembles the cast of a play or the disguises

Fig. 5.2. The image of the witch is an archetype that appears in German Carnival guising.
Two masked guisers from Rottenburg, Germany.
(See also color plate 5.)

of people who appeared in Carnivals. Plays and Carnival were banned, of course, along with Christmas, in the Scotland ruled by the Puritan fanatic government of the Covenanters.

Taxonomy of the Indeterminate

Michael Aislabie Denham (1801–1859) was a collector of folklore who published numerous erudite articles on traditional lore and practices, including articles in William Hone's *Everyday Book,* which circulated widely. After his death his abundant work was collected together by the new Folk-Lore Society and published in two volumes titled *The Denham Tracts* (1892 and 1895).

In volume 2 is a remarkably comprehensive list of terrifying mythological, magical, phantom, supernatural, and otherworldly appearances and beings from a time "seventy or eighty years ago and upward . . . when the whole world was so overrun with ghosts, boggles, bloody-bones, spirits, demons, ignis fatui, brownies, bug-bears, black dogs, specters, shellycoats, scarecrows, witches, wizards, barguests, Robin-Goodfellows, hags, night-bats, scrags, breaknecks, fantasms, hobgoblins, hobhoulards, boggy-boes, dobbies, hob-thrusts, fetches, kelpies, warlocks, mock-beggars, mum-pokers, Jimmy-burties, urchins, satyrs, pans, fauns, sirens, tritons, centaurs, calcars, nymphs, imps, incubusses, spoorns, men-in-the-oak, hellwains, fire-drakes, kit-a-can-sticks, Tom-tumblers, melch-dicks, larrs, kitty-witches, hobby-lanterns, Dick-a-Tuesdays, Elf-fires, Gyl-burnt-tails, knockers, elves, raw-heads, Meg-with-the-wads, old-shocks, ouphs, pad-foots, pixies, pictrees, giants, dwarfs, Tom-pokers, tutgots, snapdragons, sprets, spunks, conjurers, thurses, spurns, tantarrabobs, swaithes, tints, tod-lowries, Jack-in-the-wads, mormos, changelings, redcaps, yeth-hounds, colt-pixies, Tom-thumbs, black-bugs, boggarts, scar-bugs, shag-foals, hodge-pochers, hob-thrushes, bugs, bull-beggars, bygorns, bolls, caddies, bomen, brags, wraithes, waffs, flay-boggarts, fiends, gallytrots, imps, gyrtrashes, patches, hob-and-lanthorns, gringes, boguests, bonelesses, Peg-powlers, pucks, fays, kidnappers, gally-beggars, hudskins, knickers, madcaps, trolls, robinets, friars' lanthorns, silkies, could-lads, death-hearses, goblins, hob-headlesses, buggaboes, kows, or cowes, nickies, nacks (necks), wraiths, miffies, buckies, gholes, sylphs, guests, swarths, freiths, freits, gy-carlins (Gryre-carlings), pigmies, chittifaces, nixies, Jinny-burnt-tails, dudmen, hell-hounds, dopple-gangers, boggleboes, bogies, redmen, portunes, grants, hobbits,* hobgoblins, brown-men, cowies, dunnies, wirrikows, allholdes, mannikins, follets, korreds, lubberkins, cluricauns, kobolds, leprechauns, kors, mares, puckles, korigans, sylvans, succubuses, black-men, shadows, banshees, lianhanshees, clabbernappers, Gabriel-hounds, mawkins, doubles, corpse lights or candles, scrats, mahounds, trows, gnomes, sprites, fates, fiends, sybils, nick-nevins, whitewomen, fairies, thrummy-caps, cutties and nisses, and apparitions of every shape, make, form, fashion, kind and description, that there was not a village in England that had not its own particular ghost. Nay, every lone tenement, castle or mansion-house, which could boast of any antiquity, had its bogle, its spectre or its knocker. Every green lane had its boulder-stone on which an apparition kept watch at night. Every common had its circle of fairies belonging to it." (Denham 1895, 77–80)

This remarkably comprehensive list of eldritch and otherworldly powers, entities, and beings reminds us of the sheer abundance of forms that have been seen or visualized over a vast period of time. Some have been interpreted as the spirits of dead people, others as autonomous sprites that belong to an eldritch, otherworldly realm that intersects with the everyday world at particular points and times. All of them have their conventional depictions, which may appear in vernacular art and as characters in guising and mumming. The diversity of appearance and attributes of just one class of these, the Boggart or Bogey Man, may be presented as an example of the complex manifestations and ramifications of these beings in folklore, the paranormal, and popular culture.

---

*This is the first known reference to "Hobbits," later made famous by J. R. R. Tolkien.

The Bogey Man

A lifetime resident of the industrial city of Sheffield in northern England once told me that, in the 1950s, when he was a boy, he would lie in bed at night while hearing a mysterious metallic hammering noise. It was not the recognizable noise of heavy steam hammers from the steelworks. Mothers told their children, who had no idea what the mysterious noise was, that it was a warning from the Bogey Man, who punishes naughty children. So they should behave, or he would come for them and take them away. The existence of the Bogey Man was indisputable; the children had the evidence of their own ears.

In fact, the bogie man was a wheel-tapper, an employee of British Railways who worked at night in the train yards, tapping with a long metal hammer at the wheels on the bogies (trucks) under the trains. By the ring of the metal, the bogie man could tell whether the wheels were sound and serviceable or cracked, in which case the vehicle would be taken out of service and repaired. Although as a child in London, I (the present author) lived a third of a mile south of the mainline Euston station, I never heard the wheel-tappers there. They were too far away. But, even so, my mother used to terrify me with the threat of the Bogey Man, with the fiendish rhyme:

The Bogey Man is coming.
He's coming here today.
The Bogey Man is coming.
You can't get away.

The Bogey Man is coming.
He's coming to get you.
The Bogey Man will get you,
No matter what you do.

Whichever folk poet wrote this one, he or she understood well how to define the threat, escalate it, and pronounce its imminent inevitability. Contemporary politicians use exactly the same technique to drum up threats and use them as justification for extreme measures. As presented by threatening mothers, the Bogey Man was a frightening figure, the embodiment of naked terror. I was told that he was out to get me personally, that I could do nothing against his overwhelming presence, and that my inevitable destruction must follow. Sometimes, lying in bed, I felt and saw his (or its) dark presence looming in a corner on the wall, towering larger than a mortal man, menacing me with imminent attack. He was a shadowy, empty humanoid form. I could sense his indistinct penumbral outline, a liminal entry point to the emptiness of the void, whose substance is nothingness.

Folkloristically, the Bogey Man predates the days of the railway maintenance crews. He or it appears all over Great Britain under many local traditional names—Bugbear, Bogle, Boggle, Boggle-Bo, Boo-Man, Boodyman, Bugaboo, Jigaboo, the Black Ghost, Black Parr, Old Bogy, Old Blunderhazard, Miles's Boy, Simon Harcourt, the Sackman, Nut Nan, and the Clapcan—and under the generic name Boggard or Boggart. The Boggart makes its presence known through loud bumps, the noise of heavy metal weights trailing across the floor, and the rattling of chains: sounds that are somewhat similar to the metallic sounds of the bogie man testing the wheels in the nighttime yards of British Railways. The Bogey Man has been identified with Old Bogy, which, like Old Nick, Old Sam, and Old Scratch, is one of the bynames of the personification of evil, the devil. His connection with children is that, like the East Anglian demon Miles's Boy, with his big sack, he is said to capture children and take them to hell to be tormented by the devil. In this, he is a one-entity version of the Christian view of the multitude of the Furious Host or Wild Hunt riding across the land gathering up living people.

In *Lancashire Folk-Lore,* John Harland and T. T. Wilkinson gave a good definition: "What is a Boggart? A sort of ghost or sprite. But what is the meaning of the word Boggart? Brand says that 'in the northern parts of England, *ghost* is pronounced *gheist* and *guest.* Hence *bar-guest,* or *bar-gheist.* Many streets are haunted by a guest, who assumes many strange appearances, as a mastiff-dog, &c. It is a corruption of the Anglo-Saxon *gast,* spiritus, anima.' Brand might have added that *bar* is the term for gate in the north, and that all the gates of York are named 'bars,' so that a *bar-*

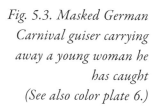

Fig. 5.3. Masked German Carnival guiser carrying away a young woman he has caught (See also color plate 6.)

gheist is literally a gate-ghost; and many are the tales of strange appearances suddenly seen perched on the top of a gate or fence, whence they sometimes leaped upon the shoulders of the scared passenger" (Harland and Wilkinson 1867, 49). The East Anglian dialect word *bogg* means "sturdy, self-sufficient, petulant." This is the unpredictable and dangerous nature of the Bogey Man. One explanation of the origin of Bogey Men is that they are ghosts of people who committed suicide or murder, murder victims, or ghosts of unjust oppressive landlords. Denied rest in the proper place, their spirits wander the Earth aimlessly, doing mischief. The Bogglebo or Bugaboo is another name for a Boggart, but this entity also appears in female form. A folktale from northeastern England tells of a witch called Old Bogglebo, who, during a storm, forced Jock the Keelman to ferry her across the mouth of the River Wear to Sunderland. When they arrived, a black cat leapt ashore, and the ferryman did not get paid his fare. Whether she was a human witch or a supernatural being is unknowable.

Harland and Wilkinson classified Boggarts into two kinds. The worse of the two are those who haunt particular places in the landscape and attack wayfarers. These include Boggarts who appear in animal form, most frequently as dogs. In East Anglia, encountering the dog called Black Shuck is an omen of one's impending death. The second kind is less dangerous but nevertheless oppressive and difficult to get rid of. They are the House Boggarts or Laboring Goblins, sprites that "are by turns both useful and troublesome to the farmers of the district where they choose to reside." This kind of Boggart revels in carrying out mad and dangerous pranks. When in a good mood, the Boggart would work to help the farmer, which in traditional times meant harnessing horses, loading carts, feeding the cattle, and gathering in the hay, but when in a bad mood, the same Boggart would smash dairy utensils, turn animals loose into the woods, tie cows together by their tails, prevent butter from churning, and sabotage the harvesters. The Boggart, sitting out of reach on one of the crossbeams in the barn, would grin with delight at the mischief he had done. Inside a house plagued by a Boggart, bedclothes are torn off in the night and invisible hands drag people down the stairs, one leg at a time. The Bogey Man appears as a capricious, malicious entity, often as an instrument of judgment and retribution. He is one who comes for those who have transgressed in some way, whether they be children who misbehave or wayfarers who stray into a locus terribilis territory where humans ought not to trespass.

Sitting on the crossbeam of the barn, the Boggart recalls the man personating the devil at initiations into rural fraternities of farm workers, such as the Society of the Horseman's Grip and Word or the Confraternity of the Plough, held in the barn called "the Horsemen's Hall." In former times in Britain, the appearance of grim, disguised, masked people at night, rattling chains and making low noises conjured up fears that Old Bogy was on the prowl. The human guisers responsible for these routs were out for a purpose, as often such disguises were used by workers on strike to terrorize and punish those who they deemed were wrongdoers, such as workers who broke a strike and continued to work. The word *bogyphobia* was coined in the nineteenth century to describe fear of the Bogey Man, for his human counterparts were indeed to be feared.

The Bogey Man also entered the sporting world. About 1890 in England, the golf club at Coventry standardized the number of shots as the ground score of each hole. This score became known as the bogey. In 1895, a writer in the *Strand Magazine* noted that "Bogey is an imaginary golfer who always plays the game as well as it ought to be played.

He is the Demon of the Links, whom it is hard to beat, Matches against Bogey are regularly played. Perhaps, in the imagination of golfers, he takes many shapes" (Anonymous 1895b, 120). An illustration of Bogey by W. A. Wickham, reproduced in figure 5.4, shows him as a pixie-like being surrounded by smaller sprites, one of whom blows the ball into the hole.

Golfing folklore tells of the name Bogey originating from a player, C. A. Wellman, who once said to Dr. Browne of Great Yarmouth golf club of an outstanding player: "That player of yours is a regular Bogey Man," the inference being (even if jokingly) of supernatural powers. The British military march written in 1914 by Lieutenant F. J. Ricketts, "Colonel Bogey March," refers to the golfing bogey. It was made infamous in World War II, with added lyrics beginning "Hitler has only got one ball. . . ." Today, in golf, a bogey is a score of one over par; with par, the number of strokes for each hole, having taken over from the ground score that gave rise to the original bogey. In soccer,

Fig. 5.4. Bogey by W. A. Wickham, 1895

supporters call a team that always appears to beat one's own team more often than it ought to statistically, a bogey team. Again, there is a hint of symbolic power about the name that emanates from bogydom, the dominion of Old Bogy.

The Bogey Man as a figure to frighten children appeared in a children's board game in the British Globe Series (proprietary games), sold from the late nineteenth century onward, called the Bogie Man. The printed picture on the box lid shows children running from a man who holds a staff on which a Halloween pumpkin lantern is fixed. It is covered with a hood and a ghostly white sheet that hangs down. The form of the frightening figure on a staff parallels the skull on a stick, usually with horns, encountered in European folk dancing and guising.

In 1932, a record made for children by British bandleader Henry Hall was titled "Hush! Hush! Hush! Here Comes the Bogey Man." The song warned children of the dangers of the Bogey Man but also gave them means to thwart his threat. Much later, the heavy metaller Yngwie Malmsteen wrote a song called "The Bogey Man," in this case the ghost of a hanged man, in which he sings, "I am the sum of all your fears." Symbolically, as a "frightening figure," the Bogey Man is none other than a personification of death, from which none can escape. We try to be somewhere else at the moment when the Grim Reaper is making his rounds. But we know that there is no ultimate escape from

Fig. 5.5. Ram's skull on pole carried by a Ramrugge morris dancer, Whittlesea, England (See also color plate 7.)

his somber power except for that short little while before he catches up with us and we are cast irrevocably into the impenetrable gloom of the abyss. The Bogey Man is thus an image of truth, even when presented in absurd form.

The Color of the Supernatural

The color of dress is significant in otherworldly beings, whether sprites, fairies, elves, trolls, or the myriad other entities enumerated by Denham. In 1860, Thomas Keightley wrote, "The Alfar still live in the memory and traditions of the peasantry of Scandinavia. They also, to a certain extent, retain their distinction into White and Black. The former, the Good Elves, dwell in the air, dance on the grass, or sit in the leaves of trees; the latter are regarded as an underground people, who frequently inflict sickness or injury on mankind; for which there is a particular kind of doctor called Kloka män, to be met with in all parts of the country" (Keightley 1860, 78). On the island of Rügen in the Baltic, three kinds of dwarfs were recognized: White, Brown, and Black. White dwarfs worked gold and silver, Brown dwarfs were capable of transformation, and Black dwarfs were blacksmiths—iron and steel workers (Keightley 1860, 174–76).

There is a story from Rügen that tells of a farmer who captured a Black dwarf and as a bargain for his release, asked him to make an iron plough. He did so, and "the smallest foal or the littlest horse could draw it through the ground," through the heaviest of clay loam (Keightley 1860, 197–200). The almost magically transformative iron plough was the foundation of the Scottish secret rural fraternity of ploughmen, the Society of the Horseman's Grip and Word, which "ploughed up the flagstones of old Aberdeen" and brought hitherto unploughable land into productive use (Rennie 2009, passim). To those who saw the remarkable transformation in agriculture made by the iron plough, it could only have come from a supernatural source.

There are many tales of shape-shifting phantoms that played tricks on people. Localized sprites such as the Hedley Kow sometimes attracted folklore collectors, such as William Henderson (1879) and

John Jacobs (1894). Henderson described this sprite's antics: "The Hedley Kow was a bogie, mischievous rather than malignant, which haunted the village of Hedley, near Ebchester. His appearance was never very alarming, and he used to end his frolics with a horse-laugh at the expense of his victims. He would present himself to some old dame gathering sticks, in the form of a straw, which she would be sure to take up and carry away. Then it would become so heavy she would have to lay her burden down, on which the straw would become 'quick' [i.e., alive —N.P.], rise upright, and shuffle away before her, till at last it vanished from her sight with a laugh and a shout" (Henderson 1879, 270–71). The Kow also appeared in other forms, as a cow, which would trouble the milkmaid before escaping with a loud laugh, and as a horse, which, when harnessed to a cart, would slip away "like a knotless thread" just as the farmer was about to drive off. This element of trickery and misrule attributed to supernatural beings is also an important part of human disguising, in which the Fool makes a fool of others.

The borderland of England and Scotland is a region that once was a lawless land of tyrannical lords, cattle thieves, outlaws, and family blood feuds. According to William Henderson (1813–1891), "sites of tyranny," especially border castles, were frequented by an evil sprite called Redcap, "a short, thickset, old man with long prominent teeth, skinny fingers armed with talons like eagles, large eyes of a fiery red color, grisly hair streaming down his shoulders, iron boots, a pikestaff in his left hand, and a red cap on his head" (Henderson 1879, 253). Redcap attacked and stoned travelers and soaked his cap in their blood. Old Redcap plays an important role in the "Border Ballad" of Lord Soulis, composed by John Leyden from a Northumbrian legend. Soulis was lord of Hermitage Castle, a strategic stronghold in the borderlands. Soulis was a cruel and hated tyrant who oppressed his own vassals, servants, and slaves as much as he did his enemies.

> *Lord Soulis he sat in Hermitage Castle*
> *And beside him Old Redcap sly:*
> *"Now tell me, thou sprite, who art meikle of might,*
> *The death that I must di(ille)"*

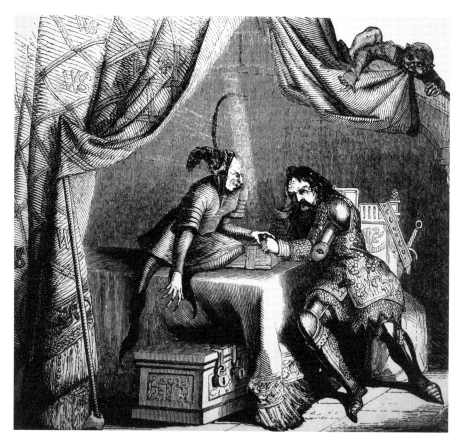

Fig. 5.6. The demon Redcap and Lord Soulis, 1847 engraving

By magic the familiar sprite Old Redcap made Soulis woundproof so he could not be harmed by edged weapons, neither could he be bound by chain or rope. But his enemies found a magical way of overcoming Old Redcap's spell by making chains of sand and chaff into ropes, binding Lord Soulis, and he was boiled to death in a cauldron inside the stone circle on Nine Stanes Rigg (Pennick 2019a, 107–9).

Butz

Pratteln in Canton Basel in Switzerland has a performance that involves *Rössli* or *zweibeinigen Pferdchen,* men dressed in horse costumes and pulling a wagon in which sits Butz. Butz at Pratteln is a *Strohpuppen*, a figure of a man made from clothes stuffed with straw and wearing a mask while sitting on a barrel. It is said that the figure represents the god of wine, Bacchus, which is appropriate for Carnival time. In Hanau, the Rölleibutzen appear at Fastnacht (Shrovetide). In Villingen, a man in a donkey mask dragging a harrow covered with greenery is called the *Butzesel*. Saint Butzewärk is also a Fastnacht character, the cry "*Katzabutzarola!*" is one of the many shouts of members of the Butzenzunft (Butz guild) in a *Butzenlauf* outing. In the eldritch dimension, a *Butzemann* is a nonhuman entity, a *Schreckgespenst* (frightening spirit or ghost)—the bogey man who makes himself known by knocking and rattling sounds. So the appearance of the Butzesel, the Rölleibutzen, and their companions is personation by humans of beings from the nonmaterial world.

Fig.5.7. Butzesel guiser wearing donkey-head mask and dragging vegetation, Villingen, Germany (See also color plate 8.)

6

The Furious Host

The Fairy Rade and the Wild Hunt

Apparitions of otherworldly processions and rides are widespread in northern European folklore. Stories of people taken away into the Otherworld by such riders reappear in contemporary accounts of out-of-body and near-death experiences. Elements of these wild processions are present in traditional customs such as the Perchtenlauf and Plough Monday. These spectral rides are variously known as the Fairy Rade, the Furious Host, and the Wild Hunt. The Fairy Rade describes rides and processions of the trooping fairies across the land in Celtic countries. This is not a terrifying rout like the Furious Host and the Wild Hunt but a stately procession. Riding on white horses, they are accompanied sometimes by music. The Furious Host and the Wild Hunt do not restrict themselves to the ground or particular pathways but also fly though the air. The Fairy Rade travels on the ground, often on roads or fairy paths, which are usually imperceptible. In Ireland, these paths are usually straight and link the ancient earthworks called Raths, which cover the underground dwelling places of the fairies. Misfortune will befall any human who disrupts or builds on a fairy path. In the west of England, such a path is called a "trod."

Fairy paths can even be underwater. In the Irish tale "The Black

Dog" we are told that sometimes the cave fairies make a straight path in the sea under the water from one island to another, all paved with coral. Fishermen told of a black band of little men with black dogs passing and repassing (Anonymous [1893] 2015, 91). A Scottish form of the Fairy Rade is the hunting of the Seelie Court. Here, the fairies rode in three groups. The first were on brown horses, the second on grays, and the third on horses "white as the driven snow." The third group contained the king and queen and sometimes a shadowy figure called Kilmoulie, who was seen by some as the devil. But the Fairy Rade appears quite sedate compared with the destructive power of the Furious Host and the Wild Hunt.

The Fairy Rade was illustrated by artist Joseph Noel Paton (1821–1901) in his painting *The Fairy Raid: Carrying a Changeling, Midsummer Eve,* now in Kelvingrove Art Gallery, Glasgow. It depicts a legend told in Scotland and Wales in which the fairies take a human child and leave a sickly fairy child in its place. By means of magical acts, the child's mother is able to force the fairies to return her child at a crossroads as the Fairy Rade passes.

> *Betwixt the haw-trees and the mead*
> *"The Fairy Rade" came glimmering on.*
> *A creamy cavalcade did speed*
> *O'er the green lawn.*

Thus wrote the Louisville, Kentucky, poet Madison Julius Cawein (1865–1914) in his book *Blooms of the Berry* (1887). Unlike the Wild Hunt, these fairy processions are enchanting rather than terrifying, though they do have a malicious dimension.

The Furious Host and the Wild Hunt are far more powerful and dangerous. In his *Teutonic Mythology,* Jacob Grimm commented, "They sweep through forest and air in whole companies with a horrible din. This is the widely spread legend of the furious host, the furious hunt, which is of high antiquity, and interweaves itself, now with gods, now with heroes" (Grimm 1888, 916). From a Christian perspective, the main protagonist is the devil. In his *The Anatomy of*

Melancholy, Robert Burton (1577–1640) wrote, "The Devil himself seems to take the opportunity of foul and tempestuous weather to agitate the spirits and vex our souls; for as the sea waves, so are spirits and humours in our bodies tossed with tempestuous winds and storms." Bands of horsemen rampaging across the country and bringing rapine and destruction to defenseless villagers were not unknown in ancient Europe. Picts, Goths, Vikings, Mongols, and Tartars operated in that way, as did the later and more organized armies that rampaged across mainland Europe from the sixteenth to the twentieth centuries. Irresistible destructive forces descending suddenly on one's home are an ever-present threat.

A vision of a supernatural host, which is often cited as the Wild Hunt, comes from the *Historia Ecclesiastica* by Ordericus Vitalis (1075–1142) of the Abbey of Saint Evroul in France, who recorded a sighting at Bonneval in 1091. Walchelin, the priest of Saint Aubin's church there, reported that on the first of January that year he was returning from visiting a sick person when he had to hide from what he thought was a rampaging military force. However, when his way was blocked by a giant knight with a club, he witnessed a purgatorial procession led by people carrying animals on their shoulders and necks, laden with household goods as if they were plunder. He recognized people from the village who had died recently, biers carrying dwarfs with barrel-shaped heads, and two "Ethiopians" carrying a beam between them on which sat a demon whipping a man hanging beneath, whom he recognized as a well-known murderer. Women riding in finery were seated on saddles studded with red-hot nails. No dogs were reported, but this cavalcade of bizarre figures and torment Walchelin interpreted as Herlechin's rabble (Joynes 2001, 66–73).

What Walchelin claimed to have seen was far from the Wild Hunt or an early French version of the animal-skin-clad guisers of midwinter festivities and certainly not a troupe of comedy actors on the way to a gig. It fits more with Christian visions of the fate of the unworthy dead, such as the horrors experienced by those who entered the cave of Saint Patrick's Purgatory in Ireland. Visions of the dead passing by are associated with a number of festal days in the year, sometimes giving the observer a glimpse of those who were bound to die in the forthcoming year.

An early sighting of an authentic Wild Hunt is recorded from England in *The Peterborough Continuation of the Anglo-Saxon Chronicle* for the year 1127 during the reign of King Henry I. "After February 6th many people both saw and heard a whole pack of huntsmen" in a royal park near to Peterborough. This was such a striking event that it warranted an entry in the *Chronicle*. (Joynes 2001, 74–76). The earliest record of King Herla's Rade is by Walter Map (ca. 1140–1210) in the twelfth century. An early name for the Wild Hunt, the Mesnée d'Hellequin, or Familia Herlequin, is possibly derived from the Wild Hunter King Herla (Old English, Herel-Cyning) of ancient British origin, the Household of Herlathing. Harlequin's antecedent appeared in the *Jeu de la Feuillère* by Adam de la Halle (1240–1287), and the demon Alichino is one of the Malebranche (evil claws) in hell in the *Divine Comedy* of Dante Alighieri (ca. 1265–1321). The character Arlecchino entered the Italian comedy about 1560, appearing in the early Commedia dell'Arte. A stock character of performances in Italy and France, he became Harlequin in the English pantomimes and harlequinades. A ninth-century French knight, Hellequin of Boulogne, who was killed fighting Norse settlers, is an unlikely origin of this tradition.

In Wales, it is the underworldly being Gwynn ap Nudd who rides with white hounds with blood-red ears. Gwynn, the guardian of the door between Abred, the world we inhabit, and Annwn, the underworld, has servants dressed half in red and half in blue, signifying hot and cold together, the principle of the union of opposites. The terrifying ride called Oskoreia, Åsgårdsreien, and the Odensjakt in various Scandinavian traditions is the Wild Hunt of Odin, an irresistible chaotic assembly of spectral beings riding through the sky in storms. In Slovenia, it is led by either Jarnik, the Slavic war god otherwise known as Jarilo or Gerovit, or by Volčjí Pastir, the wolf-herdsman.

In his *Teutonic Mythology*, Grimm wrote, "Wuotan, the god of war and victory, rides at the head of this aerial phenomenon; when the Mecklenburg peasant of this day hears the noise of it, he says '*de*

Wode tüt' . . . so in Pomerania and Holstein '*Wode jaget*,' Wode hunts. Wuotan appears riding, driving, hunting, as in Norse sagas, with valkyries and einherjar in his train; the procession resembles an army. . . . [In Scandinavia] the phenomenon of the howling wind is referred to as Odin's wagon. As that of thunder is to Thor's. On hearing a noise at night, as of horses and carts, they say in Sweden '*Oden far forbi*' [Odin drives close by]." In nineteenth-century Germany, Jacob Grimm noted people using the oath "bi Wuotunges her" (by Wotanc's Host) (Grimm 1877, 916).

Westphalia and Lower Saxony have the legend of the ghostly huntsman Hackelbarend or Hackelnberg. (There are various spellings varying with locality.) In Lower Saxony, he is identified with Hans von Hackelnberg, who died in 1521. He was in charge of the hunting hounds of the Duke of Braunschweig (Brunswick). Various versions of the legend agree that he was a huntsman who spurned the last rites on his deathbed—"The Lord may keep his heaven, so leave me to my hunting"—and so was condemned after his death to hunt night and day without rest until the Last Judgment. As with the numerous European guising traditions performed just after the winter solstice, Hackelnberg

Fig. 6.1. Woman captured in a net by Fastnacht guisers in long-trunked hood masks

is said to ride only during the Twelve Days of Christmas, which contradicts other versions that say he must ride continuously. As the baying of the hounds can be heard, a night owl called Tutosel precedes the spectral hunt. At the sound of the owl and hounds, people would lie face down on the ground to let them pass. Tutosel was a renegade nun called Ursula who joined Hackelnberg and served in owl form as his pathfinder. This is, of course, a Christian interpretation of a much

Fig. 6.2. Krampus, Pongau, Austria (A Krampus is a demonic figure played by a man dressed in animal furs and wearing a frightening carved wooden mask, often with tusks or fangs, with horns on its head. Large metal bells hang from a belt, and the Krampus carries either a bundle of sticks or a horse's tail, which he uses to whip bystanders.) (See also color plate 9.)

more ancient pagan theme, linked to the parallel idea of the furious host's leader as an agent of the devil who collects damned souls and transports them to hell.

The Furious Host is also led by powerful goddesses and the ghosts of huntswomen: Perchta, Bertha or Frau Percht, and Mad Meg are among them. Perchta came to take away the souls of babies who died before they could be baptized. One explanation is that she carried them to the lakes of souls, where they waited in the waters to be collected by storks who would fly the souls to their new mothers for rebirth. Frau Percht is associated with the Perchtenlauf of Austria, where men in animal skins bedecked with horns race through nighttime villages at New Year in a version of the Wild Hunt.

The image of Mad Meg is of a warlike woman who strides alone amid mayhem and massacre through lands devastated by deadly conflict. Otherwise known as Dulle Griet, Swatte Griet, Schwarze Gret, Booze Margriet, and Black Maggie, she is associated with Saint Margaret. She is the female dragon-slaying saint who appeared in some European dragon-guising performances, including at Norwich. In Schleswig-Holstein, she is seen as having two aspects—one beneficial and one destructive. When beneficial, she is Margaret, and when destructive, Mad Meg. In Westphalia, she is a destructive character participating in the Furious Host. A painting by Pieter Breughel de Oude, *Dulle Griet* (1562), depicts a middle-aged woman wearing armor and a steel helmet, carrying a sword. She strides through a landscape of violence and destruction, with scenes of warfare, mayhem, and killing and the Maw of Hell teeming with demons. Like the Furious Host, an infernal band is on the rampage, and toadlike goblins and humans dance together on the platform of a trained linden tree. She carries an array of containers, bags, baskets, a dish, a plate, and a dripping pan. The dripping pan appears also as an attribute of the mumming characters Old Hob and Beelzebub in English mummers' plays.

A Burgundian siege cannon of twenty-inch caliber made in 1449 by Jehan Cambier in the Arsenal at Mons (now in Belgium) was one of the earliest cannons and one of the largest and most fearsome weapons of the day. It was reputed to be able to fire a gunstone of more than three hundred pounds for two miles. Kept today in Edinburgh Castle, it is called Mons Meg. Another heavy cannon, Megge, was among the artillery of the army of King Edward IV of England in its invasion of France in 1475. (Similarly, Big Bertha was a heavy 42-centimeter-caliber siege artillery piece made by the German arms manufacturer Krupp in 1914 and used at the beginning of World War I to bombard the forts at Liège in Belgium.)

Related to Frau Percht and Mad Meg is the Fastnacht guising character Greth Schell at Zug in Switzerland, whose guise is as a woman carrying a man in a basket on her back. She is accompanied by six masked figures called Löli. Greth Schell is not what she appears to be, for her body is a life-size puppet, and the person inside the costume is the man in the basket.

As the story goes, a lady called Frau Gauden was addicted to hunting and, like Hackelnberg, thought she would rather hunt than "win heaven." One day, while she was hunting with her twenty-four daughters, they all were so entranced with it that they said "hunting is better than heaven." Suddenly, her daughters found themselves transformed into horses and hounds, four horses to pull her carriage and the rest to hunt as dogs. So they all were cursed to hunt until the Last Judgment, but only during the twelve days of Christmas. On the eves of Christmas and New Year, Frau Gauden goes through village streets, and wherever she finds an open door, she sends in a dog. The dog cannot be driven out by the inhabitants. It whines for a year, bringing sickness and death on the household and fire to the house. After a year, if the inhabitants survive, it returns to the hunt as it passes through the village. If they kill the dog, it becomes a stone that cannot be thrown away, for it returns under its own power to become a living dog that night. So doors must be kept locked when Frau Gauden is about.

In the Netherlands, the spectral hunt is called either Derk met de Hondjes (Derk with the Little Hounds) or Derk mit den Beer (Derk with the Bear). In Britain, from Saint Germans in Cornwall, comes the story of Dando and his dogs, a local version of the Wild Hunt. As with Hackelnberg and Frau Gauden, Dando was a priest who pre-ferred hunting to religious devotions. One Sunday when he should have been at church, he and his huntsmen ran out of drink in their flasks. "If none can be found on Earth, go to hell for it!" he cried (a reference to the estate called Earth, where they were hunting). At that, a stranger who had joined the hunt rode up to him and offered him his flask, which contained the best brew of the aforementioned place. Dando drank it all, and the stranger, who, of course, was the devil, took him to hell. But sometimes, Dando and his hunt are heard riding across the land in a wild tantivy (Hunt 1865, series 1, 247), the Devil's Dandy Dogs are seen without the spectral huntsman.

In Northamptonshire, Thomas Sternberg notes, "The goblin huntsman and his train, the 'wütend heer' of the German peasantry, are known to the good people of this county by the name of 'wild men,' 'wild hounds,' and so forth. Both Whittlebury and Rockingham contend for the honor of his residence; and the wild whoop with which he cheers his hounds is still to be heard among the glades of both forests" (Sternberg 1851, 142). This ghostly hunt legend tells of a knight who fell in love with the beautiful daughter of a forest ranger but was rebuffed by her. So, devastated by her rejection, he killed himself by falling on his sword. The lady soon died as well, and the ghostly knight is doomed to hunt for her with his hounds through the forest until the end of time.

Fig. 6.3. Demonic guisers in black masks and horned animal-head caps, Wilflingen, German (See also color plate 10.)

The legend of Herne the Hunter appears first in William Shakespeare's play *The Merry Wives of Windsor* (1597). Herne is a ghostly hunter who appears in Windsor Great Park by a tree "with great ragged horns." This tree, called Herne's Oak, was a major landmark in the royal park. In 1792, Samuel Ireland added to the legend by stating that Herne had committed suicide by hanging and so was doomed to haunt the area. Whether Shakespeare meant that Herne had the horns or, more likely, that the tree had great ragged horns, as some do from dieback of the crown, is questionable. The name Herne and the word *horn* are close in sound. Trees that have been struck by lightning and have ragged horns are considered to possess special virtues. Grimm added to the speculation by suggesting that Herne was connected with the Wild Hunt. In 1929, in his *The History of the Devil—The Horned God of the West,* R. Low Thompson added more to the Herne corpus by connecting him with the Gallo-Roman god Cernunnos. This god, known from a damaged inscription of the Seine boatmen on the basal part of a Jupiter Column found in Paris, has become an iconic figure in modern paganism. People personating Cernunnos or Herne today wear antlers on their head.

The Wild Horde in Music and Art

"Åsgåardsreien" is an ancient Norwegian folk song that had cultural influence during the nineteenth century. "Åsgåardsreien," a poem by Johan Sebastian Cammermeyer Welhaven (1807–1873) influenced the famous *Åsgåardsreien* painting by Peter Nicolai Arbo, painted in Paris in 1872 and now in Oslo. It depicts Odin with a sword, Thor with his hammer, valkyries, and einherjar riding horses through the sky over a desolate landscape. Opus 10 by the composer Ole Olsen (1850–1927) is titled "Åsgåardsreien," which he describes as led by Thor, who is seeking out fighters from the battlefield. Another Wild Hunt painting of that era is *Der Wilde Jagd* (1889) by German artist Franz von Stuck (1863–1928). Richard Wagner's opera *Die Walküre* (1870) includes the famous *Der Walkürenritt* (The Ride of the Valkyries). In Norse mythology, the valkyries, "choosers of the slain," rode above the battlefield in another version of the Furious Horde, selecting the most heroic fallen warriors, whom they took to Valhalla to join the einherjar. Arbo's 1869 painting, *Valkyrja,* also now in Oslo, focuses on one of them riding in the sky with two ravens and her sisters in the background. *The Ride of the Valkyries* is also a painting by the British war artist William T. Maud (1865–1903). In it, the valkyries ride through the sky on white horses accompanied by two ravens. Maud also painted other Wagnerian themes and illustrated Constance Maud's book *Wagner's Heroines* (1896). The cowboy ballad "Ghost Riders in the Sky" is a more modern version of the theme.

7

Spectral Animals beyond the Wild Hunt

Phantom Dogs and Black Shuck

Spectral dogs play a significant role in the Fairy Rade and the Wild Hunt. The hounds who run with Gwynn ap Nudd are white with blood-red ears. The Devil's Dandy Dogs have horns and eyes like fiery saucers. They may destroy any human they encounter. The Wish-hounds, Yell Hounds, or Yeth Hounds are headless spectral dogs seen in the West Country of England. In Cornwall, they hunt the demon Tregeagle (Briggs 1977, 440). In Welsh tradition, the Cwn Annwn (underworld dogs or hell hounds) are known for their howl, which portends the death of anyone who hears it (Sikes 1880, 233). The "sky yelpers" called Gabriel Hounds or Gabriel Ratchets are a pack of spectral hounds with blood-red ears like the dogs of Gwynn ap Nudd, traveling high in the air. Sometimes they appear with human heads. If they stop and appear to hover over a house, that is a bad omen for the inhabitants, bringing misfortune or death (Briggs 1977, 183). A ratchet is an old name for a hound that hunts by scent.

Animal folklore straddles an uncertain boundary between actual living things that can be seen, touched, and trapped and the vague territory of things that are glimpsed or half-seen and never caught. In the days before naturalists set up systematic biological documentation, what was actually out *in the wilds* was indeed unknown. Any animal out of the ordinary was viewed as dangerous and probably demonic. During the nineteenth century, there were naturalists' reports of unknown or exotic beasts in Epping Forest, close to London. They could have been the classic phantom animals of folklore, but at least one of these animals was flesh and blood. First identified as a wolf, but later found to be a North African jackal, it was trapped and later exhibited in London Zoo under the name Charlie (Holmes 1892, cciv–ccix).

Dogs appear as a significant component of the Wild Hunt and also in the Fairy Rade, but they also appear singly. Traditional lore of various parts of Great Britain has stories of phantom dogs. They are well documented in eastern England, though they appear elsewhere. In Lancashire, phantom black dogs are called Trash or Skriker. In his *Folk-Lore of West and Mid Wales,* J. Ceredig Davies noted the Gwyllgi, the Dog of Darkness, who appeared near Lougharne in Carmarthenshire. It was "a mastiff with baleful breath and blazing red eyes" that appeared on a particular stretch of road (Davies 1911, 182–83). Phantom animals in general and dogs in particular are associated with liminal places such as boundary walls and thresholds, passageways, lanes, crossroads, and bridges. The East Anglian name Black Shuck is now the generic term for phantom black dogs. But in 1872, when John Glyde Jr. was writing about Norfolk phantom dogs, he located Old Shuck specifically at one place on the road from Beeston to Overstrand, Shuck's Lane (Glyde 1872, 65–66).

Now generally called Black Shuck in Norfolk and Shock in Suffolk, this phantom is commonly held to be a large black dog with huge blazing eyes and dragging a chain (Bunn 1977a, 3). Charles Roper, writing in 1893, commented that in Norfolk, "Old villagers still speak of having seen Shuck, a dark, hairy, wild-looking dog with luminous eyes, that tracked the lonely traveler's steps along road-side paths by night, mostly remaining in shadow, and seldom revealing his complete shape" (Roper 1893, 793). The Reverend E. S. Taylor of Martham stated that in East Norfolk, it was a "black shaggy dog, with fiery eyes of immense size, that visits churchyards at night," and he explained the name because "*shucky* is the Norfolk dialect for *shaggy*" (E.S.T 1850, 468; Glyde 1872, 65–66). Bob Trubshaw writes that both Black Shuck and Old Shock probably derive from the Old English word *scucca,* a "demon" (Trubshaw 1994, 8).

The meaning of the appearance of a phantom dog, either collectively as with the Cwn Annwn and the Gabriel Hounds or singly as with Black Shuck, is either taken as a warning of death in the specific locality or may actually be the cause of death. Bungay in Suffolk has a story of a black dog that appeared in the church during a severe storm on Sunday, August 4, 1577. Three people who touched the dog died. On the same day, a similar or the same dog was reported seven miles away at Blythburgh, also killing three. A dog appearing during a storm and taking human life before moving on recalls the dogs of the Wild Hunt, Hackelnberg, and Frau Gauden. An 1829 account from Overstrand, Norfolk, tells of a phantom dog appearing in the churchyard. It had "a rough, hard and shaggy back, and always, after he had gone, a scar would be found on the ground as if gunpowder had been exploded" ("Demon Dogs of Norfolk and Suffolk," *Eastern Daily Press,* July 2, 1894).

Ghostly dogs have been reported recurring in many places. In Dorset, one encountered occasionally at Pimperne was accompanied with the rattling of chains. It seems to have been associated with one particular, unnamed family. At Horton in Dorset, "a black dog is reported to run across Pot lane, but nobody owns up to seeing it" (Dacombe 1935, 122). A phantom white dog occasionally appearing on Mistley Hill near Manningtree, Essex, is said to indicate a forthcoming death in the local Norman family (Newman and Wilson 1952, 100). Here, its function as summoner of death parallels that of the Irish banshee. Another association of a black dog with death is a story from Winfarthing, Norfolk, recorded in the *Norwich Mercury* on January 28, 1944, when a local woman recounted how a large black dog approached her cottage and then vanished. Her grandfather died shortly afterward, and his death was attributed to the phantom dog. In the 1930s, a similar dog was seen by William Fell, a gamekeeper at Tolleshunt d'Arcy in Essex (Wentworth-Day 1973, 11–12). How credible some of these sightings are remains in question. Even in the nineteenth century, there were people who wore disguises to play pranks on superstitious people. In 1893, Roper wrote, "Periodically these old fears are reawakened by foolish jokers, who wrap themselves round in sheets, and carry something on their heads containing light and having two holes for glaring eyes. Then the rumor goes round that Shuck is about again, or that Shiner, as the villagers call Will-o'-the-wisp, has issued from the marshes on mischief bent, and for months women and children— yes, and men, too—go abroad in the dusky twilight trembling with uncontrollable horror" (Roper 1893, 793).

The spirit called the Church Grim is part of a body of beliefs that each churchyard has its ghostly protector against harmful witchcraft and the devil. Frequently, this is in the form of an animal, in England, a black dog (Gutch 1901, 127–28). In Sweden, the Kyrkogrim appears as a lamb, and in Denmark, a "grave-sow" (Henderson 1879, 274). It is said that these guardian animals were sacrificed as the first burial when the new churchyard was first consecrated, being buried on the northern side of the church so that their spirits would remain and watch against evil. Apparitions of these beings, appearing in stormy weather, were taken as an omen of death (Gutch 1901, 127–28). The Old English word *grima,* meaning "mask," also has the connotations of a specter or ghost.

In former times, the cruel method of putting down dogs was to hang them, just as it was customary to drown cats and kittens. An East Anglian saying recorded in 1830 by Robert Forby is "to sit where the dog was hanged," and a miserable person may have a "hang-dog look" about them. The saying refers to a succession of inexplicable small misfortunes, one after the other, when the comment was "surely I sit where the dog was hanged" (Forby 1830, vol. 2, 409). This infers that the place has been cursed by a dog that was hanged there or even that the spirit of the dog remains present to take its revenge on human beings. In the Chelmsford district of Essex is the traditional saying "the black dog is at his heel," said about anyone who appears on the verge of death (Newman and Wilson 1952, 100). Hanging dogs over a pond by a rope around the body is a folk practice in Bulgaria that is associated with the Shrovetide guising of the Koukers. The dog is suspended and then allowed to fall in the pond, after which it is supposed to be immune to rabies (Fol 2004, 57).

A Terrible Reality: Bokkenrijders
and Y Tarw Scotch

The Furious Host took on a frightening reality during the eighteenth century in the southern Netherlands. Between 1730 and 1775, in the province of Limburg, gangs of bandits called Bokkenrijders roamed the countryside, attacking homesteads, farms, and small communities and robbing, torturing, raping, and killing as they went. The Bokkenrijders belonged to a secret society of initiated and sworn members who wore masks and disguises. They appeared as a version of the Wild Hunt, with their ride of plunder and destruction supposedly taking them through the air on the backs of goats, as witches were reputed to do. A saying reputed to the Bokkenrijders was "across houses, across gardens, across stakes, even across Cologne and into the wine cellar," reflecting the folklore of witches' rides through keyholes and into the wine cellars of rich people's houses to steal their liquor. Some Bokkenrijders wore goatskins and masks in the form of goats' heads (Summers 1926, 136). They were anti-religious, wrote of Satan in their threatening letters, and burned churches. They were hunted by the authorities, who treated them as witches when they were captured, tortured, and tried. Of 1,178 suspected Bokkenrijders brought to trial, 468 were convicted and executed.

Britain during the Industrial Revolution (1780–1820) experienced a period of rural turmoil and violent disputes. During strikes, bands of working men put on disguises to roam at night, visiting cottages and houses to intimidate or punish strikebreakers, and in the country, farm laborers targeted unfair masters. In the early nineteenth century, the "Black Domain" of South Wales, an area with many coal and iron mines, became a cauldron of workers' resentment and unrest. About 1808, during the shortages caused by the Peninsular War against Napoléon in Spain, acts of sabotage and violence began and then coalesced into a movement called the Scotch Cattle. The origin of the name is disputed. At that time, cattle were raised in large numbers in Scotland and driven in large herds south into England, where they were sold for slaughter. But the word *scotch* also means "to stop something," such as the use of *scotches,* wooden wedges put against the wheels of rail wagons to prevent them from moving and running away down an incline.

According to a writer who went under the nom de plume Ignotus, the original leader of the Scotch Cattle was Ned, an English iron man who came into South Wales from Staffordshire seeking work. Given that at that time violent machine-breaking was taking place in various parts of England under the banner of the Luddites, supposedly led by the enigmatic General Ned Ludd, who wore a disguise, this is an intriguing claim (Ignotus 1867, 3). However, many of the autonomous groups of Scotch Cattle intimidated "strangers"—English and Irish workers who had come to Wales to work the mines. Each village had its own group of Scotch Cattle, but there was no overall command structure, which was typical with workers' fraternities in the days before organized trade unions. There was serious violence, sometimes bordering on guerrilla warfare. Industrial unrest included using firearms in attacks on canals and railways. In 1822 at Llanhilleth, Scotch Cattle arsonized thirty railway wagons full of coal, setting a fire that burned for four days. Intimidation of strikebreakers, or *blacklegs,* began by "twisting in" with anonymous letters, sometimes written in blood, that were delivered to houses, after which a gang of Scotch Cattle made a "midnight visit."

Members of these noisy gangs wore masks or kerchiefs over their faces, dressed in cowhides, and were led by a man in a bull mask and a bull skin -Y Tarw Scotch (the Scotch Bull). Others in the group had their faces blackened with coal dust and wore jackets inside-out or women's clothing. They carried horns that they blew and chains that they rattled, also making a low cattle-like sound. "They did not speak at all, but bellowed like a bull," as one witness reported. During what was called a "scotching," they smashed windows and forcibly entered buildings to trash the interiors, often beating the inhabitants without mercy. As they left, they painted an image of a bull's head in red on the door (Wilkins 1903, 178; Jones 1971, 220–49 passim).

In October 1834, a gang of Scotch Cattle attacked the house of Thomas Thomas and his wife at Bedwelly. As they attempted to force entry, a gun went off and shot Joan Thomas, who died of her wounds two days later. Some of the culprits were tracked down, and Edward

Morgan was tried and hanged at Monmouth Prison, though it was thought at the time that the real culprit had fled to America. Although this was a stern warning of what could happen, bands of Scotch Cattle continued to appear at times of turmoil. In 1850, there was an uprising of the Scotch Cattle in Aberdare, and in 1857, an intimidating letter was delivered that threatened to "tear out the hearts of all the men" and to "fix two of them on the horns of the bull" (*Cardiff and Merthyr Guardian,* December 26, 1857). By this time, legitimate trade unionism was on the rise, but as late as 1926, during the miners' strike that culminated in the General Strike, Scotch Cattle appeared again in South Wales (Francis 1976, 250).

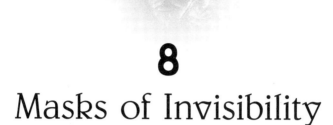

8

Masks of Invisibility

Disguise and Invisibility

Disguise and camouflage are means of not being recognized and not being seen. Literally, they produce invisibility, for someone can be in plain sight but not actually visible. The techniques of hunters and military Special Forces are intended to prevent their prey or adversaries from recognizing their presence. In guising, one becomes unidentifiable though the wearing of masks, face colorings, shape-altering costumes, and headgear. Some traditional guising costumes conceal the person's face with a mask, alter the shape of a person through padding, alter the bodily outline by means of ribbons and tatters, and alter the person's height by tall hats. It is impossible for anyone to tell the identity, age, size, or gender of a person so concealed.

An ancient tale of a helm of invisibility appears in the Greek myth of the Gorgon slayer Perseus, where it was called the "dog-skin of Hades" or the "helm of Hades," with Hades being the god of the underworld. The Old English *dernhelm* (the hidden protector) has the element *dern-*, which means "dark, hidden, secret, dire." The more modern English verb *to dern* means "to hide," from the Old English *diernan* (Old High German *tarnjan*). Derning has the sense of "darkening," as in the modern word *tarnish,* from which bright metal

Fig.8.1. Masked, padded figure, Villingen, Germany (See also color plate 11.)

becomes dull and dirty. The shiny surface becomes hidden by grime. The Old Norse word for a mask, *gríma,* also relates to darkening, as in the word grimy. In *Alvissmal* and the *Hervarar Saga, grima* also means "the shadow of night." German legend tells of the *Tarnkappe,* a cap or helm of invisibility. It appears as the *Tarnhelm* in the operas of Richard Wagner that are based on Germanic mythology.

The *Kormáks Saga* tells how Steinar Öndarson appeared at the Þórsnessþing gathering in a "bear skin coat with a mask in front of his face," the word for "mask" being *gríma* (*Kormáks Saga* 1902, 247). The bynames of Odin have several that refer to masking and disguise. He is Asagrim (the masked god), Grímnir (the masked one), Jarngrimr (iron mask), Fjölnir (the concealer), and Svipall (changing/fleeting shape). In modern English, a grim visage is a face set unmovingly in a determined way, like a mask. The Old English *egesgrima* is a mask with a frightening appearance, otherwise a horrible specter. The mask of the Terrible One, like the Gorgo, strikes fear into all who behold him. His is the same function as the Icelandic Aegishjalmur. Ysengrimus appears in the ancient tales of Reynard the Fox as a never satisfied, gluttonous wolf. According to Master Nivardus of Ghent, who was writing circa 1149,

Ysengrimus's snapping jaws sound like a sheet of iron struck on an anvil (Pleij 2001, 157). This could be a description of the jaws of a hobby animal like Snap, the dragon of Norwich.

Isengrind is a masked character who appears at the New Year at Horgen near Zürich in Switzerland. In modern English, to grimace is to "pull a face," changing one's appearance. East Anglian dialect has the verb *grimble*, "to cover with grime" (Forby 1830, vol. 2, 141). *Grime* can mean either "dirt" or "frost," as in the word *rime*. So it can refer to whitening the face with chalk or flour or darkening it with materials such as soot, dust, or clay. Darkening the face of a light-skinned person renders him or her much more difficult to recognize. It has been part of wintertime guising ceremonies since ancient times, appearing as far apart as Britain, Ireland, Scandinavia, Germany, the Balkans, and Turkey (And 1980, 88; Fol 2004, 45ff.).

Small human masks were part of larger decorative ensembles, such as on weapons, vessels, and memorial stones (Graham-Campbell 2013, 39–40). Masks and heads carved on buildings were called *búnar grímur* (Gunnell 1995, 87). A runestone dating from the tenth century with a mask carved on it was found at Århus in Jutland. It was set up, as the inscription tells us, by four warriors to memorialize their comrade Ful, who had died in battle. It bears the image of a mask in the Mammen style, with interlacing mustache and beard. A similar mask was carved on the lower guard of a bone sword hilt discovered at Sigtuna in Sweden. Its mustache is elongated to fit the shape of the guard. Another mask, similar to that on the Århus stone, was discovered in the silt during dredging of the harbor at Køge in Sjælland, Denmark. It is carved on a piece of antler fashioned as the handle of a walking stick (Graham-Campbell 2013, 107–8). An actual full-size wooden mask discovered at Stóraborg near Ejafjöll in Iceland resembles these Scandinavian mask representations in its shape and manner.

In the Norse sagas, people who put on a disguise become the role, and while they are in disguise, their true name is not mentioned. In J. R. R. Tolkien's *The Lord of the Rings,* the name Grima Wormtongue for the character who undermined King Theoden's actions reflects the mask that did not show the true face of the devious and false adviser.

Invisibility may also refer in part to the impossibility of telling the identity of a warrior dressed in armor. Standard bearers in the Roman army wore masks; it was the mark of the *signifier*. His identity could not be seen, and if a particular signifier fell in battle, another soldier could don the mask. So the appearance of the signifier, carrying the sacred standard of the legion, was unchanging. It was a form of immortality. Roman cavalry officers dressed in artful parade armor frequently had a human mask of metal as part of the helmet to cover the face. Ancient armor sometimes had a mask as a visor that could be raised.

Ysengrimus is the personal name of a mythical wolf, but the word *isengrim* also describes a mask covering the whole head, such as the mask helmet of an Anglian king that was excavated from his burial ship at Sutton Hoo in Suffolk, England. When the king wore it, he presented a grim visage to those who beheld him. He personated Jarngrimr, the iron-masked one. Vendel period mask helmets from Scandinavia are similar. In later medieval Europe, all-over plate armor included a helm with a visor, so there was no possibility of seeing the knight's face. So heraldry developed to identify individuals. The knight's shield was painted with his personal emblems, which were recorded and regulated by guilds of herals. Heraldry in England and Scotland is still controlled. In England, the College of Heralds, and in Scotland, the office of Lord Lyon, the king of arms regulate the use of heraldry. Scottish heraldry is regulated by law and strictly enforced, with penalties for those who invent their own coats of arms or add prohibited elements to shields. Several Scottish soccer clubs have been forced to change their badges by Lord Lyon or be prosecuted in the courts. It is a living tradition. Arthurian stories tell of knights who chose to conceal their identity by fighting in tournaments with a blank shield.

One of the powers ascribed to East Anglian toadmen is the ability to "walk out of the sight of men." Toadmen who followed the plough walked out of the sight of men on Plough Monday, when, with reddened, blackened, raddled, or masked faces, they wore clothes stuffed with straw to change their shape and covered them with tatters of cloth. In the darkness, they were in plain sight, but their identity was unknown to those who encountered them. Similarly, if they chose to "walk by night" as poachers, their disguises were impenetrable, and they were able to merge with the features of the darkened fields and woodland. Men in possession of the toad bone were credited with the power to see in the dark. Charles Roper tells of "a rustic living in the neighborhood of the Fen" who told him that "a team-man (horseman) living by Poppy Lot [a farm at Methwold, Cambridgeshire —N.P.] could allus do what he wanted. At night, no matter how dark the stable way, he had light enough o' his side to see what he wanted" (Roper 1893, 794–95). Toadmen were also reputed to wear magic caps that could open locked doors. "No door is ever closed to a toadman" was their maxim.

Fig. 8.2. Shapeless "flying" figure in a morris dance at Thornham, Norfolk

Actual caps of invisibility appear in folktales and magical texts. A medieval magical handbook (manuscript Clm 849) preserved in the Bayerische Staatsbibliothek in Munich, Germany, gives a means of gaining a cap of invisibility through ritual magic. It involves the magician making a magic circle and conjuring various spirits whom he compels to bring him the cap. When he gets it, he must exchange it for a white robe. The magician must return it three days later in exchange for the robe, which he must then burn. If he fails to do so, he will die within seven days (Thorndyke, 1964, 356–58; Kieckhefer 2000, 7–8). Thomas Keightley tells that on the northern German island of Rügen dwarfs wore brown caps with a silver bell that enabled them to "glide invisibly into people's houses, their caps rendering them imperceptible by all who have not similar caps" (Keightley 1860, 174). They were able to pass through the smallest keyholes, as in Patrick Kennedy's Irish folktale "The Witches' Excursion," where witches, wearing the *cappeen d'yarrag,* the "red cap," were enabled to fly on straws and enter through keyholes unseen (Kennedy (1893) 2015, 431–33).

Scientific Camouflage in Nature and Warfare

There are many examples of camouflage in nature. The coloration of birds such as the eastern screech owl blends with the patterns of the bark on trees where they roost. The patterning on many spiders and moths also resembles the tree bark on which they live, while the stick insect blends with its environment by resembling the twigs of the plants on which it lives. Living in a predominantly white Arctic environment, the polar bear is white. The white willow ptarmigan has white winter plumage that blends with the snow. The Arctic hare is white in the winter and brown in the summer.

As the natural world was catalogued by naturalists and taxonomists, nineteenth-century biologists and artists took an interest in the relationships between pattern, color, and the environment. In 1890, Sir Edward Bagnall Poulton wrote his influential book *The Colour of Animals,* in which he detailed "protective resemblances" in insects and other animals, which had arisen by natural selection. Those creatures most closely resembling the substrate on which they live were less likely to be seen by predators and eaten, leading to their survival and reproduction. Abbot Handerson Thayer's theories of "concealing-coloration" in the animal kingdom and "the laws of disguise through color and pattern" were published in 1909. These writers analyzed the forms of patterning in animals and determined several principles that were used later in designing military camouflage. Apart from patterns and colors that resemble the trees, rocks, and leaves that the animals inhabit, these included countershading or shadow elimination in which the animal's color is lighter below, such as a white underbelly, destroying the perception of a three-dimensional object that should be light above and dark below. With contour obliteration and disruptive coloration, the patterns on the body tend to obscure the outline contour and thus the perception of the shape of the animal.

These books were influential not only in biological circles but also in martial applications when camouflage became part of the military repertoire. The word *camouflage* originated from the French *camoufler,* which had the meanings of "to disguise" or "to put on theatrical makeup." The cognate Italian verb *camuffare* means "to deceive or to disguise," perhaps from *capo muffare,* "to muffle the head." During World War I, French soldiers who painted vehicles and equipment in dull colors to make them less visible to the enemy were called *camoufleurs.* Dull colors predated that war, as British soldiers had adopted dull-colored uniforms in the previous century, dyed a color called *khaki,* the Urdu word for mud.

Guisers with carnivalesque or criminal intent had camouflaged themselves for centuries before the word was coined and the military adopted the practice. The tatters, stuffed clothes, straw costumes, and be-ribboned tall hats of mummers and guisers are perfect examples of outline blurring and contour obliteration predating by centuries the theories of academics. Military camouflage, developed during World War I, included counter-shading, in which artillery barrels and aircraft were painted light below and dark above, as with animals' white underbellies. Contour obliteration on British ships was achieved in the "dazzle camouflage" devised by Lieutenant Commander Norman

Wilkinson of the Royal Navy, who was an academic marine painter. These striking patterns were intended to confuse enemy submarine crews and keep them from determining the precise position of a ship or her course (Cork 1992, 20). In 1919, Wilkinson explained that his dazzle camouflage was "a method to produce an effect (by paint) in such a way as all accepted forms of a ship are broken up by masses of strongly contrasted color."

The *Illustrated London News* for January 4, 1919, carried an article about the technique, "Camouflage against U-Boats, the Art of Dazzle Painting." The ancient Irish *liuthrindi* patterns on shields and armor that were intended to confuse the enemy can be seen as dazzle's forerunner, but clearly the theory came from the researches of the biologists. English modernist painter and woodcut artist Edward Wadsworth worked during the war, along with nine other naval lieutenants in the docks of Bristol and Liverpool, to supervise the painting of Wilkinson's dazzle camouflage on more than two thousand British ships. Wadsworth's 1917 to 1918 woodcuts in black and white of the naval optical dazzle patterns were forerunners of the Op Art movement of the 1960s (Cork 1990, 21–23). Hugh Bamford Cott (1900–1987) was from 1919 a member of the British Army's Camouflage Advisory Panel. His 1940 book *Adaptive Coloration in Animals* was a later development of the discoveries made by Poulton and Thayer decades earlier.

9

The Powers of Animal Skins

The Gorgo, the Aegis, and the Goat

Greek mythology recounts how Danaë and her son Perseus were shut up in a coffer and set adrift on the sea by Danaë's father, Acrisius. Caught in a fisherman's net, they were brought to the island of Seriphus, where they were taken before the island's king, Polydectes. King Polydectes, lusting after Danaë, sought to get rid of Perseus. At a feast, Perseus promised to accomplish anything the king desired. He was sent on a potentially fatal quest to bring back the head of the Gorgon, Medusa, whose stare turned people to stone. As the son of Zeus, Perseus gained the assistance of Hermes and Athena. His magical assistance consisted of the power of flight, a helm of invisibility, and a pouch in which to put the Gorgon's head. From the three Graiae, the "gray old women," he found the directions to the Gorgons' den. (The gray old woman was a type of mask used in Sparta; see Napier 1986, 235.) Perseus used a polished shield as a mirror when he beheaded Medusa with his sickle and, putting the head into the pouch, escaped invisibly from her two immortal sisters. Perseus gave the Gorgon's head to the goddess Athena, who afterward used it as her apotropaic aegis.

Fig. 9.1. Romano-British Gorgon-head sculpture from the tympanum of the Roman temple of Sulis Minerva, formerly at Bath, Somerset, England (See also color plate 12.)

The helm of invisibility is an attribute of the gods, used by Hermes and Athena as well as Perseus. In Greek mythology, it is the helm of Hades, the god of the underworld, more precisely the "dogskin of Hades." In the *Iliad,* Athena has a helm of invisibility lent to her by Hades. She uses it to assist Diomedes (*Iliad* 5, 844–45). Helms of invisibility also feature in later mythology in western and northern Europe. The aegis, an animal skin bearing a mask of the Gorgon, is a garment of power worn by the Greek deities Athena and Zeus (the Roman Minerva and Jupiter). It is a fearsome object, often depicted with a border of serpents or, alternatively, golden tassels. It made a roaring sound in battle and can be a goatskin shield, more magical than functional. A goatskin coat is worn by contemporary guisers in Bulgaria and Turkey, whom some see as a continuation of the Thracian cult of Dionysus. A mosaic from Pompeii in the National Archaeological Museum in Naples shows Alexander the Great wearing the aegis. Images of Roman emperors also depict them in the aegis.

Norse magic knows the aegis in the form of a magical sigil, the Aegishjalmur, or Helm of Awe. It is an eightfold starlike figure related to the escarbuncle of Anglo-Norman heraldry. Literally, its name means "shield-helm," *helm* in this context not meaning a physical helmet but literally "something at the forefront." This meaning continues today with the word *helmsman,* meaning "someone steering a ship." An Aegishjalmur marked on a Viking warrior's forehead struck fear into his opponents. It was considered to render him invincible in combat. In chapter 18 of the thirteenth-century *Volsunga Saga,* the hero Sigurd talks with the dragon Fafnir, once a man who had been a noted warrior in his youth but was transmogrified by a curse. Fafnir says that when he was young, he bore the Aegishjalmur and all feared him. Richard Wagner's operatic cycle *Der Ring des Nibelungen,* first performed in 1876, features the Tarnhelm, which magically allows instantaneous travel over long distances and is the agent of transformation. In *Das Rheingold,* Alberich the dwarf transforms first into a dragon, then a toad; at the end of that opera, Fafnir changes into a dragon and appears as such in *Siegfried;* and in *Götterdammerung,* Siegfried changes into the appearance of Gunther, who later kills Siefried.

Appearance in the form of another person is a key element in the Arthurian legend. In his *Le Morte d'Arthur,* Sir Thomas Malory tells how King Uther Pendragon was smitten with the wife of the Duke of Cornwall and made war against him. The wizard Merlin told Uther that "ye shall get a child on her" and that he would facilitate it. So he transformed Uther and his right-hand man, Sir Ulfius (whose name suggests a "wolf-warrior"). "This night," said Merlin "ye shall lie by Igraine in the Castle of Tintagil, and ye shall be like the Duke her husband, Ulfius shall be like Sir Brastias" (who was the duke's right-hand man). Uther and Ulfius were transformed by the wizard Merlin into the likenesses of the duke and Sir Brastias, and they went to the duke's castle and were admitted. Recognized as the duke, he went to Igraine and made love to her. Then the two men left. Later, news was brought to Igraine that the duke had been slain on the battlefield at the time she believed the duke to be with her (Malory [1472] 1906, vol. 1, 6–7). This is the real meaning of "impersonation," the ancient forerunner of contemporary identity theft.

The Wound-Proof Coat

In medieval Scandinavia was the practice of wearing the skin of a reindeer as a coat that rendered the wearer "wound-proof." No edged weapon could cut through the thick hide. *The Saga of Saint Olav* in Snorri Sturluson's *Heimskringla* recounts the overthrow of the Norwegian King Olav II in a slaves and peasants revolt in the year 1030. In the Battle of Stiklestad, one of the leaders of the rebellion, Þórir hundr (Thorir Hund, or Thorir the Dog) wore an enchanted reindeer coat he had bought from Sámi magicians from Finland. Thorir and his allies fought their way through the royal bodyguards to attack the king. Although the king struck Thorir with a sword named Hneitir, "the sharpest of swords, the handle of which was bound with gold," it was ineffective against the reindeer-skin coat. Thorir, Thorstein the Shipwright, and Kalv together then struck Olav's death blows (Sturluson 1967, 280). A memorial to Thorir by Svein Haarvardsholm was erected in 1980 on Bjarkøy in Norway. Six hundred years after the death of Thorir, in seventeenth-century European wars, soldiers wore a buff coat made from the stout hide of the European buffalo, elk, or ox. These could also stop the cut of an edged weapon, though they did not feature quite so well in wound-proof magic as they could not stop a pike thrust or a bullet.

Bear and Wolf Transformation

To "go berserk" now means to be in a frenzy of uncontrolled violence, losing one's sense of fear and seeming to possess superhuman strength. Going berserk means undergoing a sudden transformation without warning from a placid state of mind into an unstoppable violent rage. In Viking times, the Berserkir (Berserkers, sing.) were warriors dedicated to Odin and who had acquired the ability to go into this "red mist" condition of demoniacal frenzy through initiation rituals and training. Their name comes from the bear shirts they wore; that is, they wore the skins of bears and became like them in form and behavior. But the practice lasted a long time in many places and was not a unified and consistent practice over time or place. Some could fight as wolf warriors as well as bears. Supernatural researcher Elliott O'Donnell (1872–1965) claimed that "dual metamorphosis," taking on the forms of two different animals, was a rare phenomenon (O'Donnell 1912, 256).

Such a person was said to be *eigi einhamr*, "not of one skin" (or shape). This is the ability to transform from one shape to another, the power to take on other bodies. This is the person who puts on disguise, either by wearing the animal pelt and taking on the attributes of the animal, as in guising or by some more shamanic ability. It was believed that one could put the skin over the body and then the human spirit entered into it and the person became the animal, leaving the human body lying motionless in an apparently cataleptic state. Such a person was credited with the power of *hammrammr,* the ability to change one's shape.

In this state, whether in another body or in human form, Berserkir were "as strong as bears or oxen," howled like wild beasts, foamed at the mouth "as mad as dogs or wolves," bit the rim of their shields in a fit of frenzy, and was turned on anyone in the vicinity. Berserkir were completely out of control and could kill their friends and family if they went into the berserk state at the wrong moment. Berserkir taken on board a ship for a naval battle forgot where they were and charged overboard in their frenzy. But it is clear that not all Berserkir were untrustworthy, for some Norse kings, including Harald Fairhair of Norway, had a contingent of Berserkir as their personal bodyguards.

The bear was the source of the Berserker's power, according to the Icelandic *Hrolfs Saga Kraki.* The power was acquired in a ritual in

Fig. 9.2. Hunters in animal-skin camouflage, including one in a bearskin with the head mask turned back, Olaus Magnis, 1555

the royal hall in which the postulant had to kill the effigy of a beast and drink its blood. What this effigy consisted of is not known. The Berserker was one who did not always wear the usual chain mail shirt of the warrior and often went into battle without one or wearing a bear's or wolf's skin. However, refusal to wear armor was not a requirement. *Vatnsdæla Saga* tells how "the Berserkir who were called Úlfheðnar wore wolf-skins over their mail coats."

The Old Norse poem *Bjarkamál* tells a story about Bǫðvarr Bjarki (Bothvar Bjarki, "Fighting Little Bear"), one of the twelve Berserkir bodyguards of King Hrólf. They were summoned to fight at Lejre, Sjælland, a battle they were doomed to lose, and a young man called Hjalti was sent to wake the sleeping Berserkir but could not wake Bǫðvarr. He lay as if asleep. After the battle, Bǫðvarr told him that he had fought in the battle in the form of a bear while his body lay in a state of what is now known as unresponsive wakefulness. This was seen as a form of hammrammr shape-shifting, but also can be viewed as a classic out-of-body experience.

In Norway in 1030, Tormund Kolbrunarskald, the bard of King Olav II, was asked to recite *Bjarkamál* to his forces to encourage them to heroic deeds before they fought the peasant army at Stiklestad. It was unsuccessful, as they were defeated and the king killed. There are also traces of bear-warriors from northern Germany in Christian times. Albrecht der Bär (Albrecht the Bear, 1100–1170) was the knight who founded the Margravate of Brandenburg. His conquest of the land was the prerequisite for the foundation of the city of Berlin about 1237, whose emblem is the bear "from the cognizance of his shield."

Another form of going berserk is the divine frenzy called *wód,* or *wood* in medieval English, a word related to Woden as the god of battle, which appears in the accounts of knightly combat in Arthurian legend. The Normans, who had been Norse colonists of northern France in the tenth century, a hundred years later had the reputation of being formidable warriors, conquering both England and Sicily by force of arms. The furor Normanorum of the Christian Norman knights was as feared by their opponents as the frenzy of the Berserkir had been in heathen times.

Fig. 9.3. Helmet-panel plate depicting a Berserker in wolf-warrior mode

Being hammrammr had its hazards, as wolf-shirt warriors are closely related to the werewolf belief. In figure 9.3, an Úlfheðinn (wolf-warrior) appears next to a figure interpreted as Odin on a craftsman's die found at Torslunda on the island of Ölund in the Baltic. Such dies were used to make metal plates for the Spangenhelm type of helmet; this one shows a wolf-headed humanoid figure standing upright and wielding a spear with its left hand. Its right hand appears to be drawing a sword from its scabbard.

Voluntarily becoming a were-animal involved magic. *Volsunga Saga* recounts how Sigmund and Sinfjotl encountered two sleeping men above whom were hung wolf skins. The men had magically empowered gold rings that enabled them to put on and remove the skins at will. The Volsungs took the skins and put them on, transforming themselves into werewolves, which then went on the rampage for the prescribed ten-day period until they could "put off the wolf-shapes." Then they burned the wolf skins and "prayed that no more hurt might come to any one from them" (Magnússon 1888, 20–22).

In his commentary on *Volsunga Saga,* H. Halliday Sparling noted:

"Skin-changers" were universally believed in once, in Iceland no less than elsewhere, as see . . . the episode of Dufthach and Storwolf o'Whale. Men possessing the power of becoming wolves at intervals, in the present case compelled to so become, wer-wolves or *loupgarou,* find large place in medieval story, but were equally well known in classic times. Belief in them still lingers in parts of Europe where wolves are to be found. Herodotus tells of the Neuri, who assumed once a year the shape of wolves; Pliny says that one of the family of Antæus, chosen by lot annually, became a wolf, and so remained for nine years; Giraldus Cambrensis will have it that Irishmen can become wolves; and Nennius asserts point-blank that "the descendents of wolves are still in Ossory"; they transform themselves into wolves when they bite. Apuleius, Petronius, and Lucian have similar stories. The Emperor Sigismund convoked a council of theologians in the fifteenth century who decided that werewolves did exist. (Sparling, in Magnússon 1888, 20–21)

Transformation into a bear or wolf was long practiced in Scandinavia by Swedes and the Sámi people of Finland. It was accomplished through the power of a ring-belt. The transgressive ritual for obtaining one involved digging up the body of a man on a Thursday night and taking a belt of skin from around the corpse's waist. To become a wolf or bear, one had to creep, headfirst, through the belt three times. The first time, one's head would be transformed into the beast, the second time, one was half animal, and the third time, one became the whole animal. To undo the transformation, one had to go through feetfirst three times (Johnson 2013, 79). Anders Fjällmark, a Sámi horse-grazer, was reputed to have had such a belt and to have used it in revenge against a farmer who refused to pay him for a summer's work. Fjällmark threatened the farmer that his livestock would be devastated by a bear and a wolf if he did not pay, but the farmer laughed. Fjällmark first transformed himself into a bear and went and mauled the farmer's horses, then into a wolf to kill his cattle, sheep, goats, and chickens (Johnson 2013, 79). Another form of ring-belt for transformation into bear or wolf could be made from the sinew from the left arm of a corpse, which was then spun to be made into threads that were woven into a rope (Johnson 2013, 81).

There is a Russian invocation to the "great gray shape" or "Great Wolf Spirit" to be incanted by a person desirous of taking on a wolf form, "the terror alike of one and all." The would-be werewolf asked for not only the abilities and strength of the wolf but also the combination of powers of many animals: the wit of a fox, the eyes of a cat to see in darkness, the smelling ability of a dog, the speed of an elk, the strength of an ox, the stealth of a wolf, the jaws of a tiger, the teeth of a shark, the claws of a bear, the poison of a snake, and the ability to climb like a monkey and swim like a fish (O'Donnell 1912, 274). Eastern European magical processes for becoming a were-animal, usually a wolf, involved a different sort of magical ritual, one closer to classical magic that began with creating outer and inner magic circles with chalk on a level piece of land. Inside of the circles, a fire was lit of black poplar, pine, or larch and a cauldron set to boil. In it were thrown a combination of psychoactive fumigants that included hemlock, henbane, asafoetida, opium, solanum, parsley, poppy seed, and aloe (O'Donnell 1912, 274).

An invocation of the great gray shape was made, and the operant's naked body was anointed with an ointment made from the fat of a cat, camphor, aniseed, and opium. The parallel with witches' "flying ointment," a concoction of active substances absorbed through the skin, is clear (Valiente 1984, 142–47). Having done this, he put on a magic belt around his waist. It was three fingers in width, made of wolf skin with a buckle with seven tongues. Staying with the outer circle await the apparition of the Spirit of the Unknown. When it appeared, it was in the form of a spectral huntsman or something indeterminate, part human and part beast, usually in a state of partial materialization. The operant then offered himself to the entity and was then granted the power to take on wolf form (O'Donnell 1912, 274; Woodward 1979, 118–21).

In a section titled "Lamiarum Unguenta" (Witches' Ointments) in *Magica Natura, sive De Miraculis Rerum Naturalium* (Antwerp 1560) Giovanni Baptista Porta gave a recipe for a potion that could "make a man believe he was changed into a bird or beast." It was an infusion in wine of deadly nightshade (*Atropa belladonna*), mandrake (*Mandragora officinarum*), thorn apple (*Brugmansia stramonium*), and henbane (*Hyoscyamus niger*). Each and every one of these substances is extremely dangerous to ingest, and this recipe should not be tried by the reader (Woodward 1979, 124; Valiente 1984, 143–44).

Fig. 9.4. Krampus guisers in furs and horns, Pongau, Austria (See also color plate 13.)

Animal Skins of Traditional Dancers

Almost every disguising tradition is not a separate thing, though it may appear in seemingly specific events. Human guising characters and roles as well as people guising as animals occur in many different contexts. In his *Observations on Popular Antiquities,* John Brand wrote about performers on Plough Monday in northeastern England. "The Fool Plough goes about, a Pageant that consists of a Number of Sword Dancers, dragging a Plough, with music, and one, sometimes two, in a very Antic Dress: the *Bessy,* in a grotesque Habit of an *old woman,* and the Fool, almost covered with Skins, a hairy Cap on, and the Tail of some animal hanging down his back. The Office of one of these *Characters* is, to go rattling a Box amongst the Spectators of the Dance, in which he collects their little Donations" (Brand [1777] 1810). An early nineteenth-century manuscript by Thomas Bell, preserved at the Beamish museum in northeastern England, tells of the Fool or Gatherer of a sword-dance team who wore "a hairy cap on his head, the tail of a fox." William Henderson, noting the attendants of a sword dance in Houghton-le-Spring, recorded, "The first clown, called the Tommy, dressed in a chintz dress with a belt, a fox's head for a cap, and the skin hanging below his shoulder" (Henderson 1866, 53). Another character, Little Foxey, sometimes appeared as the Squire's son.

For centuries, the Skinners and Glovers Guild of Shrewsbury appeared along with the other guilds in the Shrewsbury Show. Along with a man guising as the King of Morocco, their ruler, at one time they had an "elaborate mechanical stag accompanied by huntsmen sounding bugle blasts" (Hibbert 1891, 118). Documented sword-dance performances were associated with skinners and furriers guilds in some locations. In Scotland, the Perth Glovers Guild performed a sword dance between 1617 and 1633 (Mill 1927, 200–201). The furriers guild as far away as Sibiu, Transylvania (Romania), also had their own sword dance (Corrsin 1997, 163). A tool used to scrape the flesh from skins may have been used in sword dances and could be the origin of the "rappers" with a handle at each end used in some dances.

The Fool of the eighteenth-century Fool Plough was dressed in animal skins, with a skin cap. Traveling players in eighteenth- and nineteenth-century Shropshire performed a repertoire that contained elements of mummers' plays and professional stage theater. Among their company was a "fool or jester" who wore bells at the knee and "a paper mask below a cap of hare skin, with the ears up" (Wakeman 1884, 385). Thomas Sternberg noted in 1851 that the "Tom Fool" of the Northamptonshire morris dancers "has generally an old quilt thrown over him, plentifully hung with rabbit-skins; his cap is ornamented with a feather, and in his hand he holds a stick with an inflated bladder attached to the end by a cord" (Sternberg 1851, 70). The North Skelton sword dancers had a Tommy (clown) dressed in an ox hide.

In 1860 in the mining village of Elsecar, a parade was held after a wedding, including mounted men in costumes, musicians, and a clown wearing a hare-skin cap. He held a staff with a bladder on the end of a string (*Sheffield Daily Telegraph*, May 4 1860). In 1895, an anonymous writer in the *Pall Mall Gazette* published an article titled "Twelfth

Fig. 9.5. English Twelfth Night sword dancers with Fool in animal-skin cap and cowhide with a tail and cross-dressed Bessie (See also figure 20.2 on page 213).

Night on the Moors: Morris Dancers in Yorkshire," which described something similar: "They danced assuredly, and did strange things. Clothed apparently in white samite, mystic, wonderful, and decked and piped with wild traditional devices in patterns of scarlet, they took the floor. Two facing rows of three, and the captain at the top, all armed with naked swords." The captain, "with a fantasy of rabbit skin about his head," started with an introductory song, and the dancing began (Anonymous 1895a, 1–2). Although the writer was clearly unaware of this, from his published drawing, the captain's skin hat is the same shape as the leather helmets worn by deputies and overmen (foremen and overseers) in coal mines. Pitmen (miners) only wore cloth caps until later regulations stipulated metal helmets (Atkinson 1968, 46–47). Clearly, to miners, the helmet was a badge of office, and the captain's hat echoed this. It had a few ribbon bows attached and a small image of a rabbit's head on the front where a military badge would be. Folk dance collector Cecil Sharp noted the hat of the captain of the

Grenoside team, describing it as "a cloth helmet covered with a rabbit's skin" (Sharp n.d. [1911], 55). Mining villages were the origin places of many sword-dance teams, and a "pitman bold" appears in some of their calling-on songs. Many pitmen owned whippet dogs that they used to hunt hares and rabbits to supplement their families' diet.

Animals' tails were part of many costumes. In 1569, Pieter Breughel de Oude painted limbless beggars with fox tails sewn to their clothing. This was a sign they were suffering from leprosy. At one time, the Dick Fools who accompanied Old Snap the dragon in Norwich were dressed as jesters in motley and decked with cats' tails. The Cormass in Dunkirk in 1759 had "men dressed in crape" who wore "masks of great hideous appearance, with tails of various kinds and lengths, some of cows, some of horses, some of hogs" (*Caledonian Mercury*, July 16, 1759, 1). In 1769, John Wallis noted in a sword dance near Hexham, "One of the company is distinguished from the rest by a more antic dress; a fox's skin generally serving him for a covering and ornament to his head, the tail hanging down his back. This figure is their chief or leader" (Wallis 1769, 29). John Brand's skin-clad Fool wore an animal tail hanging down his back. A frequently reproduced artist's impression of Plough Monday, clearly derived from Brand's account, shows, among others, the cross-dressed Bessy or Molly, the plough, and a fool wearing a conical hat dressed in a skin and holding its long tail, probably from a cow (Pegg 1981, 86). Plough Monday straw men in eastern England sometimes wore tails of braided straw, and straw tails were attached to hobby horses.

Fig. 9.6. Guiser's mask with fox tail, Rottweil-am-Neckar, Germany (See also color plate 14.)

The practices, costumes, performances, and rituals described in this book show an undivided continuity between various genres that are usually presented as separate. Elements generally associated with one genre can be found in many others. There is no fixity; the only limitation is the availability of materials and the inventiveness of the performers. In 1940, Leslie F. Newman recounted the story of how a group of witches somewhere in eastern England had "hurriedly selected a woman to take the place of an old woman who was dying." She received "the regalia of the cult," which was a collar of fur pelts with another hanging down and worn between the breasts of the wearer next to the skin (Newman 1940, 36).

Face Marking with Blood

British hunting traditions involve the initiatory rite of "blooding" a newcomer. In fox hunting, a practice, now totally banned, held that at the kill, the brush (tail) of the fox was cut off, and with it, blood was smeared on each cheek and the forehead of a person on his or her first hunt. Similarly, in shooting grouse, partridge, or pheasant during daytime or ducks and geese at night, the first bird the new hunter killed on the wing provided the blood. The head of the game bird was crushed in the mouth of the leading huntsman, and the blood and brains were smeared on the cheeks and forehead of the new hunter. Then he became a "full-blooded" game shooter. Feathers from the first bird were worn in the hatband as a trophy (Newman 1940, 41). Newman believed that the custom of wearing random feathers in country hatbands by anyone who had never shot a bird was a sham remnant of this meaningful badge of honor.

In 1830, the Reverend Robert Forby published a two-volume work, *The Vocabulary of East Anglia*. In it, under "Kitty Witch," he defined the seabird called a kittiwake and a type of crab. It also meant a female specter and "a woman dressed in a grotesque and frightful manner, otherwise called a Kitch-Witch. . . . It was customary many years ago at Yarmouth, for women of the lower order to go in troops from house to house to levy contributions . . . having men's shirts over their own apparel, and their faces smeared with blood. These hideous beldams have long discontinued their perambulations; but in memory of them, one of the many narrow rows [passages] in the town is called *Kitty-witches' Row*" (Forby 1830, vol. 2, 186). Although much of Great Yarmouth's street plan was destroyed by bombing in World War II, the narrow passage with that name still exists. Performance is often associated with very specific places, and this one records a practice whose origin and meaning are lost.

Fig. 9.7. All performance is located. This is the entrance to Kitty-witches' Row, Great Yarmouth, Norfolk, England, where the Kitty-Witches once rampaged with bloodied faces.

10
Animal Disguise—
Horses

Guising as Animals

The perception of divine or demonic beings sometimes depicts them as being a human with an animal's head. The iconography of ancient Egyptian religion is filled with such images, and medieval drawings show dancing figures with animal heads. Guising as animals at New Year was an ancient European tradition detested by churchmen who attempted to destroy indigenous non-Christian culture. Between the fourth and eleventh centuries, there are numerous documented cases from Gaul, Germany, Spain, Italy, and England of clergymen condemning the practice (Barnett 1929, 393). Their prohibitions actually recorded practices that otherwise would not be known to be so ancient. More than forty such prohibitions survive. In 370 CE, the bishop of Barcelona censured people who guised as stags (Alford 1978a, 122). Bishop Caesarius of Arles wrote, "Some are clothed in the hides of cattle, others put on the heads of beasts, rejoicing and exulting that they have so transformed themselves into the shapes of animals that they no longer appear to be men" (Miles 1912, 170). In *Sports and Pastimes of the People of England,* J. Strutt wrote, "The Bishop of Nola, Paulinus, deplored those who wore skins of cattle and put upon them the heads of beasts" (Strutt 1845, 250). Despite attempts for more than 1,700 years to ban it, the wearing the skin of a "herd animal" and "putting on the head of beasts" has carried on ever since in many parts of Europe at New Year (Summers 1926, 134). Examples are too numerous and widespread to list. The author has guised as the Horse and the Tup himself, and one's behavior is subtly altered when under ritual animal disguise.

Some of the strange beasts that appeared to people and are enshrined in folklore were clearly people in animal disguise. In the Grenaby district of the Isle of Man, an apparition called Jimmy Squarefoot appeared as a man's body with a pig's head with tusks (Gill 1929, 356–57). In England, at Wakefield, the description of the phantom beast Padfoot seems to be an animal disguise. Padfoot was the size of a calf, with twisted spiral horns in front of the head and a white furry coat (Brown 1958, 178). Witch trials frequently report the devil appearing at a witches' sabbat as a black animal. On the Channel island of Guernsey in 1617, the devil was described as a black dog with horns who stood on its hind legs and had hands like a man—evidently a guiser (Brown 1958, 186). Clearly, the motives of animal guisers range from ritual, performance, and clandestine practices to the actions of hoaxers and jokers. In 1893, Charles Roper noted "foolish jokers . . . who wrap themselves round in sheets, and carry something on their heads containing light and having two holes for glaring eyes" while pretending to be the phantom East Anglian beast Black Shuck (Roper 1893, 793). Theo Brown suggested that, at least on some occasions, Shuck may have been a pony faked up by smugglers to frighten off inquisitive people who encountered it in the darkness (Brown 1958, 186). But most animal guising is obvious, conducted as part of a ritual performance or in folk drama and pantomime.

The Horse

In ancient Europe, horses were revered as divine in their own right or as epiphanies of a deity. The horse was sacred to all the traditional religions of northern Europe. It was under the aegis of the Celtic goddess Epona and sacred to the Northern Tradition gods Frey and Woden and the Slavonic deities Svantevit and Radegast. Horses are known to have been kept as holy animals at temples in England, Sweden, and Poland. In northern England, a Christian account of their destruction of the temple at Yeavering in Northumbria approximately the year 627 CE tells how the priest, who had renounced his calling and turned Christian, rode the sacred horse, thereby desecrating both horse and temple.

It is notable, too, that Saxo Grammaticus (ca. 1200) recorded the Northern ritual practice of setting up the head of a horse on a pole: "So he first put on a pole the severed head of a horse that had been sacrificed to the gods, and setting sticks beneath displayed the jaws grinning wide" (Saxo 1905, 209). This was the *niðstong* (scorn pole), functionally the same as the apotropaic carved heads on ships' prows and building gables. On land, the intention of the niðstong was to drive away the *landvættir* and render the land of one's enemy's *álfreka*. That is, the horse head struck fear into the spirits of the land (*landvættir,* "land wights," and *álfar,* "elves"), and they fled. The land thereby lost the spirit beings who

Fig. 10.1. Reconstruction of a sacrificed horse set up over a holy lake, Lejre, Denmark. Drawing by Nigel Pennick.

supported its existence; its virtues and fertility declined, and the inhabitants starved and died as a consequence. According to Icelandic pagan belief and much later tradition in East Anglia, it was recognized that at places where helpful sprites of the land (e.g, the Icelandic *landvættir*) have been driven away deliberately, the land is spiritually dead. In pagan Iceland, the word *álfreka* was used, and this is the common technical term used today in English. (In East Anglia, it is gast land, land where protective spirits have been driven out.) When such places are no longer tended by their spiritual guardians, inevitably they will become barren; the animals and people living there will decline and die.

In countries as far apart as England and Finland, horse's heads were deposited under buildings. Forty horse skulls were discovered, neatly laid in ranks under the floor, in a seventeenth-century house at Bungay in eastern England (Mann 1934, 253–55), and in Finland a horse skull was discovered in 1993 beneath the north wall of a sixteenth- or seventeenth-century outbuilding in Helsinki's Old Town (Hukantaival 2009, 350–56). There are numerous other instances of horse skulls under and inside traditional buildings. A horse's head was used in German tradition to prevent witches from entering a house (Bächtold-Stäubli 1927, vol. 1, 143ff.). In East Anglia, a very late horse foundation rite in 1897 was recorded by a witness, W. H. Barrett, who in the 1960s recounted how his uncle had built a primitive Methodist chapel at Black Horse Drove, a remote location in the Cambridgeshire Fens. Barrett was sent to a knacker's yard to buy a horse's head. His uncle located the center of the site with a stake, dug a trench, opened a bottle of beer, and placed the horse's head in the trench. Then he poured the first glass of beer as a libation, and the men had a drink of the beer before shoveling bricks and mortar over the head as the foundation (Porter 1969, 181).

Guising as a Horse

There are a number of versions of the guiser's horse. One is a simple horse-head mask on a costumed person who stands up normally. The *zweibeinigen Pferdchen* (two-legged ponies), a number of whom pull the Butz wagon at Pratteln in Switzerland are examples of this form. A

Fig. 10.2. Morris dancer guising as a horse, Thaxted, Essex, England (See also color plate 15.)

similar morris dance horse from England is illustrated in figure 10.2.

Another form is where the guiser wears a suspended frame that has a representation of a horse's head in front. The simplest of these is the sieve-frame horse of Lincolnshire. Fabric aprons around the frame give the illusion of the operator riding a horse. The operator may be masked, such as the Brieler Rössle at Rottweil, Germany.

Fig. 10.3. Brieler Rössle hobby horse with masked rider, Rottweil-am-N   , Germany (See also color plate 16.)

Fig. 10.4. Morris dancer hobby horse at a May celebration, Northill, Bedfordshire, England

Hobby horses gave rise to the term for all guisers' animals constructed with a framework—a "hobby animal" (Shuttleworth 1994, 3).

Another name for them is "tourney beasts." Strutt classed partial imitation of animals as a different form entirely. When the animal is clearly a person standing up in an animal mask or disguise with legs that are obviously those of a human, or if it is an animal formed by the guiser bending over with a stick in front, then this is partial (Strutt 1845, 254). The traditional Old Tup "Derby Ram" is a beast of this form (see the "Rams" section on page 106). Confusingly, partial animals were later classified along with hobby animals (Shuttleworth 1994), though strictly speaking, a hobby horse was a stick with a head on the end, in German called a *Steckenpferd* (stick horse), ridden between the legs like the broom dancers' and witches' broomstick, sometimes with a skirt around it to cover the operator's legs. There exist a number of medieval graffiti in English churches depicting the framework of hobby horses made from a staff with an upper structure of sticks in the form of a horse's upper body and head. Dating from about 1300, they exist at Wallington in Hertfordshire, Shillington in Bedfordshire and Girton, and as part of the Cambridge conurbation (Behrend 1978, 4–9).

The Austrian supernatural goat called the Habergeiss is portrayed as having three legs, two at the back and one at the front. It has glowing eyes and a long beard, haunts crossroads and ditches, laughs like a goblin, croaks like a toad, and screeches like an owl. The Habergeiss takes children away in a basket on his back. Clearly, it is a guiser's costume. But perhaps this beast has escaped from the mummers and become an independent being. The third form of horse guising is a costume that covers the operator completely and has a horse's head on the end of a staff, like the ancient niðstong. The operator holds the pole and snaps the articulated jaws. The head may be a carved or papier mâché image of a horse, or it may be the skull of a real horse. Of the two latter forms, the skull is the most frightening.

Horse guising is very old; illustrations of it are known from ancient Greek painted pottery. For example, an Attic black-figure belly amphora dating from the sixth century BCE shows a performance where men in horse-head costumes of the "two-legged" form with tails are ridden by others while a musician plays a double flute (Berlin, Staatliche Museen, F1, 697). In medieval and later Denmark and Sweden, guisers in horse masks and costumes, the Hvegehors, went from door to door at New Year demanding largesse. This "quaking" or "rocking" horse (*quaeghors*) was part of the "terrifying masks and devilish guises" of Scandinavian mummers at Christmas (Gunnell 1995, 114). The tradition is ancient. An archive from Bergen, Norway, from 1307 records the personal name Arnald Jolahest (Arnald Yule Horse) (Gunnell 1995, 82). In 1543, the bishop of Zealand condemned this "unholy watchnight" and instructed his parishioners not to observe the "really evil custom." (Numerous attempts to suppress guising in Scandinavia continued with edicts every few years until at least 1808.)

In 1855, Karl Weinhold wrote about the *Schimmel* horse guised in Saxony. "The *Schimmel*," he wrote, "is a long pole to whose end a horse's head is fastened, is tied beneath the chest of a young man. Who goes on all fours and some white cloths are thrown over the whole." In Silesia, the *Schimmelreiter* was "formed by three or four youths. The rider is generally veiled, and often wears on his head a pot with glowing coals shining forth through openings that represent eyes and mouth." The Schimmelreiter was accompanied by a bear, "a youth dressed in straw who plays the part of a bear tied to a pole" (Weinhold 1855, 6). On the Baltic island of Usedom, a beast called the *klapperbock* was guised with a horse's head (Weinhold 1855, 7). In Iceland, the *heistleikur* horse dance was accompanied by ceremonial songs called *vikivakar*. The horse was covered with red material, motley tatters, and horse brasses and had a bunch of keys hanging down at the front. It was attended by two *skaldmeyjar* (shield maidens) who were men in women's clothing. In late medieval Scotland, the ragged Yule horse, the *Yullis yald,* appeared at Christmas festivities. Like the Icelandic horse, it was clothed in tatters. The court bard of King James IV (reign 1488–1513), William Dunbar, complained in a poem to the king that his clothes were as ragged as the Yullis yald, and he asked the king for some new ones, as was his right.

In 1866, the Lord of Misrule at the Yuletide festivities in the Guildhall at Cambridge was flanked by his attendants, a hobby horse and Snap Dragon. At Christmastime in 1847 in the Free Trade Hall, Manchester, Snap Dragon was brought in by two guisers dressed in straw, accompanied by a nondescript animal, "a man whose form was concealed under a long dress, bearing a large head, somewhat resembling that of a horse, the jaws of which were made to open and shut at the will of the performer" (*Manchester Times,* January 8, 1847, 5).

"At various places in North Derbyshire, such as Norton, Eckington, and Dronfield," wrote Sidney Oldall Addy in 1907, "a number of men used to go round with 'the old horse' on Christmas Eve. The body of the man who represented the horse was covered with cloth or tarpaulin, and the horse's head was made of wood, the mouth being opened by strings in the inside. When the men reached the door of a house, the man representing the horse got under the tarpaulin, and they began to sing: 'It is a poor old horse, And he's knocking at your door, And if you'll please to let him in, He'll please you all I'm sure. Poor old horse. Poor old horse'" (Addy 1907, 37). The word *horseplay* comes from its knockabout antics, for when one is guising as an animal, whether as horse, dragon, or tup, one has license to transgress social norms. In Derbyshire, the Old Horse appears at Yuletide, sometimes alongside the Old Tup, a mummer guising as the Derby Ram (Cawte 1978, 117). "It seems as if the old horse," wrote Addy, "was intended to personify the aged and dying year. The year, like a worn-out horse, has become old and decrepit, and just as it ends, the old horse dies. The time at which the ceremony is performed, and its repetition from one house to another, indicate that it was a piece of magic intended to bring welfare to the people in the coming year" (Addy 1907, 40).

The old custom of pace-egging, begging for eggs at Easter, involved guising with animal skins and sometimes as a horse. On the Thursday before Easter in Kendal in the Lake District, youths with blackened faces processed through the streets, dragging buckets and cans behind them in a noisy rout (Rowling 1976, 112–13). Easter in eighteenth- and nineteenth-century Yorkshire and Lancashire saw groups of young men come out onto the streets wearing masks and clothed in tatters of ribbons or paper streamers. As usual, cross-dressing was part of the masquerade, "young men grotesquely dressed, led by a fiddler, with one or two in female attire." In Blackburn, Lancashire, young men wore animal hides and blackened their faces. In the towns around Forest of Rossendale, a guising horse went in a procession with groups of men who had masked or blackened faces. Formed of a horse skull on a pole with sacking covering the man, the skull had snapping jaws and eyes made from bottle ends (Cawte 1978, 140–42). One of the Jolly Lads was disguised as the comic character Old Toss-Pot. He accompanied the mummers' plays and songs performed by many groups, "the fool of the party, who still jingles the small bells hung about his dress" (Harland and Wilkinson 1867, 237). He carried a pot in which donated eggs and money were collected.

A horse skull plays a significant role in rural rites and ceremonies, often being used by mummers to create the Old Horse.

Fig. 10.5. Mummers at Winster Hall, Derbyshire, England, including a horse-skull guiser under a blanket, two masked snapping-jaw hobby horses with masked riders, a crossed-dressed Bessie with a besom, and two musicians playing "bumbass" bladder fiddles (1870 photograph)

Addy noted in 1907 that in South Yorkshire, "I have been told by an old man in Eckington, now dead, and by another man in Sheffield, that formerly the mummers used to find out where an old horse was buried, and dig its head up" (Addy 1907, 39). Horse-skull guising appears in Wales in the midwinter tradition around Christmas and New Year with Y Feri Lwyd (the Gray Mary). The Mari Lwyd is made from a horse's skull with eyes made from glass bottle bottoms and jaws that have been rigged to snap together. It is attached to a pole held by the operator, who is covered by a canvas cloth. It is bedecked with ribbons, jinglers, and bells. Other names for the horse are Pen Ceffyl (the Horse's Head), Y Gynfasfarch (the Canvas Horse), Y Warsel (the Wassail), or just Y March (the Horse). Near Swansea, Mumbles has a tradition carried on by the Bowden family. Dating from 1865, it is a decorated skull. The horse, wherever it appears, is the focus of misrule and horseplay. The song "Poor Old Horse" is part of its performances.

In Glamorgan and some other places in Wales, the team accompanying the horse was made up of the Leader and his Sergeant and a Merryman (musician) who traditionally played the *crwth* (Welsh fiddle). These guisers were decorated with many ribbons and sometimes a sash around their waists. Finally, there were a pair called Punch and Judy, who had blackened faces and were dressed in tatters and carried a metal poker and a besom, respectively. The team turned up in darkness at a house and sang a song consisting of calls and answers. The first verse was sung by Mari Lwyd outside the house, when the inhabitants locked the door. During verse three, the gray mare snapped her jaws, and when the fifth verse was being sung, Punch tapped in time on the stones outside the house, while Judy swept the doorstep and windows with her besom. Trying the door, Punch attempted to gain entry. If he and Judy got in, they caused general uproar, raked the fire, and swept ashes and dirt around the floor. If they could not force entry, the song continued and the gray mare promised in verse seven that Punch and Judy would "stand in position, prepared to behave." If they got to verse twelve, they could be admitted to the house. Then the team and inhabitants all sang verse thirteen together, and the team got largesse in the form of a gallon of ale and a party cake. Then the musician played, and a party ensued until the ale and cake were consumed. Then as the revelers left, they sang the fourteenth and final verse of farewell (Owen 1987, 50–57). In Cornwall, Christmas guisers have the Penglas or Penglaz, a similar beast with either a wooden or horse-skull head. It is led by Old Penglaze, with blackened face and carrying a staff.

The Láir Bhán (White Mare) is the equivalent tradition in Ireland, where the mare was perambulated around the district, visiting farmhouses and accompanied by people blowing on cow horns (Evans 1957, 277). In 1853, William Hackett wrote, "It is not many years since, on Samhain Eve, 31st October, a rustic procession perambulated the district between Ballycotton and Trabolgan, along the coast. At the head of the procession was a figure enveloped in a white robe or sheet, having, as it were, the head of a mare, this personage was called the Láir Bhán, 'the white mare.' This figure was 'a sort of president of the ceremonies. A long string of verses was recited at each house'" (Hackett 1853, vol. 2, 308).

In southeastern England, the county of Kent has a specific custom—

the Hooden Horse. Hoodening was a Christmas ceremony usually performed by horsemen, which is known to have been performed in at least thirty-three known Kentish locations. First recorded in the eighteenth century, an early reference to hoodening (in 1807) tells that "a party of young people procure the head of a dead horse, which is attached to a pole." The party was "grotesquely habited" and carried handbells. More recent researchers have discounted the description of a real horse's head, for all the recorded examples have a wooden head with snapping jaws. Of course, the correspondent may have seen a Hooden Horse of this kind, and the practice was either an otherwise unrecorded variant or a one-off. As with other rural performances, there was and is considerable variation.

A whole team could be made up of the horse, its leader (the Waggoner) with a whip, cross-dressed Molly with a broom, a groom, a jockey, and musicians.

The hoodeners visited houses and gained entry, when the horse would indulge in knockabout horseplay. The jockey would attempt to mount the horse, but, of course, would fail, and Molly swept the house and chased any girls who were there. After largesse in the form of cakes and ale or money had been received, the party went on to the next farmhouse (Maylam 1909, passim).

Playing Old Ball was a guising horse performance in Lancashire.

Fig. 10.6. Hooden Horse and musician, Deal, Kent, England (1909 photograph)

Harland and Wilkinson's *Lancashire Folk-Lore* gives the following detailed description of literal horseplay.

> This is an Easter custom. A huge and rude representation of a horse's head is made; the eyes are formed of the bottoms of old broken wine or other "black bottles"; the lower and upper jaws have large nails put in them to serve as teeth; the lower jaw is made to move by a contrivance fixed at its back end, to be operated on by the man who plays "Old Ball." There is a stick, on which the head rests, which is handled and used by the operator, to move "Old Ball" about, and as a rest. Fixed to the whole is a sheet of white sacking-cloth, under which the operator puts himself, and at the end of which is a tail. The operator then gets into his position, so as to make the whole as like as a horse as possible. He opens the mouth by means of the contrivance before spoken of. Through the opening he can see the crowd, and he runs first at one and then another, neighing like a horse, kicking, rising on his hind legs, performing all descriptions of gambols, and running after the crowd; the consequence is, the women scream, the children are frightened, and all is one scene of the most ridiculous and boisterous mirth. (Harland and Wilkinson 1867, 234–35)

Harland and Wilkinson note also that "'Old Ball' also appeared with mummers in the Christmas festivities. Then 'Old Ball' bit anyone he could lay hold of and held its victims 'till they bought their release with a few pence'" (Harland and Wilkinson 1867, 254).

Old Ball was a favorite name at the time for a cart horse. Addy explained that *Ball* meant "a white horse," and "the folk-lore of this neighbourhood has a good deal to say about white horses, and they were supposed to bring luck. Thus, if you see a white horse, spit on your little finger, and you will be lucky all day" (Addy 1895, 102; 1907, 40). But in 2000, when the Northstow Mummers of Cambridgeshire were appearing at a folk festival at Chatteris in the Cambridgeshire Fens, I was the guiser playing the horse and had parked my car in the street some distance from the public house where the event was taking place.

I put on the white horse costume and went along the street toward the pub to join the team and perform the horseplay. A group of small boys, seeing me, shouted, "It's the horse of death!" and ran off in mock terror.

In Lincolnshire and Nottinghamshire was a form of hobby horse based on the frame of a sieve hung around the guiser's waist. It had a wooden horse's head and a horse tail attached and was covered with sacking. Horses of this kind were brought out on Plough Monday and are known from Barrington, Burton-upon-Stather, Scotter, and Scunthorpe. Soul caking in Cheshire properly takes place on All Souls' Eve (November 1, after dark) but is often performed as part of Halloween, the night before. A "curious custom which survived in certain parts of the North," it was noted in the *Wigan Observer and District Advertiser* in 1903. Men, wearing horses' heads "were a reign of terror to the neighbourhoods from their threatening attitude in demanding money. This was around All Souls' Day, November 1" (*Wigan Observer and District Advertiser* April 11, 1903, 7). On All Souls' Day, at Frodsham in Cheshire, the horse is Dick, and two drivers brought him in with a dialogue song that tells of his travels through various places and the Land of Cockaigne, and finally, as "poor old horse," his poverty in old age. E. R. Chambers noted that the horse Old Hob that was guised at Ormskirk in Lancashire was introduced by a speech from his leader, the Groom. "He's traveled through Ireland, France, and Spain, and now he's back in Old England again"—lines that appear in many mummers' plays spoken by the Doctor. Like many guising horses throughout the year, Old Hob assailed the spectators (Chambers 1933 212–13).

Hobby horses are made in many other European countries. Hobby horses called Chinchins appear in the Ducasse de Mons, of which the dragon le Lumeçon is the central character. They accompany les Hommes Blancs, who support the dragon's body, and les Hommes Sauvages, who support its long metal tail. The hobby horses called Brieler Rössle appear in Fastnacht at Rottweil-am-Neckar, Germany. These hobby horses are attached by ropes to three masked and costumed figures who wield whips. When one rope is taut, the whip man at the other end cracks his whip at the hobby horse. The whips are leather, but with thin rope ends, which cut at the feathers worn by the hobby-horse man, who is also masked. In Aix-en-Provence, France, la Fête-Dieu features hobby horses, and at Fréjus, their appearance commemorates Saint Francis of Paola, who is credited with having brought a plague to an end in 1483. Spain has the Zaldico, as in the Carnaval de Lantz, where the horse is accompanied by Ziripot, a "fat man" whose costume is stuffed with straw. In Pamplona, the Zaldico-maldico has a realistic horse's head. Its rider carries a whip. Its attendant is the Tcherro, a man carrying a horse tail and a flag. At Soule, the horse is just a fringe around the man, and its head is a stylized hook shape. In the Basque country of France, the hobby horse is the Zamalzain.

The hobby horses in southwestern Britain are more elaborate structures. They appeared on May Day at Padstow, Minehead, and Dunster and before Ascension Day at Coombe Martin in connection with Hunting the Earl of Rone. At Minehead, two horses are brought out in the first days of May. They are the Sailor's Horse and the Town Horse. The first belonged to the fishermen and mariners and the other to the landsmen of Minehead. The Minehead horse design is a boat-shaped frame made traditionally of willow withies tied together with tarred cord. The frame, which is carried on the guiser's shoulders, is pointed at each end, and a rope tail, formerly a cow's tail, hangs at the back. The masked operator's head sticks out in the middle. The upper part is covered with tatters of fabric and the lower part painted with multicolored roundels. Archive photographs show various skirts of sacking or painted cloth. The men who accompany the horse are called Gullivers.

At Padstow, the Obby Oss is made with an oval frame over which black oilskin is stretched. The head has a snapping jaw. It is attended by a cross-dressed Teaser, who wields a padded club. As in many festive parades, there is a specific tune and song that is part of the ritual. The "Day Song," which invokes Saint George, has a particular line at which the Obby Oss, having sunk to the ground as if dead, springs up again. The Obby Oss operator chases after women and covers them with its skirts, which is said to bring them good fortune. At Padstow, the earliest reference to the Obby Oss is from 1803, while the Minehead horse's earliest mention is in 1830, though a date of 1792 is quoted when a Minehead hobby horse made an appearance at Dunster Castle (Peter 1913, 248–54; Manning-Sanders 1973, 89–92).

The ritual called Hunting the Earl of Rone took place in Coombe Martin, Devon, in the days preceding Ascension Day. A masked and disguised person representing the Earl of Rone rode on a donkey and was accompanied by a hobby horse. The skirt of the snapping-jawed horse was covered with painted emblems, and the operator wore a mask. After a break of 140 years, the custom was brought back. The new hobby horse resembles that of Padstow, covered by multicolored ribbons and with a skirt similar to the Minehead horse.

11
Animal Disguise— Other Animals

Rams

The English folksong "The Derby Ram" is a song of exaggeration that sings the praise of "the finest tup that ever was fed on hay." The song increases the size of the ram as it progresses, beginning as "nine feet round," then tells how its horns stretched up to the sky, where eagles nested on them, and in another verse how his feet covered an acre of land each time he moved them. Finally, his dismembered carcass provides an oven for the old women to bake the parish bread, aprons for the women, shoes for the girls, footballs for the boys, and a rope for the men to toll the passing bell of Derby jail.

In the mummers' play, the Derby Ram is personated by a guiser beneath a cloth, fleece, or blanket. "At Handsworth Woodhouse (in Yorkshire), near Sheffield," wrote Sidney Oldall Addy, "a real sheep's head is put on the top of the sack, and the boy inside the sack walks on his hands and legs so as to look like a sheep. The butcher pretends to kill the Tup; his servant holds a basin to catch the blood, as at Castleton." At Handsworth, he reported, "The boys have an imitation of a sheep's head. It is made of wood with a pair of real sheep's horns, with two glass

Fig. 11.1. Old Tup at Handsworth, Sheffield, England (1906 photograph)

marbles for the eyes. The tongue is a piece of red flannel. The boy who is acting the old tup gets under a sack, and holds the sheep's head up with a broom handle. Here five boys go round. They begin about seven o'clock on Christmas Eve, and finish their rounds on the night of New Year's Day" (Addy 1907, 33).

The four boys played an old woman wearing a bonnet, frock, and apron, with a blackened face; a butcher with his smock and apron and his knife and steel; the Old Tup; and a Fool with his face blackened (Addy 1907, 34). Addy noted that at Castleton, Derbyshire, "A boy gets into a sack, the top of which is tied in such a way as to represent two ears or horns, or else the sack is surmounted by a real sheep's head. A second boy represents a butcher, and carries a knife in his hand; a third is dressed like a woman; a fourth, who has his face blackened, represents an old man, and carries a bowl or basin in his hand. They went from house to house singing the *Derby Ram* song" (Addy 1907, 31).

Addy also noted, "At Upperthorpe, near Sheffield, boys go round on Christmas Eve with 'the old tup.' They tie the ends of a sack to represent horns, as they do at Castleton" (Addy 1907, 35). The sack has variants. At New Whittington, a chalked face was traditional. Arthur Mayall, writing in *Notes and Queries* in 1895, tells how the Tup o' Derby's horns were often gilded. At Braithwell in the same year, for a head, the Tup

Fig. 11.2. Old Tup in a performance of the eponymous Mummers' *Play performed by the Northstow Mummers at the Strawberry Fair, Cambridge, England, with Bonny Old Lass in tatters and mob cap and Little Devil Doubt in tatters and red-horned mask (photograph by Rupert Pennick)*

had a block of wood mounted on a broom handle. It was shaped like a ram's head, with marbles* from old ginger-beer bottles for eyes, attached by a row of tacks to giving the appearance of eyelashes. The front of the head was covered in sheepskin cut from the face of a slaughtered sheep. A sack was nailed on at the back, into which the boy playing the Tup inserted his head and shoulders (Gatty 1946, 24–26). The Tup used by the Northstow Mummers, the author's side, is of the broomstick variety, having a papier mâché head with a snapping jaw operated by a cable from a bicycle.

Percy Maylam, writing in 1909, tells of the use of a real sheep's skull, and there are a number of other recorded instances from Clowne,

---

*In the nineteenth century Codd bottles solved the problem of keeping the gas in bottled carbonated drinks by using a glass marble with a rubber seal held down with a wire clip. They are collectible items now.

Ecclesfield, and Worksop. At Staveley, the Tup was usually a real sheep's head fastened on a pole, the actor being covered with a rug; a resident, Mrs. Wragg, recalled in the 1940s that in earlier times they had a real sheepskin and a ram's head with horns (Gatty 1946, 26–30). A dried ram's head was used for the Tup in Worksop, Nottinghamshire, and Brimingham in Derbyshire. There are a few records of sheep guising on Plough Monday. At Walton-le-Dale, a servant girl who was not local was alarmed by a man disguised as a sheep who knocked at the door to introduce the Plough Jags (Gutch and Peacock 1908, 186–87). As with all traditional performances, there was and is no standard form, with the mummers and guisers employing any available appropriate materials and appearing on days not commonly recognized by folklorists as customary.

At Stetten in southern Germany, ram's-head guisers appear at the Fastnacht festivities. Ram guisers appeared in the medieval Schembartlauf at Nuremberg. In Denmark, the Yuletide Julbuk sometimes had the head of a ram with a snapping jaw. The guising beast called Þingálp or Finngálpn of Iceland that rampaged in midwinter was described as a monster, though in form it has a close affinity with the Old Tup of English mumming. Its head was a carved block of wood with ram's horns attached, covered in sheepskin, and with glass eyes like the Old Ball of Lancashire. Its head was attached to a pole, and the guiser operating it was covered with a fabric cloth like a bedspread. It had a snapping jaw activated by the operator and clusters of shells that clattered and rattled as it moved (Gunnell 1995, 144–46). Its action was to chase and chastise people, especially good-looking men.

Bulls and the Ooser

The Broad was a hobby animal with a bull's head on a pole and the operator under sacking. It was guised at Hawkesbury and Leighterton in Gloucestershire in western England. Some instances of it used a hollowed-out turnip or rutabaga as the head, containing a candle like a Halloween pumpkin. In all, the custom is recorded from thirteen villages in a roughly triangular area between Stroud, Cricklade, and

Fig. 11.3. Ox guiser and Jack-in-the-Green, Oxford, May Day (See also color plate 17.)

Chipping Sodbury. Ten villages with the custom were in Gloucestershire and three in Wiltshire. A bull guiser used to accompany the wassailers at Kingscote in Gloucestershire, and a similar figure has appeared on May Day in Oxford.

In France, at Amèlie-les-Bains, a bull mask called Bou-Rouch was worn. In eastern England, at Huntingdon, was a "curious and ancient custom" of beating the bounds observed by the freemen of the borough that unusually involved an ox skull, the *Reliquary* reported in October 1892. "They assembled in Huntingdon market place and then the skull of an ox on two poles was placed at the head of the procession, then came the Freemen and their sons, a certain number with spades and the others sticks. They gave three cheers and moved out of the town to the borough boundary, then lowered it and dragged it along the boundary like a plough. They dug boundary holes afresh and a boy was thrown into each hole and struck with a spade" (Tebbutt 1984, 69). The men of Godmanchester, on the other side of the Great Ouse River, sometimes attacked the Huntingdon men and fought them for the possession of the ox skull. In Denmark, a record of midwinter guisers from 1722 included a man wearing an ox head, his body covered with a striped blanket.

Another specific instance of bulls' horns in England was on the Dorset Ooser, a unique mask that was described in *Somerset Notes and Queries* in 1891 by Canon Charles Mayo (1845–1929). It was "a wooden mask, of large size, with features grotesquely human, long flowing locks of hair on either side of the head, a beard, and a pair of bullock's horns, projecting left and right of the forehead. The mask or Ooser is cut from a solid block, excepting the lower jaw, which is movable, and connected with the upper by a pair of leather hinges. A string, attached to the movable jaw, passed through a hole, and is then allowed to fall into the cavity. The *Ooser* is so formed that a man's head may be placed in it, and thus carry or support it while he is in motion. No provision, however, is made for seeing through the eyes of the mask, which are not pierced" (Mayo 1891, 289). In his 1863 book on the Dorset dialect, William Barnes wrote, "Ooser, or oose, a mask with opening jaws, put on with a cow's skin to frighten folk" (Barnes 1863, 73). The Ooser is famous because it was photographed in the studio of M. Chaffins and Sons at Yeovil; the photo was published, but the mask was subsequently lost. Its owner, Dr. Edward Cave of Holt Farm, Melbury Osmond, Dorset, moved his home to Crewkerne and then to Bath. In his second move, he left the mask in a loft under the care of the family coachman. It seems it was sold by a groom without the owner's permission and taken away, never to appear again, but even this is uncertain (Valiente 1984, 95–96).

Nothing is known of its origin, and F. T. Elworthy noted that Osor is a byname for the devil, so the concept of frightening people is consistent with this (Elworthy 1900, 142). In the Ancient Ritual of the Buchan Ploughmen, a man in disguise personating "Auld Nick, Lucifer or the Devil presided over the initiations of new members" (Rennie and Fernee, 2009, 88). The Devil appeared in an East Anglian ploughmen's ritual, too. The Ooser's facial form resembles the pantomime giants made for the Drury Lane Theatre in London during the

Fig. 11.4. Ooser drawing by Nigel Pennick

second half of the nineteenth century. Whether the Ooser influenced the London pantomime property makers or the other way around, the resemblance is striking. It is another example of the overlap between vernacular and theatrical performance.

In 1935, a contributor to the local lore compilation *Dorset Up Along and Down Along* told of the mummers and the Bull.

> Mummers at Shillingstone survived only until the late seventies of the last century, but the men and boys of the village kept up an ancient and terrifying custom of the Bull until a rather later date. The Bull, shaggy head with horns complete, shaggy coat and eyes of glass, was wont to arrive, uninvited at any Christmas festivity. None knew when he might or might not appear. He was given the freedom of every home, and allowed to penetrate into any room escorted by his keeper. The whole company would flee before his formidable horns, the more so as, toward the end of the evening; neither the Bull nor his keeper could be certified as strictly sober. The Christmas Bull is now obsolete, but up to forty years ago, he was a recognized custom. In some parts of West Dorset, this creature was known as the Wooser, and there are those who tell us that he has his origin in Devil-worship. (Dacombe 1935, 109)

Doreen Valiente notes a report from Dorset in 1911 of a court case in which a man "dressed in a bullock's skin and wearing an ooser" was accused of frightening some girls (Valiente 1984, 96). The Bull appeared in the west of England close to South Wales, so there appears to be some connection with the violent Scotch Bull who led the disguised Scotch Cattle in their rampages against strikebreakers in the South Wales coal- and iron-producing region in the first half of the nineteenth century. In Dorset in 1978 at Holwell Medieval Fair, an Ooser made by woodcarver Tony Hawkins appeared. Later, the Wessex Morris Men brought out that Ooser mask occasionally for dance-outs, but they finally discontinued its use because it was too heavy to be carried for any length of time. Although, of course, unconnected with the Ooser, the Russian Okrutnik from the Voronezh region is a wooden mask with bison horns that has some resemblance to the Ooser.

Fig. 11.5. Habergeiss, Pongau, Austria

Goats and Camels

We have already met the Habergeiss, which hovers on the boundary between the carnivalesque and the supernatural. In Austria, the Habergeiss sometimes appears as a four-legged beast with two people inside it. This is the form of the English Pantomime Horse, played for laughs on stage. This kind of horse appears in some central European Carnivals as the Brechselschimmel. The Habergeiss has a snapping jaw that catches people and holds on to them until they make a "donation." The present author has been caught in the jaws of a Habergeiss and had to pay up. The Carnival at Braunlingen in the German Schwarzwald (Black Forest) has a goat called der Braunlinger Stadtbock. In 1555, Olaus Magnus wrote about the Julbock in connection with Shrovetide, and the guisers' Rågeit (Pole Goat) was mentioned in Jensøn's dictionary of 1646. A national law in Denmark banned the Julbukk (Yule Goat) in 1668, followed by Norway and its colony, Iceland, in 1687. The Julbock is recorded in Swedish laws against it from Malmö in 1615, Stockholm 1721, Karlskrona 1754, Örebro 177, and Gothenburg in 1786 (Gunnell 1995, 116). The Swedish Lussebock is guised by a *lussiner* with a goatskin on the back, straw around the neck, and a red hood; it goes around demanding meat and bread (Gunnell 1995, 99).

Guising and mummers' plays in Anatolian Turkey include processions of men and children dressed in animal skins with blackened faces or masks who guise at the winter solstice as camels or sheep with bells around their necks. The Tuluk Oyunu (leather play or trap play) is a performance enacted by the Tanners' Guild at Bor. Tulukçu, men dressed in white trousers and wielding inflated goat bladders, are attacked by Keçiler, goat-men with faces masked or blackened, who attempt to deflate the bladders by pricking them with large pins (And 1980, 88). The Kars mummers' play has a man dressed in white with his face whitened who is in combat with a man in sheepskin with his face blackened. There is a hobby horse and a "pig," which is killed and brought back to life by the cracking of a whip (And 1980, 87–88).

Fig. 11.6. Horn dancers and hobby horse, Abbot's Bromley,
Staffordshire, England (1897 photograph)

The Deve Oyunu (Camel Play) involves a camel operated by two
people in the manner of the pantomime horse. The head is a horse
skull covered with tatters, with mirrors for eyes. The jaws are rigged
so they can be snapped. The operators are covered with a camel skin
(And 1980, 91). The parallel with the horse guisers of northern and
western Europe and the Habergeiss of Austria is marked. Guisers at
Bèziers in France have appeared as a camel, the Chamence, since 1613.
In Turkey, the Geyik Oyunu (Deer Play) has guising as a stag, which,
as in mummers' plays and sword dances in western and northern
Europe, is killed and brought back to life (And 1980, 92). The performances of the Koukers in Volvoda, Bulgaria, similarly have animal-
skin guisers with blackened faces. The Kouker must be a poor married
man. He is dressed in a costume made from seven separate goat or
sheepskins stitched together. The skins come from seven different
households. He wears bull bells and a large false phallus and carries a
staff with tatters of leather or old cloth at the end. Some wear horns
(Fol 2004, 52–53).

Other Beasts

As a guising beast, the donkey appears in a few places in different contexts. In Zürich, Switzerland, the Gurri is a donkey skull with snapping jaws operated by a man under a white sheet. In the Shrovetide Carnival at Villingen in south Germany, the Butzesel is a head mask worn by one person in the parade. He appears with a necklace of sausages and pulls a harrow covered with vegetation. In France, l'Âne de Bessan is an eight-legged donkey with four men inside, led by a leader dressed in white. At Goathland in northern England, a fisherman riding a hobby donkey accompanied the sword dancers.

Stag guising appears as a prohibited activity in early church penitentials, but this probably did not include any horn wearing, as the devil is portrayed with them in Christian iconography (as is Moses).

Fig. 11.7. Guiser wearing a deer's head facing backward, Villingen, Germany

*Fig. 11.8. Pig mask guiser,
Rottenburg, Germany
(See also color plate 18.)*

Johannes Schefferus's famous seventeenth-century illustration of a
Sámi shaman shows a man wearing reindeer antlers and playing a frame
drum. Reindeer antlers are carried by dancers in the Abbot's Bromley
Horn Dance, though it is not suggested that these are an ancient
shamanic remnant. The Icelandic Hjartleikur (Heart Dance) involved
a man wearing a stag disguise with burning candles on the antlers. He
danced with women and sang a love song featuring deer.

In medieval Coventry, the guild of cappers and dyers appeared
in the Corpus Christi pageant with a stag and a huntsman blowing
his horn (Harris 1911, 286). Similarly, in the early modern era in
Shrewsbury, on the English side of the Welsh border, the Skinners
and Glovers Guild had an "elaborate mechanical stag accompanied by
huntsmen sounding bugle blasts" (Hibbert 1891, 118). What this was is
unknown. The word *mechanical* did not gain its modern meaning until
the eighteenth century. Before that, it referred to human skill, as in the
mechanical arts, which included blacksmithing, weaving, agriculture,
hunting, navigation, medicine, and theatrics. So it is possible that the
guild stag was a guising beast covered in deerskin. Pig guising is rare. In
Lincolnshire at the harvest supper a man would dress as the Old Sow

Fig. 11.9. Bear mask guiser, Rottenburg, Germany (See also color plate 19.)

and go on all fours around the legs of women and girls. A German Carnival pig mask is illustrated in figure 11.8.

A guiser's unicorn ridden by a female figure appeared in the Schembartlauf at Nuremberg.

The Berserkir of the ancient north were feared warriors, but bear guising did not cease when more sophisticated military organization was introduced. Straw Bears, important guising figures in Germany with two English outliers, are dealt with in chapter 12. Guising as bears in bearskins or other furs is a feature of several European festivals.

The Fêtes de l'Ours (Festival of the Bears) is held at Prats-de-Mollo-la-Preste in Vallespir in the Catalan Pyrenees of France, one of three villages with bear-guising traditions, the others being

Arles-sur-Tech and Saint Laurence de Cerdaus. At the village of Finstret in the same district, an image of Saint Columba (a woman, not the male Celtic saint of the same name) depicts her with a bear. The festival at Prats-de-Mollo-la-Preste, held on February 2, involves three groups of men dressed in different guises. The bears, after which the event is named, wear sheepskins in imitation of bear pelts, or sometimes real bearskins, blacken their faces with *suie et huile* (soot and oil), and carry large staves. The second group wears all white, with white headscarves or bonnets and whitened faces. These are the barbers, who carry heavy chains. The third group is the hunters, carrying shotguns and blanks to fire. In an outburst of misrule, the bears run loose among the spectators, threaten or hit them with staves, and smear those they can catch with black. The bears are chased by the barbers, who eventually bring them down with chains and "shave" them to return them to human form. Finally, the bears are "shot" by the hunters.

12

Straw Bears, Straw Men, and Jack O'Lent

Straw, the by-product of grain farming, had many uses in traditional preindustrial society. Straw rope or netting was used on the western seaboard of Europe to tie down roof thatch, which itself is often made of straw, though sometimes of reed. Traditional bee skeps—woven baskets used to keep bees—are made from straw rope and a spirally wound dome that are stitched together. Straw ropes were used in Scotland and Ireland for tying down the turf roofs of crofters' and fisher families' houses. Straw was also woven into hats, for which the town of Luton in England was famous, and shoes or slippers, sometimes for temporary and ceremonial use (Evans 1957, 278; Bärtsch 1993, 59–82). All across Europe, traditionally, the last sheaf of the harvest was taken triumphantly back to the community and honored in some way. An account of a Norfolk harvest on August 14, 1826, tells how "the *last* or 'horkey load' is decorated with flags and streamers, and sometimes a sort of *kern baby* is placed on the top at the front of the load. This is commonly called a 'ben'" (Hone 1827, vol. 2, 1,166). One farming family in Huntingdonshire had the tradition that the farmer carried the last sheaf home on his back (Tebbutt 1984, 72).

Straw was used to make belts, and *lalligags* of woven straw tied around trousers just below the knees were worn by men and boys on Plough Monday in the Fens of eastern England, as at Brandon Creek. At Littleport, Humpty, the broom man, wore a tail made of braided straw and a hump of straw stuffed into the back of his coat (Porter 1969, 101–2). The Burringham (Lincolnshire) Plough Jags also went around on Plough Monday with a character whose clothes were stuffed with straw and who had a goose feather in his hat. (The gray goose feather was a sign of sworn brotherhood in the Fens of eastern England.) He was called Joe Straw (Wright and Lones 1938, 94). At Whittlesea (sometimes also spelled Whittlesey) in the Cambridgeshire Fens, the day following Plough Monday was called Straw Bear Tuesday (Wright and Lones 1938, 103–4). It appears that Saint Distaff's Day or Rock Day in earlier times was January 7, the day following Twelfth Night, but in later days it became the Tuesday following Plough Monday. Robert Herrick expressed the meaning of this day, and perhaps influenced its later observance, in his 1648 poem "St. Distaff's Day, or the Morrow after Twelfth Day":

> *Partly work and partly play*
> *Ye must on St. Distaff's day.*
> *From the plough come free your teame;*
> *Then come home and fother them.*
> *If the Maides a-spinning goe,*
> *Burne the flax, and fire the tow:*
> *Scorch their plackets, but beware*
> *That ye singe no maiden-haire.*
> *Bring in pailes of water then,*
> *Let the Maides bewash the men.*
> *Give S. Distaffe all the right,*
> *Then bid Christmas sport good night;*
> *And next morrow, every one*
> *To his owne vacation.*
>
> (Herrick 1902, 292)

The straw bears were men dressed completely in straw, led by another man with a rope or chain. In England, the custom of parading straw bears through the streets is recorded only from Whittlesea and Ramsey. When the Fens were drained, the last lakes were near Whittlesea and Ramsey. Ramsey Mere was drained in 1840, along with the other smaller local lakes, Ugg Mere, Benwick Mere, Brik Mere, and Trundle Mere. Whittlesea Mere was the largest lake in eastern England, but it was pumped dry by 1852. After several years when the dead fish and water vegetation rotted in the drying lake beds, producing an unbearable stench for miles around, they were cleared by agricultural gangs recruited from elsewhere and ploughed up so that arable crops could be grown. The local Fen people who had lived off the abundance of the meres, in boat making, fishing, fowling, and gathering reeds, had their livelihoods destroyed, and they either left the area to work elsewhere or had to become employees laboring in the new fields that they did not own.

The Ramsey straw bear is mentioned in the *Peterborough Advertiser* for January 16, 1886. *Fenland Notes and Queries* records how "the custom on Straw Bear Tuesday was for one of the confraternity of the plough to dress up with straw one of their number as a bear and call him the Straw Bear" (Anonymous 1899, 228). This was referred to in the past tense, although it was a living tradition at the time. "On the day following Plough Monday," F. W. Bird tells us in his memoirs, "there was Straw Bower Day, when those who had been witches [Plough Witches —N.P.] paraded the town clad from head to foot in straw, and in that guise solicited tolls and alms. But this custom did not prevail in Godmanchester" (Bird 1911, 40).

Sybil Marshall recalls that the Ramsey straw bear appearance was a custom that used to belong to another day but got mixed up with plough witching time by chance. The straw bear was led at night on a chain from pub to pub and house to house. It appears to have been associated with a mummers' play (Marshall 1967, 200–201). Plough Monday celebrations at Ramsey were reported in 1927, but records of the bears' outings are scanty (*Peterborough Advertiser,* January 14, 1927). In Whittlesea, the custom was actively suppressed in 1909 by

Fig. 12.1. Straw bear, Whittlesea,
Cambridgeshire, England

police action (Porter 1969, 103), though in the 1990s I was told by an old Whittlesea resident that the bear was made on later occasions up until World War II and clandestinely went from house to house when the police were not looking. In Whittlesea, the custom was reinstated in 1980 as an annual event. The straw bear's design was changed from its earlier round-headed form into one resembling the bears at Wilflingen and Hirschau in Germany, with a sheaf on top. The bear's outing expanded into the Straw Bear Festival, when special ale was brewed and special sausages made. Unlike former times, when it was for the ploughboys and ploughmen, the festival featured numerous morris, Molly, and sword dance teams as well as a visiting straw bear from Walldürrn in Germany. Similarly, in Ramsey, the straw bear custom was brought back and sustained by a local school, Molly dancers, and broom dancers. The author has played in the bands of the straw bear parades at both Whittlesea and Ramsey.

In the whole of England, straw bears are recorded only from these two towns, where the way of life went a drastic and irreversible turn in a short period in the mid-nineteenth century when the lakes were drained. The tradition of straw bears and straw men exists in a much

Fig. 12.2. Mepal broom dancers at Whittlesea. (Mepal is a remote village in Cambridgeshire, close to the drainage canal known as the Hundred Foot.) (See also color plate 21.)

wider area in Germany and former German territories, where they are recorded in 218 towns and villages. In Catholic parts, straw bears are made for Fastnacht, but in Protestant areas they appear at various other times of celebration, such as the Kirmesbär of Grosseicholzheim. According to Hanns Bächtold-Stäubli's collection of "superstitions," with the straw bear tradition in Saxony, the bear is made from the last cut of the harvest and then led through the village; it's called Cornbear, son of Corn Mother (Bächtold-Stäubli 1927, vol. 1, 893). In the Schwarzwald tradition, the bear is said to represent winter, which the people of the village are driving out.

Bears can be made of various kinds of corn straw or pea straw, which affects their shape. Many straw bears have no visible face at all, with the guiser seeing through gaps in the straw, but some leave the guiser's face

Fig. 12.3. Straw bear and masked keepers, Wilflingen, Germany

visible. However, in most places, it is almost concealed by the straw, as at Empfingen and Hirschau.

Some wear bear masks, as at Buchen (Odenwald), Epfendorf, Osterburken, and Wellendingen. At Hettingen, some of the straw bears have bear masks, while others show the guiser's blackened face amid the straw. At Singen, the guiser of the Hoorige Bâr wears a red human-faced mask with a lolling tongue. The straw bear at Wilflingen, which has a woven basket without a bottom around its head, is tied to a rope held by two masked figures in spotted costumes with tall pointed hats and is accompanied by devil guisers in black masks with horns. In Silesia, the guising horse called the Schimmelreiter was accompanied by a straw bear that was tied to a pole (Weinhold 1855, 6). This description resembles the heraldic emblem of Warwick in England, the Bear and Ragged Staff.

The tallest straw figures of all are the Kloas, straw bears with a massively extended upper part above the guiser's head that may rise to fourteen feet in height. These are traditional at Ebershardt and Waldorf, where they are billed as "Germany's tallest straw bears." The Hisgier of Sulzberg-Laufens wears a neat straw suit with a hat that comes down

Fig. 12.4. Straw bear, Wilflingen, Germany (See also color plate 20.)

over the shoulders to make a mask with holes for the eyes. The Hisgier, which also appears at Betberg and Seefelden near Buggingen, wears garlands, a sash, and bells. It is associated with decorative pace-egging at Easter. The Pelzmärtle that appears at Nonnenmiss and Sprollenhaus near Bad Windbad has its straw arranged in neat rows, some actually woven, unlike the normal uncut straw of most straw bears, which gives them a ragged outline. These figures also wear a belt and iron bells. The Pelzmärtle at Gaistal wears a straw suit with long straw plaits as horns with red ribbons at the top. In 2011 at Empfingen, Baden-Württemberg, to celebrate 60 Jahre nei da Flegga, the sixtieth anniversary of the Narrenzunft (Fools' Guild), straw bears from towns and villages all over Germany appeared in the parade, one of the largest assemblies of straw bears anywhere.

Fig. 12.5. Walldürrn, Germany, straw bear performing at Whittlesea Straw Bear Festival

In France, the Butzimummel is made at Attenschweiler and l'Iltis at Buschwiller. L'Orso di Paglia is a straw bear guised at Valdieri in Piedmont, Italy. Other straw figures appear at Epiphany in Nicolospiel at Mitterndorf, Steiermark, Austria, and as the Strohbutz with a tall, ribbon-bedecked headpiece at Ailringen and Zaisenhausen. Straw men appear at Stary Hrozenkor in Slovakia, Hlinsko in the Czech Republic, and in Germany as the Urstrohmann at Leipferdingen, with long, pointed straw bundles bound to the arms and over the head. Similar straw men are made at Unterwittstadt and Sigmaringendorf, where ribbons top the tall mask-hat. In 1933, Ethel Rudkin reported an account of the straw man formerly made at Holton-le-Clay in Lincolnshire. There, the straw man appeared on Plough Monday with the Plough Jags, who did not take a plough with them but performed a mummers' play. The straw man appeared to be a dummy with a long straw tail that dragged behind him along the ground. He was carried from place to place by the other men in the group. They carried the straw man into a house and set him down. Suddenly, he would come to life, for there was a man inside, and he began to speak, and the play commenced (Rudkin 1933, 282). This is the classic instance of the seemingly empty figure who suddenly comes to life. He is the Dudman, a hollow man whose human identity is questionable, who crosses the borderline between otherworldly spirit, puppet, effigy, and disguised human as an embodiment of the incorporeal. His scarecrow-like appearance emphasizes his link with the land. Straw men appear in Shrovetide customs in Slovakia, Slovenia, Serbia, Croatia, and Romania.

The straw man is also a figure associated with the Christian fasting season of Lent. Jack O'Lent was made and set up on Ash Wednesday. Sometimes the straw man was covered with fish emblems, signifying the season of fasting. (During the six weeks of Lent, he was occasionally pelted and stoned, and he was finally burned on Palm Monday.) The straw man, once known in England as Jack Straw or Jack O'Lent, appears on windowsills in southern Germany to this day during the period of Fastnacht, the days leading up to Shrove Tuesday. Pieter Breughel de Oude's 1559 painting *De Strijd tussen Vasten en Vastenavond*

(*The battle between Carnival and Lent*) shows a clothed stuffed straw figure sitting on just such a ledge. The fate of the straw man, clothed in ragged castoffs, is to be dragged through the streets and shot to pieces or cast into the fire. Jack O'Lent was beaten, kicked, stoned, shot at, or burned, for in Cornwall, he is identified as Judas Iscariot (Wright and Lones 1936, 38). In former times, effigies of Judas Iscariot were burned at street corners in Liverpool, and at Kirton-in-Lindsey, Lincolnshire, a straw man was burned on November 5 in place of the usual effigy of Guy Fawkes (Peacock 1907, 450). Jack O'Lent appears as a target figure in Ben Jonson's play *Tale of a Tub*.

> *Thou cam'st but halfe a thing into the world,*
> *And wast made up of patches, parings, shreds:*
> *Thou, that when last thou wert put out of service,*
> *Travaild'st to Hamsted Heath, on an Ash-wensday*
> *Where thou didst stand six weekes the lack of Lent,*
> *For boyes to hoorle, three throwes a penny, at thee.*
> (JONSON [1633] 1816, VOL. 6, 207)

The most celebrated Jack Straw was one of the leaders of the English Peasants Revolt of 1381, who disguised himself as the archetypal maukin. The connection of straw with rebellion is known from thirteenth-century France, where the rebels called Paillers carried about a bottle of straw called a *paille* with which they burned the property of their oppressors (O'Neill 1895, 296). (This practice also existed in England, where one Cambridgeshire Plough Monday chant recalls it.) It is likely that Jack Straw's name comes from the connection of the straw man with rebel incendiarism. He was a well-known figure in the folk tradition, and a play from 1593, *The Life and Death of Jack Straw, a Notable Rebel in England,* recounts his struggles against the royal tax collectors, taking the cause of the poor and dispossessed against the rich overlords: "Neighbors, neighbors . . . but marke my words, and follow the counsell of John Ball, England is gone to such a past of late, that rich men triumph to see the poore beg at their gate." The rebel Jack Straw was killed in 1381, but his example lived on. He appeared as a character in mummers' plays and was banned by an ordinance of King Henry VIII in 1517, "that Jack Straw and all his adherents should be henceforth utterly banisht, and no more be used in this house." Jack Straw is a character in a number of mummers' plays from Ireland (Gailey 1972, 136–37).

> *With my whim wham whaddle O!*
> *Jack Straw straddle O!*
> *Pretty boy bubble O!*
> *Under a broom.*

Straw figures also appeared as accompanying figures in Christmas guising. In 1847, a Christmas party in Manchester's Free Trade Hall for members of the Mechanics' Institution included all the traditional elements of Christmas, the rustic processions and mummeries. "The rustics and mummers," a correspondent for the *Manchester Times* wrote, "forming what was called The Procession of Father Christmas, the Wassail Bowl and Snap Dragon." When the Yule log was brought in, "the merrie, merrie boys cracked their whips, and the Snap Dragon was ushered before the company, by a man and his wife dressed in straw garments, masked and attended by a party of mummers" (*Manchester Times,* January 8, 1847, 5).

Straw men are ambiguous; they may be just a dummy or there may be a person inside, ready to leap into action. Scarecrows are dummies traditionally made from old clothes stuffed with straw with the intention of frightening off birds. But they recall the figures of spiritual guardians set up in fields in former times to ward off evil spirits and harmful forces that might cause the harvest to fail. Made from the straw of the last harvest, they looked forward to the next. Butz at Pratteln in Switzerland, who rides astride a barrel on a wagon pulled by men dressed in horse costumes, is a Strohpuppen, a masked dummy of a man made from clothes stuffed with straw. Straw-stuffed clothes worn by real people were a feature of traditional parades on Plough Monday in England. In Germany, the masked Wuscht guisers at Villingen, the Ausgestopfen (Stuffed Ones) at Villingen, and the

Lumpenhunde (Ragged Dog) at Gegenbach all feature clothes stuffed with straw.

A painting by Francisco Goya (1746–1828), *The Straw Manikin,* made in 1791 and 1792, depicts four women tossing a masked straw figure in a blanket, either an effigy or a person. A similar Goya etching from about 1820 shows five women tossing two small, puppet-like figures in a blanket. The Straw Boys of Ireland, dressed in straw suits with their faces obscured by conical hats of straw, turned up at weddings uninvited and claimed food and drink and the right to dance with the bride. In some places, they appeared with a hobby horse (*Kerry Evening Post,* December 29, 1886, 3). Similarly, the Irish Biddy Boys of the festival of Saint Bridget appear in straw masks and suits bound with ropes

Fig. 12.6. Verschmanndl guiser and goat, Sankt-Johann, Austria (See also color plate 22.)

of woven straw. The name of the clownesque French character Paillasse, often depicted in a Pierrot-like costume, means "straw man," and a straw man, the Bonhomme de Paille, appeared at Mezilles. The title of Rugerro Leoncavallo's famous opera, *Pagliacci,* has the same meaning. The American folklorist Charles Godfrey Leland saw this character, on sale as doll-like figures in Florence, Italy, in the 1890s, as an image of a goblin (Leland 1897, 8). To dress in straw is to assert our spiritual bond with the Earth. Albert Bärtsch, the Swiss expert on central European masking traditions, likened straw men, straw bears, and figures covered with shredded tree bark with *die Wilden;* that is, with Woodwoses (wild men), though this interpretation is challenged (Bärtsch 1993, 93–98).

In Britain, the straw man was not only a Christmas, New Year, and Lenten custom. He also was made for rantanning, otherwise known as "rough music," a ritual of shaming and punishment of villagers who had transgressed the accepted morality of the day. If any man had offended the community by behaving badly to his wife, such as beating her, he would be given a warning to stop, but if he continued, then his neighbors "took the law into their own hands" and the person was rantanned. Sometimes it was a woman who beat her husband or couples who indulged in an extramarital affair who were rantanned. Even couples who decided at the last minute not to get married could be rantanned. In 1895, Sidney Oldall Addy noted that in 1888 "a man and a woman living at Cold Aston, in Derbyshire, were engaged to be married, the wedding ring was bought on Saturday, and the marriage was to be celebrated the following Monday. But, in the meantime, they quarreled, and the wedding did not take place. On the Monday evening the boys of the village made a straw image of the man, which they burned in the street opposite to his door, and they also burned a straw image of the woman opposite her door in the same manner" (Addy 1895, 76).

In 1933, an incident was recalled by a "Mr. L" from Holton-le-Clay in Lincolnshire in which a schoolmaster beat a boy severely and left him tied by his thumbs to a clothesline. Even by the rough and brutal teaching standards accepted as the norm in 1933, this treatment so enraged the villagers that they rantanned the schoolmaster. The locals got their kettles and cans from their houses and borrowed a piece of sheet iron from the blacksmith. Two people held the sheet, and others beat it with sticks and hammers. The people made a straw man and carried him to the schoolmaster's house. Then they made rough music for the schoolmaster for three successive nights. After the third rantanning, they took the straw man to the green outside the public house and burned it (Rudkin 1933, 292). A rantanning song from Willoughton, Lincolnshire, which threatened to put a wife beater "in the news" (i.e., the obituary column of the local newspaper) went:

> *Ran tan tan!*
> *The sound of an old tin can.*
> *He did lick her,*
> *He did kick her,*
> *He gave her a sad bruise,*
> *And if he does the likes again,*
> *We'll put him in the News.*

Usually, the rantanned man stayed indoors and dared not show himself. Anyone who was taken out of the house was beaned—that is, beaten with short-stocked whips with five thongs—then thrown in the pond. The straw man presided at the punishment (Rudkin 1933, 292–93). The making of a straw man for rantanning is recorded in several Lincolnshire villages, including Langwith, Willoughton, Winterton, and Holton-le-Clay, places where the straw man also appeared on Plough Monday. In West Wales, a similar rite to punish and shame adulterers used a straw man on a straw horse, the Ceffyl Pren.

It was carried around the village or town in a noisy procession with blowing horns and hitting metal. After the parades, which may have been made over a three-week period, the straw rider was shot and effigies were burned outside the front doors of the guilty.

Sometimes, as in the Lincolnshire example quoted above, the people were dragged from their houses and paraded in ridicule on a ladder (Davies 1911, 85–86). In some places in Britain, straw effigies were not made, but the "tin can band" came out. In East Yorkshire, "to excite public opinion against a wife-beater it is customary to 'ride the stang' for him. A 'stee' (ladder) is procured, and a noisy procession perambulates the streets, singing and shouting and making the night hideous with the braying of horns, clashing of iron pans, screaming of whistles, and banging of drums. This must be done on three successive nights to make it legal, or the 'riders' believe they could be summoned for breaking the peace" (Nicholson 1890, 33). Thus, a ritual was made legal in the eyes of its participants so long as it was performed according to the proper ceremonial form. Another name for this rite is skimmington, or the skimmington ride. In the west country, a Wooset was made to accompany the rough music for village offenders (*Wiltshire Archaeological Magazine,* 1, 88, quoted in Chambers 1933, 213–14). Those going Ooset hunting or Wooset hunting used a horse's skull with snapping jaws on a pole with a pair of horns attached (Read 1911, 302).

13

Dragonry

Legendary Dragons and Dragon Legends

The dragon is a mythical earthly beast, unlike Boggarts, Bogey Men, Goblins, and their ilk. Even phantom animals like the Hedley Kow, the Habergeiss, or Black Shuck do not possess the archetypal resonance of the dragon. Although many of these beings are embodiments of disruptive and destructive forces, they are not general images of universal chaos, which the dragon is. Dragons are images of the awesome power of chaos that can intrude at any time on the seemingly determinate world of human activities. The dragon is a manifestation of turbulent cosmic powers, the irresistible flow of water, and the wind-driven firestorm. In the Northern Tradition, it appears both as the watery Midgard serpent Iormungandr, writhing on the ocean bed, triggering earthquakes and tsunamis, and as the terrestrial dragons that must be overcome by the self-sacrificing action of brave warriors.

What are generically called dragon legends encompass beasts of several forms. It is telling that in parts of Britain that culturally have Scandinavian elements, they are all referred to as *worms*. This comes from the Old Norse word *ormr*. In the headlands at Llandudno in North Wales, they are called the Little Orme and Great Orme. The English word *vermin* is related to *worm,* an animal considered so

135

harmful that it ought to be exterminated. Worms, which are not in the class of dragons, are not just the legendary worms but also earthworms, tapeworms, woodworms, and so forth. A worm can be a dragon, a wyvern, an ask, or a serpent, fiery or otherwise. Serpents and dragons merge with each other in myth. The Irish Péiste, or water horse, sometimes appears in serpent form. Dragons were literally monsters, the word coming from the Roman spiritual concept of the *monstrum,* something disturbingly errant from the natural order that served as a visible sign of the gods' displeasure. Remains of dragons were preserved as relics by city authorities and in churches.

The beasts called Lyngvi or Lingorm appear in *Volsunga Saga.* A *lindwurm* is a central European beast that is said to live for 270 years. The first ninety are spent in the earth, the second in linden trees, and the third ninety in the desert. Catholic images of the Queen of Heaven show her trampling a lindwurm. It was traditional to set such images on notable linden trees as well as in sacred contexts. A skull identified as belonging to a lindwurm was unearthed at Klagenfurt in Austria in 1335. At Brno, in the Czech Republic, an object believed to be a stuffed lindwurm used to hang above a passage that led to the city hall. It had been killed by a knight who filled a calf's skin with quicklime, which the lindwurm ate and died. The Great Dragon of Malpasso on the Mediterranean island of Rhodes also was preserved.

Medieval legend has many sagas and stories featuring slayers of worms, serpents, and dragons. The Arthurian hero Sir Percival (a.k.a. Peredur or Parzifal) has various accounts in which he kills serpents. In *The Mabinogion,* the tale "Peredur, Son of Evrawc" tells of his encounter with a serpent who guarded a gold ring and how he later killed the Addanc of the Lake, another dragonlike beast. Finally in this story, he kills the Black Serpent on the Mound of Mourning. In *The High History of the Holy Grail,* Percival kills a serpent that "had issued from a hole in a mountain" and later a dragon with yawning jaws that "casteth forth fire and flame in great plenty."

Several Christian saints and prelates are credited with the destruction of dragons. The Celtic saint Samson killed both a serpent at Ynys Pyr in Wales and a dragon at Lewannick in Cornwall.

Saint George is the most famous dragon slayer of all. In medieval times, festival days of these saints featured dragons paraded through the streets and sometimes "killed" by a knight on horseback personating the saint. Pope Sylvester I (Saint Sylvester) is depicted leading a dragon whose jaws he bound with a consecrated rope. Saint Donatus killed a dragon living near Arezzo in Italy. Saint Martha, vanquisher of a dragon, is personated at Tarascon in France by a woman who leads the Tarasque through the streets. Saint Margaret is also shown with a tamed dragon on a lead. In Croatia, Saint Hilarion ordered a dragon to go into a bonfire, where it was burned, which appears to be the fate of some guising dragons at the end of their parade.

Local legends credit local heroes with ridding their districts of marauding worms and dragons. In Austria, Herzog Karast of Klagenfurt rid the marsh there of a lindwurm that was devouring cattle and people. The Lindwurmbrunnen Fountain in the city, erected in 1590, has an image of the dragon he slew. Its head was modeled from the lindwurm skull found in 1335. Thomas Percy's *Reliques of Ancient English Poetry* (Percy 1891, vol. 3, 107–13) contains "The Legend of Sir Guy," an ancient story mentioned by Geoffrey Chaucer. In 1823, R. Surtees wrote:

Sir Guy of Warwick is a local hero who was more than a mere dragon-slayer. He fought and killed a number of threatening figures including the giant Amarant, Colebrand or Colbronde, the champion war-rior of the Danes, whose bones were kept as relics in Coventry and Warwick, the dreadful giant Dun Cow of Dunsmore Heath, and the Longwitton Dragon in northeastern England. Also in Northumbria the Sockburn Worm was killed by a knight, Sir John Conyers who, as *Bowes's Manuscript* tells us "slew that monstrous and poisonous vermin, wyvern, ask, or werme, which had overthrown and devoured many people in fight: for that the scent of the poison was so strong that no person might abyde it." (Surtees 1823, vol. 3, 243)

To kill the worm, Sir John Conyers used a falchion, a type of sword with a broad blade two and a half feet long. This thirteenth-century weapon is still in existence.

Not only legendary and symbolic figures were dragon slayers. The feat was ascribed to real historic knights of great prowess. Gilles de Chin (died 1137) killed a dragon in 1133, and the feat was celebrated in the city of Mons and at Wasmes, where there was an annual dragon procession. The Provençal knight Dieudonné de Gozon was the grand master of the Knights of Saint John at Rhodes from 1346 to 1353. He killed the Great Dragon of Malpasso, which some claimed to be an outsize crocodile (Hasluck 1914, passim).

Dragon Parades

In 1859, Frederick William Fairholt (1814–1866) wrote:

In many churches in France before the great Revolution, it was customary, three days before Holy Thursday, for the clergy to carry in procession a dragon, whose long tail was filled with chaff. The first two days it was borne *before* the cross, with the tail *full;* the third

Fig. 13.1. Le Lumeçon, Mons, Belgium

day it was borne *after* the cross with the tail *empty.* This was to signify that on the first days the Devil reigned in the world; but on the last, he was dispossessed. The local dragons abounded, and were realizations of those believed to have been conquered by the patron saints of the various places. M. Bottin in his *History of the North of France,* has noted twenty-one such in that district alone; and M. Delmotte in his *Recherches sur Gilles Chin et le Dragon de Mons,* added seventeen others. (Fairholt 1859, 95–96)

The majority of dragon appearances in European culture are in association with Saint George. In the Netherlands, Flanders, France, and England in medieval times, dragons were made and brought out on Saint George's Day, April 23, by Saint George's guilds, which represented fighting men. The thirteenth-century London Guild of St. George later became the Honourable Company of Pikemen, traditionally the body-guards of the lord mayors of London. St-Joris Doelen existed in many towns in the Low Countries, guilds of crossbowmen dedicated to Saint George, which were the cities' defensive militias. They existed in Aalst, Bruges, Ghent, the Hague, Middelburg, and a number of other cities. Several are still in existence, practicing the sport of crossbow shooting. A print by Pieter Breughel de Oude, *De Sint-Joriskermis* (the fair of Saint George; ca. 1559) shows a number of activities, including dancing, drinking, and feasting. As well as this being one of the oldest known pictures of longsword dancing with two bagpipers providing the music, there also is a dragon on wheels being pushed by a man and a knight on horseback attacking it with his lance. In the background, the marksmen are shooting at a target atop a long pole set on top of a windmill.

The only surviving English dragon is also associated with a guild of Saint George, for the East Anglian city of Norwich has a tradition of dragon parading that dates at least from the fourteenth century. In 1342, the city had its own defensive artillery in the shape of thirty *springards* (bolt throwers) (Howlett 1907, 60–61), and by 1385, fifty guns were mounted on the towers and gates of the city wall (Maddern 2004, 193). The wickerwork and canvas dragon called Snap or Old Snap is a symbol of local identity, an instance of long cultural continuity at a particular place. Old Snap is a hobby animal, made to be carried by an operator inside it. The operator's head is visible. Like the related hobby horses, hobby dragons are a little-recognized element of the repertoire of the basket maker.

Old Snap began as part of a religious performance; it was the property of the Norwich Guild of St. George, which dated from 1385. The guild assembly records for the year 1408 record money being voted to provide copes for the priests to wear, "and the George shall go in procession and make conflict with the dragon." As with all traditional processions, it always took a particular route through the city, ending at the cathedral for a Mass in Saint George's Chapel. The dragon, being a symbol of evil, was not taken into the cathedral but left on a flat stone, called *the dragon's stone,* by the door (Porter 1974, 60–61). In the 1429 performance, the dragon's operator was paid danger money as gunpowder was used to make the dragon breathe fire.

In 1417, King Henry V awarded the Guild of St. George a royal charter, and in 1430, the guild attempted to fix the election of the lord mayor of Norwich. By then, the Guild of St. George was the most powerful organization in the city, and in 1452, a legal ruling called Yelverton's Mediation led to the guild taking complete control of the city. Norwich was ruled by the guild for the next 279 years. Most religious guilds were suppressed at the Reformation, but the Guild of St. George, having a royal charter, continued to exist as the Company of Saint George. Dragon parades continued every year, but no longer did the dragon slayer Saint George or Saint Margaret, who had been added at some time, appear. "There shall neither be George nor Margaret; but, for pastime, the Dragon to come and shew himself as in other years." The dragon, not

Fig. 13.2. Old Snap, Norwich, England (1901 drawing)

being a Roman Catholic saint like George and Margaret, outlived them.

In 1584, the City Assembly amalgamated the Saint George's Day festival with the inauguration of the lord mayor. Old Snap appeared annually in the lord mayor's parade from 1585 until 1731, when the Company of Saint George was finally abolished. The dragon, however, continued to appear at the inaugurations of lord mayors. In the eighteenth century, it was accompanied by "a train of Whifflers" who juggled with their swords and Dick Fools, dressed in motley and decked with cats' tails and small bells (Chambers 1933, 174). But in 1835, the Municipal Corporations Act abolished many ancient traditions and usages, and the parading of dragons by the Corporation of Norwich was one of them. However, even this did not stop the dragon from appearing on the streets on Saint George's Day until 1850 (Porter 1974, 60–61). During the early part of the twentieth century, reflecting the puritanical antifestive stance of utilitarian uniformity of the time, the dragon did not appear on the streets. As with Plough Monday elsewhere in England and the Fastnacht revels in Germany, the authorities frowned on the alcohol-fueled merriment and misrule inherent in these traditions. With its snapping jaws, Old Snap

Fig.13.3. Old Snap on an outing in nineteenth-century Norwich

Fig.13.4. Old Snap in the Norwich lord mayor's parade, 1996

grabbed people's hats and caps and then demanded money for their return: "Snap, Snap, steal a boy's cap; give him a penny, he'll give it back."

In 1951, as part of the Festival of Britain celebrations, one of the old dragons was brought out onto the Norwich streets again for a brief outing. After that were further sporadic appearances, but not for the lord mayor. In the 1980s, Snap was reintroduced to the lord mayor's procession by the Kemp's Men morris dancers.

There were other dragons around Norwich. Two city suburbs had their own unofficial guilds that paraded dragons. The Pockthorpe Guild, founded in 1772, had a dragon that traveled from inn to inn on each April 24, the day after Saint George's Day. Another dragon was paraded during Whitsuntide at Costessey when a "mock mayor" was installed. That tradition was suppressed in 1895 (W. H. Jones, in Andrews 1898, 182–95). Three complete Old Snaps have been preserved, as well as the head of a fourth. The oldest Norwich dragon is preserved in the Castle Museum. It dates from 1795. Two others are Pockthorpe Snaps, which were kept in public houses when not on parade, and the head is from a Costessey dragon. The 1795 municipal dragon has a wickerwork frame and is covered with painted canvas. "The body was five feet in length," wrote Fairholt, "and was sometimes used to secrete wine abstracted from the Mayor's cellar. The neck was capable of elongation (measuring three feet and a half when extended); was supported by springs attached to the body, and was capable of being turned in any direction at the will of the bearer" (Fairholt 1859, 98). The head is carved from wood and has a snapping jaw mechanism fitted with horseshoes to make the noise. In the 1880s, Back and Company, wine and spirit merchants, acquired one of the old Pockthorpe dragons and hung it in the shop doorway as trade sign for the Norwich liquors Old Snap whisky and gin. Old Snap whisky was advertised by a color illustration of the dragon in front of Saint Andrew's Hall.

There are number of other performing dragons documented in the eastern counties of England, but they did not continue to become part of local identity in the way that Old Snap has. In Hertfordshire, at Bishop's Stortford, a dragon is mentioned in the churchwardens' accounts (Jones-Baker 1977, 175). It appears to have been part of a play of Saint Michael and the dragon. Made of hoops and canvas like Snap in Norwich, it was hired out to Braughing and other neighboring

Fig. 13.5. Morris dancers' dragon, King's Lynn, Norfolk, England (See also color plate 23.)

parishes. At Wymondham in Norfolk, an indenture of 1519 refers to the construction of an image of Saint George and a dragon for a guild procession on Saint John the Baptist's Day, June 24 (Harrod 1872, 271). The Tuesday before this day was known there as Snapdragon Day (W.C.B. 1908, 481). At Burford in Oxfordshire, a dragon and a giant were carried "up and down" on midsummer's eve (Fairholt 1859, 61). The medieval guild at Little Walsingham in Norfolk also had a dragon, but nothing is known of it. Until World War II put an end to the custom in 1940, small dragons were sold at the fair at Henham in Essex each July, and a special festival ale called Snakebite was brewed and sold. All that is known about the Henham dragon comes from seventeenth-century pamphlets that may be allegorical or satirical in intent, such as *The Flying Serpent, or, Strange News out of Essex*. But the dragon appeared at least once in theatrical form. In May 1910, it was featured in the lavish *Saffron Walden Pageant*. In scene eight, titled "Scenes from Old Walden," Hugh Cranmer-Byng presented "The Flying Serpent of Walden," beginning with the lines:

> *When Sol his refulgent beams*
> *Above the mount of Henham gleams,*
> *A grisly Dragon stalks abroad*
> *And preens himself upon the sward.*

The dragon appeared as a pantomime animal in this performance. Hugh Cranmer-Byng quotes his source in the published text of the pageant, which was a 1669 pamphlet by Peter Lillicrap, which tells of the dragon, or rather a cockatrice, "who by his very sight killed so many." After the usual heroic knight, clad in armor of "Christal Glass," slew the monster, "the effigies of the Cockatrice, set up in Brass, and a Table hanged close by wherein was continued all the story of the adventure" were set up in the church at Saffron Walden. But, "in these late times of Rebellion, it being taken for a monument of Superstition, was by the lawless Soldiers broken in pieces" (Cranmer-Byng et al. 1910, 37–39).

In Bavaria at Furth im Wald, *Der Drachenstich,* a mummers' play dating from the fifteenth century, was performed on the first Sunday after Corpus Christi. It featured a fire-breathing wooden dragon. In England, theatrical dragons appeared in mummers' plays with titles like *Saint George He Was for England* and in the Shropshire traveling players' outdoor stage play *Saint George and the Fiery Dragon,* in which the dragon, like the Furth im Wald dragon, was made of wood and breathed fire. Snap Dragon was a feature of Old English Christmas and sometimes appeared outside of the context of the mummers' plays. At Christmas feasts in Victorian Britain, Snap Dragon appeared along with Old Father Christmas. Similar events took place in other places in the mid-nineteenth century, including Cambridge, where the Lord of Misrule was attended by Snap Dragon and a hobby horse.

In Belgium, a larger relative of the Norwich dragon is paraded in the city of Mons. Gilles de Chin was a real twelfth-century knight who became a tournament champion before taking the cross as a crusader. He was killed in 1137 and buried in the Abbey of Saint Ghislain. Gilles de Chin was commemorated in the dragon festival of the Ducasse de Mons, of which the dragon le Lumeçon is the central character, slain by the valiant knight, but later Saint George supplanted him. The dragon is carried by les Hommes Blancs, dressed in white, who support the body, and les Hommes Sauvages, otherwise called Hommes de Feuilles (Wild Men or Leafy Men), who carry and manipulate the long metal tail. The earliest note of them is in the town records from 1723. As in many such parades, such as at Whittlesea and Rottweil-am-Neckar, there is a ceremonial tune that is played repeatedly during the Mons event, called "El Doudou." In its form, le Lumeçon closely resembles Old Snap at Norwich. The wild men's costumes are covered in more than two thousand fabric ivy leaves. The men are accompanied by hobby horses called Chinchins. (De Tournai 1941, passim). In Belgium, dragons were also formerly paraded at Namur and Brussels, and in the Netherlands in the Draakestaken at Beesel.

In France at Metz, the guising dragon called le Graully was paraded on April 23, Saint George's Day. However, it did not commemorate the dragon slayer Saint George but rather a mythical first-century bishop, Clément, who was credited with having killed a dragon in the year

LE GRAULLY

(LÉGENDE MESSINE)

Dragon effroyable, aux proportions gigantesques, qui répandit dans la cité Messine la terreur, l'épouvante et la mort. Il fut vaincu par saint Clément, 1ᵉʳ Évêque de Metz, en l'an 47 de notre ère.

(Voir la Notice qui se vend au profit du Bureau de Bienfaisance.)

Fig.13.6. Le Graully poster, Metz, France

47 CE. Le Graully was carried on a decorated vehicle pulled by horses. The poster reproduced in figure 13.6 depicts it with only two legs, so it was a wyvern. Bakers made small bread dragons for sale at the festival.

At Draguignan in France, an effigy of the dragon slain by Saint Hermentaire was paraded. Another French parade dragon of note is the Tarasque. Brought out at Pentecost and on Saint Martha's Day, July 29, this dragon is the emblem of the Provençal city of Tarascon. According to legend, the Tarasque, a scaly, six-legged dragon with a spiky carapace resembling a turtle, lived on the banks of the River Rhône between Arles and Avignon. It was vanquished by Saint Martha. The festival dates from 1474, when King René chartered a guild of Tarascaires to organize and oversee the festival. The guild's motto was Anen Beure ("let us drink"). The Tarasque is a wickerwork and canvas construction comparable to that of the dragons of Mons and Norwich and the Obby Oss of Padstow. It was carried by three men, making it six-legged. It has snapping jaws, and fireworks in its nostrils provide its fiery breath. There is a stone sculpture of the Tarasque near King René's Castle in Tarascon. Other Tarasques appear in Corpus Christi processions in Spain, at Madrid, Granada, Toledo, and Valencia.

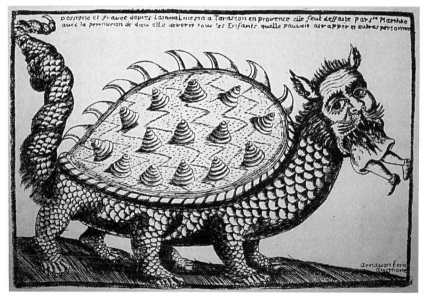

Fig. 13.7. Tarasque, Tarascon, France

14

Civic Giants

The custom of parading various giant figures that represented people of local importance was widespread in medieval Europe on various saints' days and the feast of Corpus Christi. European civic giants often recalled founders and spiritual guardians of cities as well as the opponents of the founding heroes they commemorated. Writing about civic tradition in northern France, Marie-France Gueusquin noted that the giants of the festival parades in Flanders were representations either of barbarians who had been converted or annihilated or of defenders of urban institutions (Gueusquin 1985, passim). In London, giants made of wickerwork and pasteboard were originally called Gogmagog and Corineus, the former after the Cornish giant slain by Brutus's champion, Corineus. For hundreds of years, they appeared as the guardians of the city in pageants and civic parades. Later, when the founding legend was no longer celebrated, they became known as Gog and Magog.

In 1859, Frederick William Fairholt wrote, "When the old Lord Mayors' shows consisted of a series of pageants, invented by poets of no mean fame, the Civic Giants were part of the great public display. On occasions of Royal progresses through the city, they kept 'watch and ward' at its gates. In 1415 when the victorious Henry V made his triumphant entry to London from Southwark, a man and woman giant stood at the entrance to London Bridge" (Fairholt 1859, 27). In 1432,

King Henry VI was greeted by "a mighty giant" when he entered the city. Giants were made or brought out for later royal visits, including for Queen Elizabeth I at her coronation in 1554. John Marston (1576–1634), in his play *The Dutch Courtesan* (1604), has the line "the giants stilts that stalk before my Lord Mayor's pageants" (Fairholt 1859, 30). The figures continued to appear at lord mayors' shows each November. In 1708, new figures were commissioned from Captain Richard Saunders, whose business was carving ships' figureheads. Unlike the earlier wickerwork and pasteboard figures, this time Gog and Magog were carved from solid wood, too heavy to carry easily, as their forerunners had been. They stood in the London Guildhall until, in 1940 during World War II, they were destroyed when the Guildhall was burned during the London blitz.

The Salisbury giant, Saint Christopher, is first recorded from 1496 when he was brought out to lead the mayor and the corporation to meet King Henry VII. The Salisbury Guild of Merchant Tailors, whose charter dated from 1447, were the patrons of the giant, whom they brought out in parade on the eve of the Feast of Saint John, the old Midsummer Day. As with all dragons and giants, new ones were made to replace older ones when they wore out. The hobby horse called Hob-Nob, first recorded in 1572, accompanied the giant along with morris dancers, first mentioned in 1544, and whifflers (bodyguards) to part the crowds (Fairholt 1859, 62). At some point in the long history of the giant, he was also accompanied by a beadle, three black boys, and the devil. The beat of a bass drum signified the lumbering footsteps of the giant. As with the visit of King Henry VII, the giant was paraded to celebrate national events. In 1746, a twenty-five-foot giant was paraded to celebrate the defeat of the Jacobite rebels at Culloden. In 1856, the end of the war in Crimea was commemorated, and in 1919, a peace parade was held with the giant to mark the official end of World War I. The twelve-foot-high giant preserved in the Salisbury Museum along with a hobby horse was purchased from the Saint Nicholas Tailors' Guild in 1873.

The most widespread and tenacious giant tradition is in Flanders, whose ancient boundaries straddle northern France and Belgium. Most cities and towns have a giant or a series of giants. Some are representations of ancient traditional founders and liberators, such as Lydéric at the French city of Lille (Flemish name Rijsel) and Sylvius Brabo in the Belgian city of Antwerp. Others represent the giants overthrown by the heroes as well as biblical and mythological figures. Fairholt noted that these giants were brought together sometimes at great religious festivals such as that of Saint Rombaud at Malines (Mechelen) and Saint Macaire at Mons (Bergen). These "reunions of giants" paraded figures "lent by the corporations of each town to swell the public show" (Fairholt 1859, 65). The photograph reproduced in figure 14.1 below is from one of these reunions that took place in Brussels in 1897. "It was a lively sight," wrote Emile Dessaix. "The wooden giants, with their rough-hewn faces and costly raiment, towered high above the crowds. . . . At Antwerp, Ath, and Cambrai the giants appear in might; and at Mons, as well as Brussels, Bruges, Tournai, and a few other places, the giants are accompanied by different ridiculous wooden figures—

Fig. 14.1. Saint Nicholas Tailors' guild giant and hobby horse, Salisbury, England, circa 1890

burlesque representations of local by-words and people of traditional or current notoriety. . . . The Hasselt giant is merely the traditional pet of the little Belgian town. His figure is seen everywhere, just as the bear is seen in Berne, or the little monk in Munich. His relation to Hasselt is very like that of Gog and Magog in London" (Dessaix 1898, 343).

Lydéric is celebrated as the giant of Lille. Pierre D'Oudégherst (1571) records how in the year 620, Sylvaert, the duke of Dijon, was traveling across Flanders to England with his pregnant wife, Ermengaert, when he was attacked and killed by the dreadful giant Phinaert. Ermengaert escaped into the forest and was rescued by a hermit, gave birth, and died. Her son, Lydéric, was brought up by the hermit and at the age of twenty learned his true identity. He hunted down Phinaert and killed him. King Dagobert awarded him the lands owned by the giant, and there, in the year 640, Lydéric founded Lille. Lydéric is also regarded as the founder of les Forestiers de Flandre, the foresters.

Antwerp's giant legend tells that the giant Druon Antigoon (Antigonus) oppressed merchants by levying a heavy toll on all ships entering the Scheldt, cutting off the right hand of anyone who refused to pay and throwing it into the river. A captain of the Roman army, Silvius Brabo, fought the giant, cut off his right hand, and rid the port of its tyrannical master. Two hands formed the coat of arms of Antwerp, and the giant figure had a symbolic hand on his breastplate (Dessaix 1898, 347). A giant's head dating from 1535, made by the noted Flemish artist Pieter Coecke van Aelst (1502–1550), has been preserved. It is made from pasteboard (papier mâché), fabric, metal, and hair. On its helmet is a long-necked black bird with a red mouth. In 1887, the Brabofontein Fountain was set up in Antwerp's Grote Markt square. Made by sculptor Jef Lambeaux (1852–1908), it shows Lambeaux's artist's impression of Silvius Brabo triumphantly holding up the severed hand of Druon Antigoon. In the English play *Locrine* (1595), Antigonus appears as a giant fought and killed by Brutus the Trojan in Greece.

The Ducasse d'Ath has biblical and ancestral figures—Goliath and Madame Goliath, Samson, and Ambiorix. The ancient Gallo-Germanic king Ambiorix, whose forces resisted the inroads of Julius Caesar, was seen as a Belgian hero and a symbol of national resistance when the nation-state of Belgium was established in 1830. An artist's impression statue of him stands in the Belgian town of Tongeren. In contrast with the rich mythology of many Belgian giants, Emile Dessaix noted in 1898 that some of the giant effigies had no name. They were not deliberately the Sansnom (No Name) of the Valentine and Orson story, intentionally without identity (see page 227, in chapter 20). An unnamed Flemish writer quoted by Dessaix had noted that "they represent neither the founder, nor the liberator of the city, neither the heroes of Scripture, nor of mythology, neither an inhabitant of Heaven or Hell. They have no character, sacred or profane, and no significance, good or bad; they are simply 'the giants'—that is to say, the puppets of a people who have forgotten almost the traditions connected with them" (Dessaix 1898, 349).

A correspondent to the *Caledonian Mercury* in 1759 gave an account of the Cormass in Dunkirk, a procession of civic worthies and floats with giants and attendant guisers that was held on Saint John's Day, June 24, each year. One was "an enormous figure somewhat resembling an elephant; the head and eyes were very large, and it had also a huge pair of horns, on which sat several boys dressed as devils, with frightful masks and crepe dresses. The monster was hollow within, and the lower jaw was moveable, so that when pulling a string, it opened, and discovered more devils that were within. These devils who worked the jaw, were also employed to pour out liquid fire through a spout contrived for that purpose" (*Caledonian Mercury*, July 16, 1759, 1).

The French and Belgian giants and dragons are now classified by UNESCO as "intangible cultural heritage" that deserves protection as part of world culture. Paradoxically, comparable traditions north of the English Channel—the Norwich dragon, the Whittlesea Straw Bear, the Hobby Horses of Cornwall, and other English, Welsh, and Scottish guising customs—are not listed by UNESCO. In the early twenty-first century, mechanical giants have been paraded in Liverpool and Sheffield, and giant articulated and internally illuminated lantern figures have been paraded in towns in the west of England. Incidentally, the Géant de Flandres is an outsize breed of rabbit, but whether this is also a protected species is unknown.

Fig. 14.2. Antigonus, giant of Antwerp, Belgium

ANTIGONUS,
THE GIANT OF ANTWERP.

Fig. 14.3. Pallas giant paraded in Brussels, Belgium (1893 photograph)

15

Misrule, Comedy, Masks, and Puppets

The Lord of Misrule and His Merry Rout

In his Puritan polemic, *The Anatomie of Abuses,* Philip Stubbes vilified every aspect of sports, games, customs, and enjoyment. In so doing, he recorded certain details that otherwise might have been lost. Ironically, some have served as templates for later performances, the exact opposite of Stubbes's objective in publishing the book. His attack on the entourage of the Lord of Misrule, who oversaw Christmas revels, records interesting details: "Everie one of these his men he investeth with his liveries of green, yellow, or some light wanton color," and they "bedeck themselves over with scarfs, ribbons, and laces hanged all over with gold rings, precious stones, & other jewels; this doon, they tye about either leg xx or xl [20 or 40] bells then al things set in order, they have their hobby horses, dragons and other antiques, together with their handy pipers and drummer to strike up the devils dance whereal" (Stubbes [1584] 1879, 147).

Court jesters are well known from the courts of medieval monarchs. In his *Curiosities of the Church* (1890), William Andrews noted the employment of full-time fools in Old England:

Fools found a place in the great halls of the nobility until the period of the Civil War [1642–1651 —N.P.], when they appear to have fallen into disfavor. Records of their deaths appear in parish registers. The following is from Saint Anne's, Blackfriars [London —N.P.]:

> 1580. William, foole to my Lady Jerningham, bur. 21 March.

The one as follows is from St. John's, Newcastle-on-Tyne,

> 1589. Edward Errington the Towne's Fooll, bur. 23 Aug. died in the peste. . . .

A famous fool, named Dicky Pearce, died in 1728, at the age of 63 years, and was buried at Beckley, and [Jonathan] Swift [1667–1745] wrote the following epitaph for his gravestone:

> Here lies the Earl of Suffolk's Fool,
>   Men call him Dicky Pearce,
> His folly served to make men laugh,
>   When wit and mirth were scarce.
> Poor Dick, alas! is dead and gone,
>   What signifies to cry?
> Dickys enough are still behind
>   To laugh at by and by.

The last fool retained in an English family was the one at Hilton Castle, Durham, who died in the year 1746 (Andrews 1890, 163–64).

In England, jesters, fools, and clowns are significant players in traditional performances. As servants of the Lord of Misrule and characters accompanying morris dancing, ploughboys, and dragon parades and as characters in mummers' plays recorded from the eighteenth century onward, there appear Tom Fool, Dick Fool, Blather-Dick, Happy Jack, Saucy Jack, Fat Jack, Humpty Jack, Hump-and-Scrump, Silly Squire, Old Squire, Tosspot, Billy Buck, Big-head-and-little-wit, and Tommy Twing-Twang. Some, such as Harlequin, Punch, and Pierrot, originated in the Commedia dell'Arte. Big Head, whose name comes from the over-the-head masks that became the

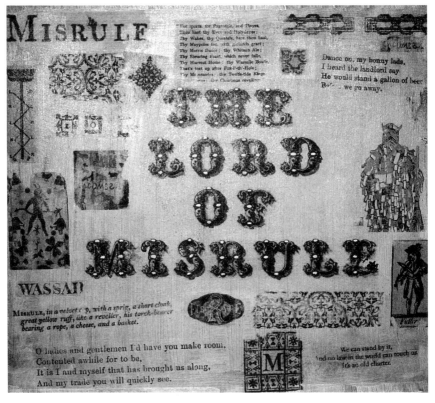

Fig. 15.1. The Lord of Misrule *acrylic transfer print on Masonite (Nigel Pennick, 2012)*

stock-in-trade of Victorian pantomimes, even when the character was not masked, also appeared as Head Per Nip, I as Ain't Been Yet, Mazzant Binnit, Fiddler Wit, Old Father Scrump, Boxholder, Little Man Dick, and Little Dick Nipp (Chambers 1933, 64). Victorian pantomime characters like Buttons, Widow Twankey, and Wishee-Washee are within the same tradition.

Masks and Influence of the Commedia dell'Arte

The Commedia dell'Arte is a dramatic form that originated in Renaissance Italy. It has the other, more descriptive, names of

Commedia all'Improvviso, its original name before the eighteenth century, referring to the instantaneous, improvisational format of the plays, and Commedia alle Maschere, because of the masks worn by actors. Originating in entertainments at markets and fairs, it became a professional art of considerable complexity, hence its present name. It flourished between 1550 and 1750 but never died out completely. Its influence on popular entertainment and folk customs alike is enormous. Performers had to be versatile, being, in addition to actors, accomplished acrobats and musicians. The Commedia dell'Arte is famed for its stock characters in recognizable costumes and masks. Companies of about ten actors, each specializing in one character, performed plays that were not scripted but had scenarios, a series of acts with particular characters playing out a story with comic sketches. The actors improvised their performances and ad-libbed their spoken parts. Comic voices and exaggerated local accents and thick dialects were

Fig. 15.2.
Commedia
dell'Arte
character
Scaramouche

identified with particular characters. The earliest plays consisted of a master and a servant. The servant character may be the oldest, as there had been comic poems and performances from the fourteenth to the sixteenth centuries that featured a mistreated, unhappy servant and his schemes to get even.

There were three sorts of character in Commedia dell'Arte. The Lovers and Servants, without masks, played the straight parts and drove the plots of the play; the Old Men were quirky characters who, while part of the plots, were masked comic caricatures; and there were the Zanni, the servants of the Old Men. The Zanni appeared to break up the action with slapstick routines and comic dialogues, sometimes obscene. They could serve as go-betweens for the Lovers and carry the plot forward in other ways. The masked valet character Mezzetino, whose name means "go-between," wore a costume of red and white stripes and used lazy tongs to deliver letters to ladies on balconies. This

Fig. 15.3. Lazy tongs wielded by a guiser in Donaueschingen, Germany also color plate 24.)

amusing tool also appears in central European carnivals and has been an instrument of misrule in England.

Of the main characters, there was the Doctor, a pedantic Old Man character sometimes named Graziano who spoke in a garbled Bologna dialect and pig latin, boring the other characters. He was dressed from head to foot in black except for a white collar. Played with a false potbelly and wearing a black semimask that covered his nose, he had a red spot painted on his cheek. Pantalone (Pantaloon), another Old Man character, bent over with age, was a merchant from Venice. He was an incompetent authoritarian, often outwitted. Married to a beautiful wife who cheated on him, he pursued other women without success. He wore a dark-brown mask with a hooked nose and a long, pointed beard. His costume was a tight-fitting one-piece red outfit, covered with a large

Pantalon.　　　Harlequin.　　　Francifquina.

Fig. 15.4. Commedia dell'Arte characters: Pantalone, Harlequin, and Francesquina

black cloak. He carried a large white handkerchief and wore a black cap, a sword, and a money pouch. Il Capitano (the Captain), sometimes called Spavento del Vall'Inferno, was a boastful bully and coward. He was played as a vainglorious Spanish soldier with a characteristic black mask with round eyes and a large nose. He wore a flowing cape and a large plumed hat and carried an outsize sword.

The Old Men characters were accompanied on stage by two Zanni, one of whom was clever and cunning and the other who was unintelligent and naive. The Zanni talked in a lower-class dialect with the local accent of the towns from which they were supposed to come. The English word *zany* comes from these characters. The Zanni performed comic double-act slapstick routines called *lazzi,* which interrupted the ongoing scenes of other characters. There were several Zanni characters, though some are immediately recognizable while others were never as popular. Most of them had names that indicated their character. Brighella (Troublemaker) came from Bergamo. He was a cynical, violent character involved in theft and seduction. He wore a green-striped jacket and white trousers and a brown mask with upturned eyebrows and a hooked nose. He carried a dagger, which he thrust through curtains and into wine barrels. Scapino (Escapee) was similar to Brighella and also wore green and white and a hooked-nosed mask. Performances by the actor Tiberio Fiorillo popularized the character Scaramuccia (Skirmisher), and he ceased to be masked. Otherwise called "Scaramouche," he was a black-garbed Zanni from Naples who loved wine and women. In his actions, he resembled the Captain's argumentative braggadocio. The Zanni Pulcinella (Little Chicken) was a humpbacked, potbellied scoundrel who combined stupidity with cruelty in his acts of gluttony and lust. He was played as a peasant from the country near Naples, wearing a conical hat, multicolored striped costume, and a broken-nosed mask. He was the prototype of Punch in the English Punch and Judy puppet shows.

Of the lesser characters, Beltrame was a servant from Milan, Franca Trippa (Tripe) was from Bologna, and Coviello, from Naples, played music and performed acrobatic feats wearing a light-brown mask and dressed in a white costume with bells. He was sometimes accompanied

Fig. 15.5. Commedia dell'Arte characters

by a character called Bertolino, a servant. Pasquariello, a sword-wielding schemer, had a long-nosed mask. Other characters appeared at various times and places, including Truffalidino (Trickster). The innocent Zanni Pedrolino (Little Peter) was a simpleton who often mimicked the actions of Il Capitano while pretending to be mute. This character was transformed in France by the playwright Molière into Gilles, a sad character dressed in a baggy white costume with a large, floppy collar and big buttons. He is not masked but has his face whitened. The image of unrequited love, he was played as Gilles in France, where Antoine Watteau (1684–1721) produced several paintings featuring him.

Michael Byrom asserts that there is some evidence that the masks of the Commedia dell'Arte were originally derived from puppets. He quotes the historian P. C. Ferrigni, who noted that puppet shows existed before the Commedia dell'Arte and showed characters that became the models of the masks. Francesco Cherea and Andrea Calmo, actors in Venice in the late sixteenth century, also were famous *marionettisti* (puppet masters). Cherea staged puppet plays with sacred themes for Pope Leo X in the Vatican (Byrom 1988, 84). The Venetian puppet master Antonio da Malin (1540–1580) was the actor who created the character Brighella. Another Commedia dell'Arte Zanni character, Burattino, an ever-hungry flat-nosed fool, has a name that means "glove-puppet" (Byrom 1988, 85). Only some of the characters in the Commedia dell'Arte are masked. They are the various Old Men and Zanni mentioned above. Of course, a nonmasked character may still have been derived from a puppet. In England, the Italian Zanni became a character in its own right as the "whachum or zany" who performed in markets and fairs as the comic foil of the quack doctors, called mountebanks, whose silly routs attracted customers for their remedies (Thompson 1928, 129).

The best known and certainly most influential character of the Commedia dell'Arte is Arlecchino, better known as "Harlequin." Possibly, his name is derived from earlier devil figures in medieval plays and ultimately from the ancient British king Herla, who rides in a version of the Wild Hunt. Whatever his antecedents were, his character was introduced to the Commedia by Zan Ganassa in the late sixteenth century. Originally, he was dressed in a peasant's shirt and long trousers covered with multicolored patches and tatters, and he spoke with a deep parrot-like squawk corresponding with Pulcinella's chicken-like voice. A master of disguises, wearing a black half-mask with a snub nose, he feigned stupidity. A hare's tail hung down from his small gray cap. His most characteristic costume was patterned all over with equal-sized lozenges or diamonds in blue, green, and red. He carried a wooden *batte* (sword or slapstick).

As Harlequin, this character became the main focus of the "ancient pantomime" slapstick performances staged by John Rich (1692–1761) at the Covent Garden Theatre in London. Harlequin's costume was transformed from beggar-like patches of the Commedia dell'Arte to a splendid outfit patterned with diamonds and circles and fringed with tassels and ruffs (McConnell Stott 2009, 109). In the pantomime, his batte became the means, like a magic wand, to transform scenes and objects, as in stage magic. Perhaps this element of the performance was imported from the zanies of the mountebanks, who performed tricks to bring in the customers for their masters' dubious medicines.

The names of earlier versions of two Commedia dell'Arte characters—Pantalone and Arlecchino—have been suggested to be derived from different sources: one a Christian saint and the other an infernal demon. Saint Pantaleon (a.k.a. Pantaleimon) is a legendary martyr from Nicomedia, a physician supposedly killed in the pogrom of Christians by the emperor Diocletian that began in 303 CE. Six different ways of killing him were attempted, all of which failed until beheading succeeded. His name is supposed to mean "all lion" (Edwards 1968, 6). He is venerated as a wonder worker, one of the Vierzehnheiligen, "the fourteen holy helpers" revered in German and

Fig. 15.6. Arlecchino

Austrian Catholicism (Delahaye 1912, 181 ff.). The word *pantaloon,* supposedly derived from his mode of dress, has gone out of use, both to describe a kind of trousers and also its earlier meaning, from the Commedia dell'Arte, of "a foolish old man"—"the lean and slippered pantaloons," as Shakespeare called him. A definition of *pantaloon* from an early eighteenth-century edition of *Chambers's Cyclopaedia* is "the name of an ancient garment frequent among our forefathers, consisting of breeches and stockings all of a piece." Saint Pantaleone was never depicted in that way, having an iron nail as his attribute along with physician's instruments, a urinal (vessel for inspecting urine), and an ampulla of ointment (Lanzi and Lanzi 2004, 231). Arlecchino only gave his name to his spangled costume, though his Malebranche antecedent, Alichino, as a demonic denizen of hell according to Dante Alighieri, is the opposite of Saint Pantaleon and his heavenly destination.

Punch and Judy

The "Punch and Judy Show" is a British puppet show conducted in a tall booth with a small proscenium at the top. The professor—

Fig. 15.7. "Punch and Judy Show": final scene, Punch fights the devil (engraving by George Cruikshank) (See also color plate 25.)

all operators of Punch and Judy shows are called professor—stands unseen and operates the glove puppets. The center of the action, Punch, is derived from the Commedia dell'Arte character Pulcinella, a humpbacked, potbellied scoundrel who embodies mindless folly and cruelty. The Italian prototype is played with a cackling, chickenlike voice, often speaking in the garbled dialect *grammalot,* and the professor of Punch and Judy has a special device called a *pivetta* or *swazzle* in the mouth to distort the voice in a similar way. In his book *Tolondron,* Giuseppe Baretti explained that the English name Punchinello is in Italian Pulcinella, which means "a hen-chicken" (Baretti 1786). Little chicken Chicken's voices being squeaking and nasal and chickens being timid and powerless, so the character, both on stage and in the puppet show, expresses its cowardly—"chicken"— nature (Byrom 1988, 85). Punch is depicted in the "Punch and Judy Show" as a bully and a coward. The play is a cavalcade of characters whom Punch disposes of violently with the repeated line "That's the way to do it!" The puppet Punch has a truncheon or club derived from the batte carried by certain characters in the Commedia dell'Arte. Essentially, the story is that Punch has a series of encounters with varied characters, and after some comic exchanges, he beats and kills them—and usually gets away free at the end.

The characters in the "Punch and Judy Show" have varied over the years. The Museum of London has a set of puppets made around 1830: Punch, Judy, Baby, Beadle, Policeman, Doctor, Scaramouche, the Hangman, Jones, Publican, two boxers, and Priest (Byrom 1988, 100). Professor Smith's script published in *The Book of Punch and Judy* by London's leading toy shop, Hamley's, in 1906 includes in the "figures" Punch, Judy, Dog Toby, Joey the Clown, Mr. Marwood the Executioner, Policeman, Ghost, and Crocodile. William Marwood (1818–1883) was the public hangman in mid-Victorian England. The character of Joey was based on the celebrated clown Joseph Grimaldi (1778–1837), who appeared in harlequinades in London in the early nineteenth century. Mr. Punch clubs everyone he encounters. Finally, he tricks and hangs the hangman about to execute him for murder. In some plays, the devil then comes for him but is killed by Punch. At the end, Punch is the only survivor and rides off on a hobby horse. An engraving by George Cruikshank (1792–1878) shows the final scene of Punch killing the devil: "Huzza! Huzza! The devil's dead!" In a 1734 scenario for *Pulcinella, the False Prince,* in scene 16, Pulcinella gains a spell to control the devil and forces him to carry him on his back (Gordon 1983, 72).

Punch as a political scoundrel appears in William Hogarth's 1754 painting series *The Election,* now in the Sir John Soane Museum in London. It depicts the cynical corruption and partisan violence that getting elected to Parliament entailed. In the second painting, *Canvassing for Votes,* the scene is outside an inn whose sign depicts the Royal Oak. From the crossbar supporting the sign, a canvas hangs showing the Treasury in London at the top and Punch at the bottom. Punch is pushing a wheelbarrow laden with gold coins, which he throws with a ladle to the bystanders. Below is the text "Punch candidate for Guzzledown." Apart from caricaturing the bribery and corruption inherent in politics, the fictitious place-name Guzzledown has echoes of the Land of Cockaigne and the gluttony of Pulcinella in some Commedia dell'Arte scenes.

In 1841, the first edition of the satirical periodical *Punch, or The London Charivari* was published in London by Henry Mayhew and Ebenezer Landells. It was a great success, lampooning contemporary mores and politics. The cover, by Richard Doyle, was used well into the twentieth century. It depicted Punch sitting in a chair, holding a dripping quill pen, and Punch's dog, Toby, with ruff and hat. Beneath them was a frieze in parody of an ancient Dionysiac procession, with Punch riding on a donkey, holding a young woman under one arm and wielding a very phallic slapstick in the other. He was accompanied by dancing women and musicians. Other figures, some masked and some demonic, flew beside and above and through the masthead title letters. The magazine was a great success, being published from 1841 to 1992. A brief revival in 1996 was unsuccessful, and *Punch* finally folded in 2002.

There is, as usual, overlap between genres. Elements of mummers' plays as well as Commedia dell'Arte banter survive in recorded

Punch and Judy scripts. Byrom suggests that the lines spoken in Mr. Mowbray's 1887 version of the "Punch and Judy Show," "Ha ha, good morning this afternoon, ladies and gentlemen. It's not so cold as it is, was it?" might have come straight from Beelzebub in a mummers' play (*Pall Mall Gazette,* June 15, 1887; Byrom 1988, 50). Human guisers appeared as Punch and Judy in Wales in the midwinter guising with the horse Mari Llwyd (see chapter 10). In Glamorgan, the team consisted of a Leader and Sergeant, a Merryman (musician), and Punch and Judy. The latter appeared dressed in tatters with blackened faces, Punch carrying a poker and Judy a besom. The pair were the agents of disorder. Forcing entry to a house, Punch raked the fire with his poker, and Judy swept the ashes all over the floor.

16

Masquerades

In the realm of urban entertainment, masking was separated from its appearance in Carnival and theater. The masquerade or masked ball emerged as a fashionable amusement for the upper classes. A Swiss diplomat, Johann Jacob Heidegger (1666–1749), promoted his first masquerade in London in 1710. (Later, he was appointed master of the revels by King George II.) The events at the Haymarket Theatre were so successful that they were extended to the pleasure gardens at Ranelagh and Vauxhall, where "midnight masquerades" were staged by "the Swiss

Fig. 16.1. Bat masks in a German masquerade (See also color plate 26.)

Count," as he was known. Costumes were many and varied. Characters from the Commedia dell'Arte mingled with characters from Greek mythology, literary fiction, and rustic traditions. People wearing lavish and daring costumes competed to see who could outdo everyone else.

Masquerades were staged to celebrate great national events, such as the Rejoicings for the Peace of Aix-la-Chapelle in 1749, where Horace Walpole (1717–1797) noted a troop of Harlequins and Scaramouches and a Maypole around which masqueraders, all in masks, danced. Masquerades gave those who could afford it an opportunity to have anonymous encounters. This included forbidden sexual activity. There were clandestine gay masquerades where "He-Whores" in masks cross-dressed in "gowns, petticoats, head-cloths, fine laced shoes and furbelow scarves" and groped their willing partners as they danced. By 1755, the scantily clad Miss Chudleigh had scandalized "society" by appearing topless as Iphigenia. In May of that year, a Naked Masquerade where women would appear as Water Nymphs and Graces and men as Satyrs, Pans, Fauns, and Centaurs was proposed in the *Connoisseur*. Later that year in Portugal, on All Saint's Day (November 1), a major catastrophic earthquake struck Lisbon, devastated the city, and killed a large part of the population, a modern estimate being between thirty thousand and fifty thousand dead. The shock of this natural disaster was reported all over Europe, and churchmen seized this as an opportunity to suppress frivolous revelries, which they viewed as having caused God to destroy Lisbon. At the time of the earthquake, being All Saints' Day, most of the population of Lisbon was in church. But the zealots did not let this detail spoil a great chance to exercise their power. So the bishop of London and the archbishop of Canterbury ordered masquerades banned. But the bans, in the absence of any effective police force, were ignored, and as Walpole wrote, "Happily the age prefers silly follies to serious ones."

The London Masquerades appeared in the art of the period. In 1724, the satirical artist William Hogarth (1697–1764) lampooned the events in an engraving titled *A Satire on Masquerades and Operas*. It depicts masked and costumed people standing in line waiting to enter a theater. They are being led in by a devil carrying a bag with "£1000" written on it. The Chelsea pottery, which produced editions of fine porcelain figures, produced a series that depicted Ranelagh Gardens masqueraders from 1759 to 1763. There are a number of characters. A set of eleven is displayed on the mantel of the dining room of the Governor's Palace in Colonial Williamsburg, Virginia. Chelsea porcelain women mainly wear the black oval Moretta mask associated with the Venice Carnival, which they hold with one hand to their faces. A masked man playing an end-blown flute appears frequently in sales of antiquities.

In 1783, Wolfgang Amadeus Mozart appeared as Arlecchino in a masquerade pantomime with music written by him (K446), coming onstage during an intermission between dancing at the Redoutensaal in the Hofburg Palace, Vienna (Lawner 1998, 7). In Britain, Archecchino and Pulcinella became Harlequin and Punch. Harlequin branched off to become a lead character in pantomimes and then a circus clown, while Punch became a puppet. Matthew Sully, who was the first circus clown in the United States in Ricketts's Circus in Philadelphia in 1793, began his career in London as Harlequin. *Harlequin and Mother Goose, or the Golden Egg* by Thomas John Dibdin (1771–1841), which was staged in London in 1806, set the mold for pantomime as performed today, and Harlequin pantomimes went well on into the nineteenth century. In *Harlequin and Mother Goose,* the Mother Goose witch figure was a man in drag, and ever since, pantomimes have featured cross-dressed characters: the Dame, such as Widow Twankey, played by a man, and the Principal Boy, such as Prince Charming, played by a woman. A century later, Harlequin appeared at the Garrick Theatre in London in a pantomime written by W. S. Gilbert titled *Harlequin and the Fairy's Dilemma.* By then, Harlequin was far away from the Commedia dell'Arte, appearing among "supernaturals" (fairies and the like) and "unnaturals" (human characters).

The storyline of the harlequinade was the comic and futile pursuit of Harlequin and his lover, Columbine, by her father, Pantaloon, and his servant, who, as Clown, often stole the show. In England, of the four, only Harlequin was masked.

The most famous English Clown was Joseph Grimaldi (1778–1837), who in the early nineteenth century appeared in London harlequinades

Fig. 16.2. Characters of the harlequinade (1947 print)
(See also color plate 28.)

Fig. 16.3. Joseph Grimaldi as Clown (See also color plate 27.)

and later as a character outside the harlequinades. For many years after Grimaldi, clowns had the generic name "Joey."

Harlequin also had a servant, Pierrot, derived from Gilles and Pedrolino before him. In Britain, the white-faced Pierrot also escaped from the harlequinades and concert parties; musical shows featuring him became popular seaside entertainment in the early part of the twentieth century. They were staged by troupes of identically dressed Pierrots with no further reference to their origin in their musical performances. Pierrot shows ceased with the advent of World War II.

The character also became a literary figure. *The Pierrot's Library,* a series of books illustrated by Aubrey Beardsley (1872–1898), was named after the first book in the series, *Pierrot* (1896) by Henry de Vere Stacpoole (1863–1951) (Calloway 1998, 130). Beardsley's drawing *The Death of Pierrot* appeared in issue 6 of the *Savoy* magazine in 1896. One of the figures approaching his deathbed is masked, and masks appear in several other of Beardsley's drawings.

The oil painting *Sweeps' Day in Upper Lisson Street* (ca. 1835) by an anonymous artist, now in the Museum of London, shows a May Day scene in London. A Jack-in-the-Green is surrounded by figures

Fig. 16.4. Caitlin's Royal Pierrots, Scarborough, Yorkshire,
England (1906 postcard)

that include a clown, complete with red-and-yellow mask and asses' ears, along with a drummer, male dancers in white and green bedecked with red ribbons, grimy-faced sweeps' boys, and a milkmaid with a ladle. Chimney sweeps and milkmaids were long associated with May festivities in English urban settings. It is likely that the clown in *Sweeps' Day in Upper Lisson Street* was an impersonator of Joseph Grimaldi. Similarly, well into the twentieth century, Charlie Chaplin impersonators as well as Harlequins and Pierrots appeared randomly at festivals, carnivals, and parades in Britain. Later, Elvis Presley impersonators and tribute bands for acts including the Beatles, Genesis, and Abba continued the tradition.

The Commedia dell'Arte was very influential in art in many genres. Franz von Bayros (1866–1924), best known for his erotic drawings for which he was prosecuted, produced several artworks in which Commedia figures appeared, including the pornographic *Der Fetischist* 1908), which depicted an erect Harlequin about to penetrate a half-dressed lady while her husband looked on from behind a screen. Another, a copy of which is in the Museum of Modern Art in New York but not on show, is titled *Woman in Bed Observing a Donkey* (1911), which has a Pierrot in the foreground. A nonerotic painting from 1910 is titled *Tänzerin und Pierrot.*

Gino Severini (1883–1966) was an Italian futurist before and during World War I, but afterward with *The Return to Order,* his painting became neoclassical and he favored themes from the Commedia dell'Arte. In 1922, Sir George Sitwell commissioned Severini to paint a whole room with frescoes of Commedia characters at his residence, Castel de Montegufoni near Florence in Tuscany. The result was *La Salla delle Mascheri.* Three of the walls have Commedia characters. The north wall shows Pulcinella with a fiddle and two Arlecchini seated at a table pouring wine. The east has two Pulcinelli, one in blue playing a clarinet and, on the other side of an end window, one in white with a four-string tenor guitar. The south wall has three figures. Arlecchino is dressed in red and green, wearing a half-red-half-blue mask and playing a large mandolin or bouzouki. Beppe Nappa is dressed in gray, wearing a helmet with a red-faced mask with a long black nose. He plays a similar instrument. Severini's depictions of musical instruments are inaccurate and, in practice, would be unplayable. The third figure is probably Tartaglia, who wears large round spectacles and a black mask with a long nose. However, he wears a white and not a black hat, and his costume is a green Pulcinella one. He plays a melodeon.

Also in 1922, Severini drew the frontispiece for Edith Sitwell's book *Façade.* It depicts a snow scene with a red-and-green clad Arlecchino with a lute slung over his back and accompanied by a Pulcinello with a guitar slung over his shoulder. *Façade an Entertainment* was the presentation of a series of poems by Edith Sitwell (1887–1964) with music by William Walton (1902–1983). The poems were read through a Senger Megaphone that was invented by opera singer Alexander Senger, who used it when singing the part of Fafner in Wagner's *Ring* cycle. It was of fibrous paper construction, a forerunner of loudspeaker cones that avoided the metallic sounds of earlier megaphones. The narrow end covered the mouth and nose of the singer or reciter, and in *Façade,* the wide end of the Senger Megaphone was the mouth of a mask in the middle of a stage curtain painted by Frank Dobson (1886–1963). The musicians and the speaker could not be seen by the audience—this was the *Façade.*

Dobson's stage curtain was used for the first performance at a private venue and subsequent performances at the Chenil Gallery in London. Another, for the International Music Festival at Siena, Italy, in 1928 was painted by Gino Severini (Sitwell 1949, 183). The best-known image of this is from a subsequent performance in 1942, when John Piper (1903–1992) painted the scene, in which the mask appears more like a classical bust. The mouth, although circular like the previous two, was not the end of a megaphone, because a microphone and loudspeaker were used instead. It was issued as a print in 1987. Sitwell, Walton, and his musicians made a recording of *Façade* in 1929, though despite the high technical quality, the inability to record in stereo at the time reduces the effect that a live performance must have had.

Severini's twentieth-century work at Castel de Montegufioni had two illustrious forerunners. The older, and among the earliest representations of Commedia dell'Arte figures, is at Burg Trausnitz near Landshut in Bavaria, Germany. Designed for Duke Wilhelm V by Friedrich Sustris and painted by Alessandro Scalzi detto il Paduano (?–1596), the work was carried out between 1575 and 1579. It depicts various Commedia scenes with life-size characters climbing up the Narrentreppe (Fools' Staircase). It was damaged by fire in 1961 and restored. The other great castle murals of the Commedia dell'Arte are at Český Krumlov in Bohemia, Czech Republic. Painted by Josef Lederer in 1746 and 1749 for Joseph Adam zu Schwarzenberg (1722–1782), the Masquerade Hall includes trompe l'oeil architectural features thronged with life-size human figures. A group of aristocrats mingles with people of various ethnicities in characteristic costumes—Turks, Moors, Armenians, Spaniards, and others. Andreas Altomonte (1699–1780) oversaw the architectural reconstruction, and a painting in the Museum of Modern Art in New York, *A Masked Ball in Bohemia* (ca. 1748), is attributed to him, so he may have designed the mural scheme. Of the three castle murals with Commedia figures, this work is the largest and most impressive.

Eighteenth-century European porcelain from the major centers included exquisitely detailed figures of Commedia dell'Arte characters. About 1740, Johann Joachim Kändler of the Meissen pottery modeled the Harlequin Family in hard-paste polychrome porcelain, and a few years later at the Capodimonte pottery in Naples, Giuseppe Gricci made a group that showed Harlequin and Pulcinella playing cards while Pantalone watches. In England, the Chelsea pottery produced a series of Ranelagh Gardens masqueraders from 1759 to 1763, several of which were Commedia dell'Arte characters.

17

Carnival Characters, Mumming, and Mummers' Plays

The irresistible appeal of Commedia dell'Arte characters meant that they soon found their way beyond the stage and into carnivalesque and vernacular performances. The German version of Pulcinella is Kasperle, otherwise Hanswurst, sometimes given the mock-aristocratic title of Hans Sausakh von Wurstfeld (Hans Sausage from Sausagefield), who sometimes wears necklaces of sausages. An eighteenth-century engraving in the Nationalbibliothek in Vienna shows aristocratic dancers in tall headdresses dancing hand in hand in a circle while Commedia dell'Arte characters stand looking over an ornate baroque fence. Arlecchino and Hanswurst are on ladders looking over the fence, while Pantalone, Scapino, and Pedrolino peer over the fence. Behind Hanswurst, who wears a mask over his mouth and nose but not his eyes and who doffs his conical hat, is another local character, Knofel Moferel, in a white half-mask over the nose and eyes (Lawner 1998, 105). Hänsele (Hansel, Hänsele, or Hansili) is a masked character, often wearing bells, who appears in many places in the German and Austrian

Carnivals. The masked figure Hänsele appears in the sword dance at Überlingen in southern Germany, the place with the oldest continuously performed sword dance in Europe, the organization that performs it dating from 1538 (Corrsin 1997, 169). He carries a whip with "a lash of three to six meters length" that he cracks "like a pistol shot" (Künzig 1950, 24).

Characters in central European sword-dance troupes have included Commedia dell'Arte figures, such as Harlequin, recorded in 1833 at a festival in Linz, Austria. There, Harlequin was conflated with Hanswurst as derived from Pulcinella, as this one wore a "wide belt of ringing bells" (Depiny 1933, 132–33). In Sibiu, Transylvania, in 1848, the furriers' guild performed a sword dance with a Hanswurst carrying not a sword but "the usual wand" and wearing "the usual multicolored

Fig. 17.1. Whip cracking on horseback at New Year, Pongau, Austria

Harlequin's clothing" (Wittstock 1896, 352). This may mean colored tatters. It is always difficult when the description is not precise and assumes knowledge in the reader that he or she may not have. The sword dancers of upper Austria in the nineteenth century personated specific characters: Junger Gsell, Schöllnerfriedl, Hanstrumpet, Grünerwald, Raubdunst, and Rauhbein, with the fool being called either Edlas Bluat (Noble Blood) or Kasperl. Edlas Bluat and another fool, whose name, Praschenweibl, (German *Weib*—woman, female, so *weibl* is the dialect diminutive of *weib*, *praschen* possibly a dialect word for a sound such as crackling or drumming) infers cross-dressing, wore a long, loose, multicolored "Pierrot costume" (so-called, though Pierrot was invariably dressed in white) (Corrsin 1997, 145). Prior to the expulsion of German-speaking people in 1945 from the Český les (Böhmer Wald)

Fig. 17.2. Masked and costumed characters on Fastnacht in Rottweil-am-Neckar, Germany (See also color plate 29.)

of Bohemia (Czech Republic), the sword dancers of the Kaplitz (now Kaplice) district traveled from village to village to perform. The teams had two fools, Foschai (Shrovetide), otherwise called Edles Blut, and the Mehlweib (Flour Woman), who wore a clownesque costume with bells. In later years, at least, the female figure was a cross-dressed man (Corrsin 1997, 150).

The relationship between characters in the Commedia Dell'Arte, the themes of mummers' plays, and the practices of the mountebanks is close. The mountebanks traveled around the country, setting up at markets and fairs to sell their quack medicines, which invariably were promoted in the most flowery gobbledygook with exaggerated claims of their effectiveness. The quacks and their assistants put on a show, which often involved songs and a practical demonstration of the medicine on a clownish assistant. Sometimes the assistant would handle a supposedly poisonous snake or pretend to eat a toad and then fall dead on the stage from their poison. At which point, the "doctor" would produce his elixir and set it to the "dead" man's lips, and he would rise again to the acclaim of the crowds, who rushed forward to buy the miracle product.

According to C. J. S. Thompson, the word *mountebank* was mentioned by Richard Stanyhurst in his 1577 "Description of Ireland," describing "the traveling quack who from a platform appealed to his audience by means of stories, tricks, and juggling, often attended by a clown or fool" (Thompson 1928, 14). Thomas Coryat in 1611 was said to have derived the word *mountebank* from the Italian *monta'in banco,* someone who mounts or climbs on a bench and "hyperbolically extoll[s] the virtue of his drugs and confections." Coryat mentions mountebanks being accompanied by jesters (Lawner 1998, 79). In 1646 in *Pseudodoxia Epidemica,* Sir Thomas Browne mentioned "Saltimbancoes, Quack-salvers, and Charlatans" (Thompson 1928, 14). "Quack-salver" meant a mountebank who sold salves, ointments, and eye lotions at fairs. Ben Jonson, in his 1605 play *Volpone,* tells of "quack-salvers, fellowes who live by selling oyles and drugs" (Thompson 1928, 23).

A 1610 engraving by Giacomo Franco of Piazza San Marco in Venice shows the "entertainment that every day charlatans offer in Piazza San Marco to the people of all nations who crowd there morning and night." In the foreground, we see the backs of spectators who are watching a bearded man in drag playing the lute. They are labeled as Greek, French, Capalletto (an Albanian mercenary), Spanish, Turkish, and English. All are wearing their respective national dress. On one side of the lutenist is a pair of mountebanks holding snakes, and one, the quack doctor, offering his elixir to would-be customers. On the other side, a Pantaloon in a mask leers toward the she-male musician while another masked figure stands beside him. Behind are two more stages with spectators watching actors and singers performing to a harp-playing woman. In the center of the piazza, a circle has formed around a man with a performing monkey. This is the milieu in which quackery, Commedia, and mumming arose and flourished.

In England in 1511 under King Henry VIII, an act was promulgated to suppress quack doctors and restrict medicine to registered practitioners. Seven years later, the College of Physicians was founded with a royal charter that gave powers to suppress "Mountebanks, Runnagate [renegade —N.P.], Quack-salvers, and women." Subsequently, any woman who attempted to practice any medical activities ran the risk of being numbered among the witches and killed. However, as with any attempt to suppress disapproved activities, it was almost impossible to police the practice of quack doctors, and their traveling shows remained popular and profitable, as many records from the following centuries show. This did not mean there were no prosecutions, but they were few and sporadic.

An obituary from the end of the seventeenth century of Jack Edwards, a versatile London quack and street performer, tells how he "combined the callings of Quack-Doctor, Ballad-Singer, and Merry Andrew, but was particularly successful in treating horses for various disorders. When trade in selling his medicines in the markets and at street corners fell off, he would turn Zany to some fellow practitioner, sing ballads, or distribute bills, and afterward return to his mountebank pranks and sell his own pills and potions" (Thompson 1928, 138). In 1733, a songbook called *The Merry Mountebank, or,*

Humorous Quack Doctor was advertised in Derby, "containing various never failing Receipts against Spleen and ill Nature. Exemplified in a choice collection of Old and New songs." The author was credited as Tim Tulip, of Fidlers Hall in Cuckoldshire (*Derby Mercury,* January 18, 1733, 1).

The spiel of mountebanks is reproduced in most English mummers' plays. A satirical seventeenth-century broadside titled *The Infallible Mountebank,* printed by H. Hills in London, has a woodcut depicting the mountebank with a monkey and his zany peeping out from behind a curtain. The spiel of the Doctor could be used as the text of a mummers' play, for which it may actually be an origin. "Sirs, sirs, sirs here (he cries), a Doctor rare who travels much at home. Here take my pills, I cure all ills, past, present, and to come; the cramp, the stitch, the squirt, the itch, the gout. The stone, the pox; the mulligrubs, the bonny scrubs, and all Pandora's box." And on it goes (Thompson 1928, 76–77). Enterprising quacks would enunciate eloquently garbled names of newly emergent diseases, which their elixirs, they claimed, would prevent or cure, such as "the Strong Fives, the Moon Pall, Marthambles, and the Hockogrockle" (Thompson 1928, 110). Similarly, the "doctor" part of mummers' plays has a humorous dialogue between one of the characters who was involved in the earlier killing of another character and the Doctor, who has been summoned. The Doctor is questioned as to his qualifications, talks in a garbled way like the Doctor in the Commedia and the English quacks, in which he tells of his extensive traveling and what he can cure. Finally, from his bag he produces a miraculous elixir that raises the dead.

Below is part of *The Play of the Old Tup* as performed by the Northstow Mummers at various places in the eastern counties of England in the latter years of the twentieth century and the first years of the twenty-first century. In this play, the masked character of Little Devil Doubt, who carries a broom, is the interlocutor of the whole play and first causes the Old Tup to be killed and then to be brought back to life again. The Old Tup is the Derby Ram, played by a mummer in a hobby animal with snapping jaws. After Little Devil Doubt calls up the

Butcher, who kills the Old Tup, Old Lass, who is leading the Tup to the market in Derby says:

Old Lass: Now look what you've been and gone and done! How am I going to get him to market now?

Butcher: Ah, that's no business of mine. That's Doctor's work, that is, and it's a good Doctor you'll be wanting, too.

Little Devil Doubt: Our Ben's a Doctor.

Old Lass: Well, call him up!

(All the cast call for the Doctor. He enters with a flourish. He is dressed in a black suit with a top hat and carries a doctor's bag).

Doctor: Here am I!

Little Devil Doubt: Are you the Doctor?

Doctor: Yes, yes, as you can plainly see.

Little Devil Doubt: What by?

Doctor: By my art and activity.

Little Devil Doubt: By your arse and cap of the knee? (Peers round at Doctor's behind)

Doctor: No! No, you foolish blockhead. By my art and activity.

Little Devil Doubt: How came you to be a doctor?

Doctor: By my traveling.

Little Devil Doubt: How far have you traveled?

Doctor: Oh—Ittalty, Tittalty, High, Low, France, Germany, and Spain, and now back to cure old England again.

Little Devil Doubt: So far and no further?

Doctor: Oh yes, a great deal further!

Little Devil Doubt: How far?

Doctor: From the fireside, cupboard-head, upstairs and into bed, where I stole many a lump of cheese and bread.

Little Devil Doubt: What sorts can you cure?

Doctor: All sorts! Itsy, pitsy, palsy, gout, the pain within, the pain without, the pain that flies all round about!
(Finally, after further banter between Little Devil Doubt and the Doctor, the latter produces his elixir.)

Doctor: This elixir beats the old man himself! Surely, poor Tup, if I can't cure you! Take a sup of my bottle and let it run slowly down your throttle, and if you're not quite dead, rise up and bay! (The Old Tup rises from the floor, alive again. Musician plays, and the cast, including the Tup, circle round and sing the last three verses of "The Derby Ram." The End.)

Plate 1. Demon or guiser? Medieval stone carving fragment, Wisbech Cambridgeshire, England

Plate 2. Ancient Greek mask

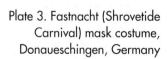

Plate 3. Fastnacht (Shrovetide Carnival) mask costume, Donaueschingen, Germany

Plate 4. Eighteenth-century mask of Saint Edmund. Stone carving Bury St Edmunds, Suffolk, England

Plate 5. The image of the witch is an archetype that appears in German Carnival guising. Two masked guisers from Rottenburg, Germany.

Plate 6. Masked German Carnival guiser carrying away a young woman he has caught

Plate 7. Ram's skull on pole carried by a Ramrugge morris dancer, Whittlesea, England

Plate 8. Butzesel guiser wearing donkey-head mask and dragging vegetation, Villingen, Germany

Plate 9. Krampus, Pongau, Austria (A Krampus is a demonic figure played by a man dressed in animal furs and wearing a frightening carved wooden mask, often with tusks or fangs, with horns on its head. Large metal bells hang from a belt, and the Krampus carries either a bundle of sticks or a horse's tail which he uses to whip bystanders.)

Plate 10. Demonic guisers in black masks and horned animal-head caps, Wilflingen, Germany

Plate 11. Masked, padded figure, Villingen, Germany

Plate 12. Romano-British
Gorgon-head sculpture
from the tympanum of the
Roman temple of Sulis
Minerva, formerly at Bath,
Somerset, England

Plate 13. Krampus guisers in furs and horns, Pongau, Austria

Plate 14. Guiser's mask with fox
tail, Rottweil-am-Neckar, Germany

Plate 15. Morris dancer guising as a horse, Thaxted, Essex, England

Plate 16. Brieler Rössle hobby horse with masked rider, Rottweil-am-Neckar, Germany

Plate 17. Ox guiser and
Jack-in-the-Green, Oxford, May Day

Plate 18. Pig mask guiser,
Rottenburg, Germany

Plate 19. Bear mask guiser,
Rottenburg, Germany

Plate 20. Straw bear, Wilflingen, Germany

Plate 21. Mepal broom dancers at Whittlesea

Plate 22. Verschmanndl guiser and goat, Sankt-Johann, Austria

Plate 23. Morris dancers' dragon, King's Lynn, Norfolk, England

Plate 24. Lazy tongs wielded by a guiser in Donaueschingen, Germany

Plate 25. Punch and Judy show:
Final scene, Punch fights
the devil (engraving by
George Cruikshank)

Plate 26. Bat masks in a German masquerade

Plate 27. Joseph Grimaldi (1778–1837), the most famous English Clown, who appeared in London Harlequinades and later as a character outside the Harlequinades.

Mr GRIMALDI, as Clown.

Plate 28. Characters of the harlequinade (1947 print)

Plate 29. Masked and costumed characters on Fastnacht in Rottweil-am-Neckar, Germany

Plate 30. Midwinter Mummers at Whittlesea, Cambridgeshire, England

Plate 31. The author guising as Beelzebub in the Huntingdonshire Mummers' Play at the White Swan, Conington, Huntingdonshire (1998 photograph by Rupert Pennick)

Plate 32. Molly dancing at Comberton, Cambridgeshire

Plate 33. Mepal Molly men dance at Wilburton, Cambridgeshire, England, on Plough Monday 2019

Plate 34. Foliated head, stone carving, Oxford

Plate 35. Fastnacht witches burn their besoms at the end of Carnival.

18

Mummers

Characters, Disguises, and Costumes

"*Mumm* is said to be derived from the Danish word *mumme* or *momme* in Dutch, and signifies to disguise oneself with a mask," wrote J. Strutt in *Sports and Pastimes of the People of England* (Strutt 1845, 251). Or to mumm is "to wear the mask with cunning art and mummer and deceive" as the *North Wales Chronicle* put it (January 29, 1839, 4). In Britain, *mummers* is a generic term, but in some places, they are called *guisers* or *guizards,* which in the Cockney dialect of London became the word *geezer,* meaning an unnamed or unrecognized person. The word *guy* has a similar derivation, conflated with the popular name of Guido Fawkes (Guy), but that's appropriate when his effigy is wearing its customary mask. The Sussex word for mummers is *tipteers* or *tipteerers,* and in Cornwall they were *geese-dancers* and their play was called the *Giz-Dance.* Performers of a specific mummers' play in Kent are called the Seven Champions, which is the title of the play as well, and the same for the Christmas Boys on the Isle of Wight and also in Wiltshire. In the north of Ireland, they are Rhymers, and they are White Boys on the Isle of Man (Chambers 1933, 4–5). Although they perform particular plays at midwinter, mummers are not associated with the Carnival season, and the characters and their costumes are

Fig. 18.1. Mummers' play, Yorkshire (1895 photograph)

part of the same milieu as Plough Monday, sword dancing, and morris dancing, where characters deemed "supernumerary" by uncomprehending folklorists played a pivotal role in warming up the audience and collecting money.

Fig. 18.2. Midwinter Mummers at Whittlesea,
Cambridgeshire, England. (See also color plate 30.)

Mummers' plays are only one particular aspect of mumming. Writing about them in 1930, Alice B. Gomme noted the costume of some Plough Bullocks: "The smock had represented upon it in colored cloth the men, house, barn, horse, plough, dog, sheep, pig, animals, and objects of farming" (Gomme 1930, 195). An almost identical nineteenth-century mummer's costume with the emblems and the classic mummers' entry line—"in comes I"—is illustrated in figure 18.3.

Traditionally, mummers have worn costumes cobbled together from old cast-off clothes, improvised weapons and masks, hobby animals, and other properties. Ragged Heroes is a name sometimes given to mummers who perform what folklorists describe as the "hero-combat" play.

Mummers performing their play would travel from place to place

Fig. 18.3.
Nineteeth-century
mummer's costume,
Nottinghamshire,
England

to perform. The typical mummers' play takes only a few minutes to perform, and after thankfully receiving a drink, food, money, or all three, the mummers moved on to the next farmhouse or inn and repeated the performance. Traditionally, there was no written text for the play. It was an oral tradition transmitted by word of mouth, with new performers learning the words and action from existing members who had learned the play in the same way. In his *Notes about Notts* (1874), C. Brown wrote of the South Nottinghamshire *Plough Bullock Day Play* on Plough Monday: "The men generally met at some appointed rendezvous, and visited the residences of the tradesmen and farmers. . . . After being admitted into the farmer's kitchen, they would proceed with a novel play, at which frequent rehearsals had made them proficient. . . . Immediately at the close of the performance contributions are solicited from the spectators, and the band proceed elsewhere to repeat the doggerel and to again go through the same antics. When the last place has been visited the treasurer accounts to his comrades as to the state of the exchequer, and a supper and jollification generally closes the proceedings on 'Plough Bullock Day'" (Brown 1874, 83–85).

Historic descriptions and photographs from the nineteenth century concur. In the Scottish mummers' play *Galatian,* an 1841 account tells us that "Galatian is (at the royal burgh of Peebles) dressed in a good whole shirt, tied round the middle with a handkerchief, from which hangs a wooden sword. He has a large cocked-hat of white paper, either cut out with little human profiles, or pasted over with penny valentines. The Black Knight is more terrific in appearance, his dress being, if possible, of tartan, and his head surmounted by an old cavalry cap, while his white stockings are all tied round with red tape. A pair of flaming whiskers adds to the ferocity of his aspect. The doctor is attired in any faded black clothes, which can be had, with a hat probably stolen from a neighbouring scarecrow" (Chambers 1841, vol. VII, 299). In England, Leicestershire performers were "the mummer boys who dress themselves in paper armor and paper masks and went from house to house at Christmas time performing interludes for the entertainment of gentlemen's servants" (*Leicester Journal,* January 10, 1845, 4).

A PARTY OF MUMMERS.

Fig. 18.4. Mummers, an artist's impression, 1828

In Cornwall, Uncle Jan Trenoodle recorded an account of mummers in 1846. "Most of the company were in white with ribbons tied upon their shirt sleeves with napkins and swords and such caps as I never saw. They were half a fathom high made of pasteboard with rows of beads and mirror glass . . . strips of old cloth strung upon slivers of pith hanging down." The character of Old Father Christmas came wearing a mask and a long white wig, the Doctor "with a three-corner hat, and his face all redded and whited" [original in Cornish dialect, rendered into standard English by N.P.] (Uncle Jan Trenoodle, *Specimens of Cornish Provincial Dialect*, 52, cited in Chambers 1933, 83). Near London, G. W. Septimus Piesse wrote in 1860: "About this time of year the inhabitants of Chiswick, Turnham Green, and neighbourhood are entertained . . . by a set of boys calling themselves 'the Mummers.'

They dress in masks and bedizen themselves in colored ribbon and paper, then go from shop to tavern reciting the following jumble." Piesse then gave the text of the mummers' play, beginning "(enter Girl with a broom. A room! a room! pray guard us all. Give us room to rise and fall come to show you activity."

Then other characters enter: Swish Swash and Swagger, King George and "3rd Boy," who kills George in a fight. The Doctor then appears and brings George back to life. Lord Grubb then appears, and there is a finale with music and dancing (Piesse 1860, 466).

In 1861, the Reverend Edward Bradley (1827–1889), writing as Cuthbert Bede, described a Worcestershire mummers' play.

In the Christmas of 1856 to 1867, I witnessed several performances of a set of mummers, who lived in the hamlets of Upper and Lower Howsell, in the parish of Leigh, Worcestershire; and went the round of the Malvern district with their Masque. . . . The lads were well up in their parts, and were spirited performers. The Valiant Soldier wore a real soldier's coat; Old Father Christmas carried holly; the

Fig. 18.5. Islip Mummers at the Cherry Orchard, Holton, Oxfordshire, 1894

Turkish Knight had a turban; and all of them were decked out with ribbons, and scarves, and had their faces painted. Little Devil Doubt had a black face, and carried a moneybox, a besom, and a bladder; with the bladder he thwacked the performer whose turn it was to speak. . . . Little Devil Doubt, having brushed away the snow and cleared a space, the performers ranged themselves in a semicircle, and the play began. (Bede 1861, 271–272)

Despite the comical and often ramshackle appearance of the mummers, mumming always has an air of ceremony and magic about it. Alex Helm noted that in mumming plays there was a fundamental necessity to preserve anonymity for the actors. If one was recognized, then the "luck" was broken (Helm 1981, 37). However, with other nonplay disguising, the same principle applied. In the mumming on Cakin Neet (Caking Night), which was localized to the city of Sheffield, the participants had to not be recognized or the cake they sang for at house doorsteps would not be forthcoming. The disguise had to have local significance, and contests were held (anonymously) in public houses with a prize for the best costume. Guisers drank beer with a straw through their mask so as to remain anonymous. Red masks with slits for eyes, similar to traditional Guy Fawkes masks, were favored, along with carnivalesque costumes of local origin. Held on the night of November 1, however, Cakin Neet died out in the 1990s, overwhelmed by the commercialized Halloween.

Old Father Christmas, Tom Fool, and the Devil

Three significant characters who appear in mummers' plays around Christmas are Old Father Christmas, a fool, and the devil. The personification of Christmas appeared as a character in 1616 in Ben Jonson's royal court masque *The Masque of Christmas,* which begins with the instructions: "Enter *Christmas,* with two or three of the guard, attired in round hose, long stockings, a close doublet, a high-crowned hat with a brooch, a long thin beard, a truncheon, little ruffs, white shoes, his scarfs and garters tied cross, and his drum beaten before him." The character first introduces himself: "Why gentlemen, do you know what you do? Would you have kept me out? Christmas, old Christmas, Christmas of London, and Captain Christmas? Pray you, let me be brought before my lord chamberlain, I'll not be answered else: *'Tis merry in hall, where beards wag all*" (Jonson [1616], 1816b, vol. 7, 273). Later, he appeared again in another royal masque by Thomas Nabbes in 1638 as "an old gentleman in furred gown and cap" (Hutton 1996, 117). Less than six years later, in 1644, the celebration of Christmas was banned by Parliament in the whole of Great Britain. When the revolutionary Puritan regime was collapsing in 1659, the festival reemerged. Old Father Christmas, who is not Santa Claus, appears in many mummers' plays. His long beard is a characteristic, as in the mummers photographed in 1901 at Newbold, reproduced in figure 18.6.

Old Father Christmas always refers to being uninvited and unwanted, as in Jonson's masque. "In comes I, Old Father Christmas. Wanted here, or wanted not, I hope Old Father Christmas will never be forgot." Killjoys' attempts to suppress merriness are always a threat.

A specifically British character who appears in morris dancing, sword dancing, carnivals, and other places is Tom Fool, Tom, or Tommy. The expression *tomfoolery,* meaning "absurd antics," comes from this character, just as *horseplay* comes from the animal guisers. Tom Fool is connected with a legendary character, Mad Tom of Bedlam, who

Fig. 18.6. Beelzebub and Old Father Christmas mummers at Newbold (1901 photograph)

had a song written about him in about 1600, of which there is a core with numerous differing verses. Bedlam was the Bethlehem Hospital in London, where mentally ill people were incarcerated. Some of the inmates, who were not considered a danger to the public, were allowed out as "ticket-of-leave-men" who carried papers of authorization. Beggars of the era were supposed to be organized into guilds that allocated pitches in the streets and categorized them into different forms. Some who were not out on leave from Bedlam took on the persona of Mad Tom in their begging, making outrageous and absurd claims for themselves in the hope of receiving a donation. The song "Mad Tom of Bedlam" describes his fantastic delusions. One version begins with the spoken declamation, which refers to supernatural and magical beings:

> *By the Hag and hungry Goblin*
> *That into rags would rend ye,*
> *And the Figure that stands by the Naked Man*
> *In the* Book of Moons, *defend ye!*
> *That of your five sound senses*
> *You never be forsaken*
> *And wander out abroad at night*
> *With Tom to beg your bacon.*

The song then begins and tells of Tom's claims and delusions, for example, "my staff has murdered giants," and his outrageous threats, such as "and when that I have murdered the Man in the Moon to powder, his staff I'll break, his dog I'll bake, there'll howl no demon louder." Tom visits Satan's kitchen to beg food, and "there I got souls piping hot, all on a spit a-turning." His clothes are composed of things he stole on his trip to the heavens, such as "the rainbow there is this I wear" and a patched and tattered coat resembling that of Arlecchino, with pieces of many colors.

Fools are not only called Tom. Among many other foolish characters, Judas appears as an unlikely clown in the Scottish New Year's mummers' play *Galatian,* published in 1841 (Chambers 1841, vol. VII, 299–384). In a text from the next year, *Christmas: His Pageant Play, or*

Mysterie, of "St. George," Judas enters to collect money from the audience and says:

> Here comes in Judas—Judas is my name, come, drop some silver in the bag, it was for that I came; I have been in the East, I have been in the West, at many a castle gate, but you will treat me the best; I've seen geese going in pattens; I've seen clouds, all day pour peas and beans in torrents down, you could not find your way; I've seen the farmers thatch their barns with needles and with pins, swine flying in the troubled air, like peelings of ingins [onions]. Our hearts are made of steel, but our bodies soft as ware, if you've anything to give, good folks, why put in—there. (Slight 1842, 183)

Another variation comes from the *Christmas Guisers' Play* performed at Newport and Eccleshall, which was recited in 1879 by mummers to folklorist Charlotte Burne. She had two manuscript copies of the play, "written down (from memory) for me in 1879 by Elijah Simpson, chimney-sweep, of Newport, Shropshire, and John Bates, sawyer, of Eccleshall, Staffordshire, both habitual actors." In it was a version of Beelzebub who wore tatters and a bell, showing another of the countless possible variations on a single character. "Billy Bellzebub, the Fool, who is dressed in white calico garments, sewn all over with many-colored bits of ribbon, etc. He has a bell fastened in the middle of his back, and within my memory always carried a club in the left hand, and a long ladle fur basting roast meat in the right, as described in his speech. He rushes upon the scene with a leap and a bound, runs up and down all the time he is speaking, and takes care to turn his back to show his bell when he mentions his name" (Burne 1886, 483).

Aspects of Impersonating the Devil

The devil appeared as himself in medieval mystery plays, often portrayed as a figure burned red or black in the fires of hell. His function was to tempt the "virtuous" actors who rejected him, a lesson to the audience to reject temptation to do wrong. In the medieval

Fig. 18.7. Fourteenth-century devil wall painting in the church at Melbourne, Derbyshire (1860 engraving)

Doomsday Play at Coventry, the devil presided over the blackened-faced damned dressed in the black-and-yellow "Devil's Livery" who appeared to be burning among the flames of hell, while the saved shone in white-leather costumes. Mary Dormer Harris noted that an interlude by John Hayward "had often played the role of the devil in Corpus Christi play performed at Coventry" (Harris 1911, 306).

The actual nature of the devil as an objective being has always been fluid. The devil himself must be a single entity, as pointed out by Daniel Defoe in his withering critique, yet, seemingly, he can appear in many places at the same time. Additionally, beings with fewer powers that "the man himself" are also called "devil." Demonologies postulated hierarchies of hell with various named demons or devils. The three most popular devils—Satan, Lucifer, and Beelzebub—have different historic origins, and the latter appears in English mummers' plays along with a character called Devil Doubt. Some devils were ancient gods demonized by the Christian Church. The English "Old Harry," a euphemism for the devil, was identified by Osbert Sitwell as a byname of Odin. The popular figure Harlequin, who gave rise to the circus clown, began as a leader of the Wild Hunt and then became a devil, appearing in the thirteenth-century *Jeu de la Feuillière* and as Alichino in Dante's *Divine Comedy*.

In mummers' plays, Beelzebub appears as a disruptive, killer figure—"In comes I, Beelzebub, and under my arm I carries a club"—but also as a Fool figure.

In various mummers' plays, Beelzebub becomes Beelzebub the Fool, Old Billy Beelzebub, Belcibub, Belzeebug, Bellzie Bub, Billy Bellzebub, Bellsie Bob, Bellesy Bob, Bells Abub, Baal Zebub, Hub-bub-bub-bub, and Lord Grubb (Chambers 1933, 65). Such is the nature of transformation. Little Devil Doubt appears as an interlocutor trickster who, in *The Play of the Old Tup*, causes the death of the Derby Ram and then helps to bring it back to life again. Little Devil Doubt's weapon is a broom, with which he demands money from the audience: "In comes I, Little Devil Doubt. If you don't give me money, I'll sweep you all out.

Fig. 18.8. The author guising as Beelzebub in the Huntingdonshire mummers' play at the White Swan, Conington, Huntingdonshire (1998 photograph by Rupert Pennick) (See also color plate 31.)

Money I want, and money I crave; if you don't give me money, I'll sweep you all to your grave!"

The devil was also impersonated not as a character in drama but as the real thing in initiation rituals of British secret societies and rural fraternities. The Society of the Horseman's Grip and Word was a secret society that existed mainly in Scotland and East Anglia, which taught the secrets of horsemanship to initiates and also functioned as a kind of clandestine trade union. Like other rural fraternities, it had rites that were magical in character (Newman 1940, 32). Taken at night to "the Horseman's Hall" (a barn), the initiate underwent a series of physical and mental ordeals that culminated in him being forced to swear the "Horseman's Oath" (Evans 1971, 230–31). Then the "Horseman's Word" was given to him. It varied in different regions, but was always imparted to the initiate by shaking hands with a masked man in the guise of the devil, "a grip o' the Auld Chiel's hand" as it was called in Scotland. The devil's hand was really a stick covered with a hairy skin, or a cow's foot with its cloven hoof. It glowed in the dark from a luminous substance that added to the disorientation and terror of the initiate (MacPherson 1929, 291; Singer 1881, 8).

The Oddfellows originated in England in the eighteenth century. Its oldest record is of a "Loyal Aristarcus Lodge No. 9" from 1748 that met at three different inns in London. Like other orders, the Oddfellows had several grades or degrees, and each had its own initiation ritual. The first degree's ritual involved the candidate being stripped naked and blindfolded and tied to two ropes by which he was pulled in various directions through a series of circuits around the room: bumping into various things, being pulled close to the fireplace, and being doused with water. During this, frightening noises were made by gongs and shaken sheets of metal. The candidate was then made to swear an oath, after which his blindfold was removed and he was confronted by a human skeleton or a real skull, while around him the officials stood, wearing devilish "fright masks." The initiate was given an explanatory talk about mortality and his duties, the lights were lit, and his nudity was covered with a lambskin apron bearing the emblems of the Oddfellows, thus admitting him to the order.

Traveling Players in the Welsh Borderlands

Most events in history remain unrecorded. The documentation of events in royal, municipal, military, ecclesiastical, and legal history is more or less complete for many centuries. Most performance, however, was never documented. It was an immediate experience that needed to leave no record. Nevertheless, we have fragmentary knowledge of many "unofficial" happenings and practices, and fragments can be gleaned from remaining documents. From the seventeenth century, there are records of plays performed by traveling players at village wakes and fairs (Chambers 1933, 190). A Shropshire tradition was recorded by Sir Offley Wakeman in 1884 from the eighteenth and nineteenth centuries. In various villages, traveling players performed from two wagons in the open air to audiences of up to one thousand. The plays performed were *Prince Mucidorus, Rigs of the Time, Saint George and the Fiery Dragon, Valentine and Orson,* and *Doctor Forster* (Wakeman 1884, 384–85). The presentation was partly in the manner of stage plays and partly in the milieu of mummers' plays. "In all of them the Fool or Jester seems to have been a very important character," wrote Wakeman. "In the local phraseology, he is reported to have 'played all manner of megrims'" (Wakeman 1884, 385). This Fool's opening is reminiscent of a mummers' play.

> *Good morrow, gentleman, every one,*
> *From half an hour to three score and ten.*
> *We've come here today some pastime for to show,*
> *But how we shall behave, indeed I do not know.*
> (WAKEMAN 1884, 384)

Properties in common with other events appeared in the plays. Bear guising in *Mucedorus and Amadine* involved an actor in a "shaggy skin" who fought with and was killed by the hero. (This play is known from editions of the ballad publisher Francis Coles before 1668.) *Saint George and the Fiery Dragon* involved a wooden dragon "worked from the side scenes by means of a long pole; the effect of the fiery breath was produced by a gunpowder squib place in its mouth." The actor playing Saint George "struck off its head with his sword, to the great amusement of the spectators" (Wakeman 1884, 386). *Doctor Forster,* which was a version of *Doctor Faustus,* was considered, like *Macbeth,* to be bad luck. Wakeman reports that it was "wholly acted in the sly and not at the regular wakes" (Wakeman 1884, 385–86). When the play was over at the wake, the fiddler struck up and dancing ensued. In the 1860s, these performances were stopped "by the law" (Wakeman 1884, 383).

Hunting the Earl of Rone: The Combe Martin Revels

From an unknown date until 1837 at Coombe Martin in Devon the ritual of Hunting the Earl of Rone took place in the days preceding Ascension Day. After a break of 140 years, the custom was brought back. In the nineteenth century, the actor personating the Earl of Rone wore a grotesque mask, a laborer's smock padded with straw, and a string of twelve hard sea biscuits strung around his neck. He was accompanied by a hobby horse covered with painted emblems, whose operator was masked. The horse had snapping jaws. A masked Fool, dressed in a colorful costume, carried a besom. A number of men, carrying guns, wore Grenadier costumes with paper hats. A real donkey accompanied the group.

The event began when the Grenadiers went to Lady's Wood, accompanied by spectators, to hunt for the Earl of Rone. There, they took him prisoner, to the lamentations of the hobby horse. The Earl was sat on the donkey, facing backward, and was accompanied back to the village in triumph. At certain customary places, the Grenadiers fired a volley and the Earl of Rone fell from the donkey. As in many mummers' plays, the Earl was resurrected, not by the customary Doctor but by the Fool. The Earl was then hauled back onto the donkey, and the procession resumed until the next place where a volley was fired. Money was collected from bystanders. Those who did not pay were grabbed by the hobby horse's jaws until they did. The same thing happened at the next stopping place, the volley of shots, the Earl's fall, and his resurrection. At nightfall, the procession reached the sea, and he was shot into the sea.

The restoration of the tradition in the late twentieth century saw a hobby horse resembling the Padstow one with the round section covered by multicolored ribbons and a skirt like that of the Minehead one with a small black-painted "snap" head. The Earl of Rone is dressed in a coat made of sacking, and his red-black-and-white mask has some resemblance to the Padstow hobby horse mask. The Grenadiers wear British army ceremonial red coats but with a tall hat with colored streamers.

19

Rural Ceremonies, Performance, and Disguise

It is necessary to keep up the day: Plough Monday.

In Britain, farmworkers were hired at special hiring fairs where, if the farmer's agent took them on, they signed on to work for a whole year. If the farmer had work after that, the worker might be kept on for another and subsequent years. Those who could not find work had to travel around from place to place seeking the odd day's work here or there. Casual work was available, especially at harvesttime. But it was unreliable, and the specter of poverty was ever present. There are a number of traditional songs about hiring fairs, such as "Copshawholme Fair," which describes a negotiation between a worker and a potential employer. The Scottish bothy ballad "The Barnyards of Delgaty" warns would-be workers not to go to work there because of the atrocious conditions.

Sometimes laborers who could not find work took to performance in disguise. In 1890, John Nicholson described the custom in East

Yorkshire: "Martinmas time being over, some of the unhired men disguise themselves by dressing in motley garb. One will dress as a woman, and, carrying a besom, is known as 'Besom Bet'; another having his hat covered with strips of all kinds and colors of rags, has a 'blether' (bladder) attached by a string to the end of a stick, and is called 'Blether Dick'; the others adopt other devices, and going from village to village, collect odd pence" (Nicholson 1890, 17). This guising is better known from the period after Christmas, especially on Plough Monday.

In England, Plough Monday is the first Monday after Twelfth Night, January 6. It was the first day that farmworkers resumed work in the fields after the Yuletide period, the Twelve Days of Christmas. To mark it, a procession of workers took a plough around the locality, visiting the larger houses, shops, and public houses to demand largess, "a penny for the poor ploughboy." The plough was decorated with ribbons and accompanied by men in disguise. It is an ancient custom observed for a long time in England from the north to the midlands. It was observed in Northumberland, Durham, Yorkshire, Lincolnshire, Nottinghamshire, Warwickshire, Leicestershire, Northamptonshire, Cambridgeshire, Huntingdonshire, western Norfolk, and Bedfordshire.

There are several theories about its origin. One is that it was brought to England in the ninth century by Danish settlers in continuation of the heathen tradition of Midvintersblót, celebrating "midwinter's day" (winter running from October 13 to April 14 in the Old Norse calendar). It might have included the Danish celebration of their victory against the Saxons in Wessex in the year 878 that took place "at midwinter after Twelfth Night," which is Midvintersblót or Tiugunde Day, January 13, twenty days after the Yule. The Danelaw was established in that year, when half of England was under Danish rule. However, counties outside the Danelaw also have Plough Monday traditions.

Another theory is that the festival was established by the archbishop of York in the eleventh century. In the early nineteenth century, it was thought to originate in religious devotion. "Anciently, a light called the Plough-Light was maintained by old and young persons who were husbandmen, before images in some churches, and on Plough Monday they had a feast, and went out with a plough and dancers to get money to support the Plough-Light. The Reformation put out these lights, but the practice of going about with the plough, begging for money remains, and the 'money for light' increases the income of the village alehouse" (Blomefield [1736] 1805–1810, vol. 9, 212). The earliest historical record of Plough Monday is in the sixteenth century in a religious tract of 1543 by John Bale (1495–1563). In his *Five Hundred Points of Husbandry* (1557), Thomas Tusser (1524–1580) wrote, "Plough Monday. Next after thet Twelf-tide is past, Bids out with the plough, the worst husband is last" (Frampton 1989, 3).

In his *Norfolk Garland* (1872), John Glyde Jr. tells of the medieval tradition of the Confraternity of the Plough. "Plough Monday was the name given to a rustic festival held on the Monday after the feast of the Epiphany, commonly called Twelfth Day, on which day, after the festivities of Christmas, it was in olden time customary to resume the labor of agriculture. There is in the tower of the church at Cawston a gallery called the Plough Rood, and on this the following lines are carved.

> *God spede the plow,*
> *And send us ale corn enow,*
> *Our purpose for to make*
> *At of the plow lite of Lygate,*
> *Be merry and glad;*
> *What good ale this work mad."*

This is believed to refer to those celebrations of Plough Monday, which prior to the Reformation were not unusual in connection with guilds in agricultural districts. The members of the guild would go on Plough Monday to church, and kneeling before the plow rood, they would say, "God spede the plow, and send us ale corn enow our purpose for to make," that is, to carry on their labors on the land and to spend a joyful day at the plow light of Lygate. And there, to show their belief in the need of good ale to enable them to work, they say, "Be merry and glad, 'twas good ale this work made." After which they, gaily dressed, passed in procession through the village, dragging a plough that had been blessed and censed with incense by the priest, gathering largess as they went along. It seems strange to us to pray for ale, but in those times, ale was everywhere the common beverage of the country and was thought as necessary for the support of life as bread, and therefore it was thought as natural to pray for ale corn to make ale with as to pray for daily bread. "Bread and ale gave them strength to plough the land" (Glyde 1872, 110).

"At Hull the Miracle-plays were usually performed on Plough Monday, by the members of the trade guilds," wrote William Andrews of the Humberside port.

> The representatives of each guild had their peculiar dresses, badges, banners, &c, and as they marched through the streets to the sound of music and the pealing of church bells, they must have presented an imposing and brilliant sight. After parading the principal streets they proceeded to the Holy Trinity Church, where, for the entertainment and instruction of the people, a play was performed. It was, as a rule, the play of Noah. In the church was suspended an Ark, which was brought out, and in it the piece was acted. It was covered with paintings of animals, which were supposed to have been in the Ark at the time of the Flood. (Andrews 1890, 10)

It is possible that, after the suppression of the Catholic Church, Plough Monday remained as the last trade guild parade of all.

There are a few early records of Plough Monday customs outside the guild parade context. In Huntingdonshire in 1684, two Fenstanton men, Thomas Martin and Emmanuel Offley, were arraigned for the manslaughter of John Banson of Little Shelford, who was riding in a shortcut across the Great Doles between Fenstanton and Saint Ives when he was stopped for money, which he refused to pay. He was killed in the fight that ensued. The defendants claimed that it was customary on Plough Monday and Whitsuntide to take a penny from anyone who rode across the common land there (Tebbutt 1984, 55). At Fowlmere,

William Cole was visited by the ploughboys on January 11, 1768. "Plow Monday. All the boys in the parish with Hurdy Gurdy's, black'd faces, Bells and Plows," George Frampton noted (Frampton 1993, 6).

The boys and men who went out on Plough Monday were called variously Ploughboys, Plough Witches, Plough Stots, Plough Bullocks, and the Fool Plough. In Hertfordshire, Cambridgeshire, Huntingdonshire, and Northamptonshire, some of the participants in Plough Monday ceremonies were called Plough Witches (Sternberg 1851, 123; Jones-Baker 1977, 124; Tebbutt 1984, 52). Samuel Page Widnall, writing in 1875, described Plough Monday in Grantchester, upstream from Cambridge: "Boys go round the village in a party of 30 or 40, and at each door shout in chorus 'Pray bestow a ha'penny on the poor plough boy—woa-ho-up,' repeated with a loud cracking of whips. Some of the young men go 'Ploughmondaying,' but they usually go into Cambridge for the day and make the round of the village in the evening. They deck themselves in ribbons and one of their number is dressed as a woman. A fiddler accompanies them and at intervals they stop in the street and dance, one or two going round to beg of passers-by. Only men and boys take part" (Widnall 1875 quoted in Porter 1969, 97). In some parts of Hertfordshire, they were accompanied by morris dancers and "Guisers" and the "Wodehouse," the legendary wild man, bedecked all in greenery. The appearance of the Wodehouse in Hertfordshire on Plough Monday was terminated in 1914 by the outbreak of World War I (Jones-Baker 1977, 124).

Disguise in various forms is a significant element of Plough Monday. Although they were lumped together under a single name, such as Plough Stots or Ploughboys, the participants played different characters. Each played a specific character, signified by different forms of facial disguise. All detailed accounts describe various forms of costume, face painting, and masks, which appear in other contexts such as sword dancing and molly dancing on other traditional days of the year. Costume-characters from the Italian Commedia dell'Arte, most especially Harlequin, appeared in British folk performance far away from their place in the comic scenarios and the mountebanks' stages. In the Commedia, Harlequin wears a black mask. In 1817,

George Young described Plough Monday at the fishing port of Whitby, Yorkshire. The plough was accompanied by Clowns or Toms (Tom Fool) dressed as Harlequins "having their faces painted or masked," and cross-dressing men "called *Madgies* or *Madgy-Pegs,* clumsily dressed in woman's clothes, and also masked or painted who went from door to door collecting money. Some walked on stilts to cadge money from spectators looking out of upper windows" (Young 1817, vol. 1, 880–81; Holt 1890 , 21).

In 1825, in a letter to *The Every-Day Book,* the "peasant poet" John Clare recounted how at Helpston, north of Peterborough, the local ploughboys went to the blacksmiths to blacken their faces with soot and grease before doing their rounds (Deacon 2002, 293) This was an identical technique to that recorded in Bulgaria (Fol 2004, 53). Plough Bullocks all blackened their faces, while only some of the Plough Witches did. The cross-dressed She-Witch had his face raddled (smeared with patches or streaks of red and white). Thomas Sternberg quotes a report of 1848 of the Northamptonshire Plough Witches being "decked with ribbons and daubed with paint" (Sternberg 1851, 124). In Nottingham in 1838, William Howitt wrote of the motley team: "This consists of the farm-servants and laborers. They are dressed in harlequin guise, with wooden swords, plenty of ribbons, faces daubed with white-lead, red-ochre, and lamp-black. One is always dressed in woman's clothes and armed with a besom, a sort of burlesque mixture of Witch and Columbine. Another drives the team of men-horses with a long wand, at the end of which is tied a bladder instead of a lash; so that blows are given without pain, but plenty of noise" (Howitt 1838, 471–72).

In 1873, a newspaper reported what it thought to be the demise of Plough Monday in Ramsey, which it called "this licensed system of begging and the attendant foolery of disguised villagers in the bloom of red-ochre, the sickly pallor of whiting, or the orthodox demoniacal tint of lamp-black" (*Peterborough Advertiser,* January 18, 1873, 3). A record from Eye, to the east of Peterborough, in 1894, tells how on Plough Monday "a large number of plough-boys attired in the most grotesque manner, having faces reddened with ochre or blackened with soot, waited on those known to be in the habit of remembering the poor old *ploughboy*" (*Peterborough and Huntingdonshire Standard,* January 13, 1894, 8).

Clare's 1825 letter reports the element of misrule, vandalism, or settling of scores that was facilitated by Plough Monday. Boot scrapers were ripped out of the ground, people were "wound up" in the ropes used to pull the plough, and sometimes gardens had a plough driven through them, pulled by the Ploughboys (Deacon 2002, 293). To "wind up" someone is to make them angry, still a common expression. At Ramsey, it was said to be the custom to settle scores on Plough Monday by playing practical jokes. This might involve ploughing up the garden or the front step, moving the water butt so it would flood the house when the front door was opened, or taking gates off their hinges and throwing them in the nearest dyke (Marshall 1967, 200–201). At Great Sampford is a record from the early twentieth century of a "pickaxe man" ready to dig up boot scrapers: "Up with the scraper, Jack!" (Wortley ms., May 28, 1944). Stone-throwing that broke a plate-glass window on Plough Monday 1871 was blamed on the Plough Witches (*Cambridge Independent Press,* January 14, 1871, 7). In Nottingham in the 1880s, the Plough Bullocks were active. As the correspondent "Old Timer" recalled in 1925, "in some streets of Nottingham in the 80s men with blackened faces went from yard to yard threatening to plough up doorsteps, although they had no plough, and demanding money for ale" ("Old Timer" 1925). This element of misrule led to repeated attempts by the authorities to suppress the festivities.

In his 1911 memoirs, F. W. Bird recalled "Plough Monday was a great institution at Godmanchester. Farming men, many of them dressed as women, and having their faces besmeared, paraded the streets. Not content with assuming grotesque costumes, and beadaubed faces, they stuffed bundles of straw between their shoulders, which gave them a hunch-back appearance." Clare noted the same use of straw in 1825. Bird continues, "They dragged a wooden plough behind them, and men, all more or less hideously attired, accompanied the procession with money boxes. They halted at all the principal houses of the town and asked for toll. If nothing was forthcoming from a call, rumor said that the plough witches made no more ado but ploughed up the front part of the houses and departed, but no such damage was remembered in Godmanchester" (Bird 1911, 39). When two groups of Ploughboys from neighboring villages met, fights between them broke out. According to Bird, "severe encounters" between the Ramsey and Benwick Plough Witches "often took place."

Various versions of Plough Monday chants are known. At Pampisford, Cambridgeshire, it is:

> *Up with the scraper*
> *And down with the door.*
> *If you don't give us money,*
> *We'll plough no more.*

One ominous chant referred to a form of retribution carried out by laborers on masters who had treated them badly. The chant probably dated from the Laborers' Revolt of 1832, when gangs of disguised men who were followers of the mythical Captain Swing burned hayricks and houses. It went:

> *Sifting the chaff*
> *A bottle of hay*
> *See the poor crow*
> *Go merrying away*
> *Hi! Nickity Norny.*

The "crow" was the band of rebellious men with faces blackened with soot so as not to be recognized. A bottle of hay is a small truss, easy to carry, which was set alight and thrown through smashed windows into houses to burn them down. A traditional tune written by Clare is called "Smash the Windows" (Deacon 2002, 140). The author has played it as part of the repertoire of the Traditional Music of Cambridgeshire Collective. Often a threat rather than an action, nevertheless the song represented an assertion of potential by the members of the rural fraternities who carried it.

The newspapers of the period, far more meticulous than modern journalism, reported in detail the Ploughboys' outings, such as this one in the *Cambridge Chronicle:* "Plough Monday—Last Monday was a wretched day for the display of rustic masquerading in the streets of our town. It was a thorough wet day, and the streets were ankle-deep in mud; so that the 'plough-boys' cut a very sorry figure indeed. Nevertheless they made their appearance as usual, and were as eager in their efforts to levy contributions as if they had had the advantage and excitement of a bright day and a sharp frost" (*Cambridge Chronicle,* January 13, 1849).

The Cambridge press of the 1850s has several references to the disguises of the Plough Witches, who were "disguised in women's clothes or with blackened faces" or "dressed in a bonnet and petticoat and hat the same time had a black face." At Helpston, north of Peterborough, Clare recorded that the Plough Bullocks all blackened their faces, while only some of the Plough Witches did. The She-Witch had his face raddled. In 1888 at Elton, Northamptonshire, the day was kept up by thirty men "dressed in fantastic costumes, some in women's attire, others with large hats and streaming ribbons, and some with darkened faces, [who] paraded the streets" (*Peterborough Advertiser,* January 14, 1888, 5). Blackened faces, which were easily made with dirt, lamp-black from oil lamps, or soot from burned straw or from up a chimney, were used at some time or another at Saint Ives, Eye, near Peterborough, Great Gidding, Kimbolton, Warboys, and Yaxley between 1872 and 1940 (Frampton 1996, 17–18, 20–21). Plough Witches were recorded with blackened faces at Holywell around 1910, in Easton up to 1939, and at Spaldwick in 1943. At Sawtry, faces were blackened and coats worn inside-out (Tebbutt 1984, 53).

At Brandon Creek, the male participants wore belts and lalligags made of woven straw (Porter 1969, 101). At Littleport in the early twentieth century, the broom man was called Humpty. He wore a tail made of braided straw hanging down his back (Porter 1969, 102). Sybil Marshall reported that at Ramsey, the Molly dancers of the early twentieth century put on the traditional disguise and used devil masks (Marshall 1967, 84), and in the Ely district, darkened faces and motorcyclists' goggles are recorded (Needham and Peck 1933, 6).

Any group of people going about in unusual circumstances can pose the threat of violent behavior. In Cambridgeshire, there was threatening activity (Lomping, or Mumping) on some particular dark winter nights, including Plough Monday. At Barnwell, "at night, too, a large number of these ugly ruffians black their faces and provided with large sticks, they beat at doors and calling themselves *Mumps* are clamorous for halfpennies" (*Cambridge Independent Press,* January 18, 1851). In his manuscripts in the Cambridgeshire Collection, Russell Wortley (1912–1980) tells of stave-wielding men at Fulbourn on Plough Monday and Bottisham on Dowlan Day, December 21, who went around chanting, "Lomp, Lomp. If you don't give us something we'll give you a good crump" (Wortley ms., March 26, 1938; August 8, 1975). Men called Mumpers, carrying staves and threatening passers-by at night, are known from nineteenth-century Cambridge. In one example, recorded in 1963, eighty-two-year-old Hannah Gawthrop, recalling her younger days, told how at night on Plough Monday in Cambridge, Mumpers would come with blackened faces, knocking on doors and chanting the verse used at Bottisham, but with "Mump, mump" at the beginning (Porter 1969, 103).

In post–World War II Plough Monday outings, there was neither lomping nor whipcracking, although whips played an important part in Plough Monday in earlier times. Wortley records one or more whip-men on Plough Monday at many villages: Cheveley, Fulbourn, Ickleton, Horseheath, Madingley, Snailwell, Weston Colville, West Wratting, Wimpole, and Whaddon. In Essex, whips were cracked at Saffron Walden (Wortley ms., 1938).

20

Molly Dancing and Garlanding

In Warwickshire, the Ploughboys had two who cross-dressed to represent Molly, who carried a ladle to collect money, and Bessy, who carried the can and gave out beer to every good man. There was also a Clown who blew a horn (Palmer 1976, 45). In addition to taking around the plough, there is a particular form of dancing connected with Plough Monday, Molly dancing. Villages around Cambridge had their own teams, also called *sets*. Needham and Peck list Comberton, Coton, Girton, Grantchester, Histon, and Madingley (Needham and Peck 1933, 2). The sets left home early in the morning and danced at various locations, ending up in Cambridge marketplace around midday, where they "danced against each other" (Needham and Peck 1933, 2–3). Wortley records the teams dancing on Market Hill circa 1938 from Madingley, Dry Drayton, Girton, Hardwick, Comberton, Barton, Grantchester, and Haslingfield (Wortley ms. 1938). Each set had six dancers, one a she-male—Molly or Bessie—as well as a musician (fiddle or melodeon) and the Umbrella Man. Accompanying the Molly set was a team of men dragging a wooden plough and men with whips that they cracked. In the evening the sets returned to their home villages,

Fig. 20.1. Molly dancing at Comberton, Cambridgeshire (See also color plate 32.)

where they drank and danced into the night. Women accompanied the men in these dances (Needham and Peck 1933, 3). The umbrella, called a *dickey-shud* (donkey shade) in Suffolk (Jobson 1966, 173), is a sign of the Cunning Man, who is associated with historical figures like Cunning Murrell and Old Winter.

On September 8, 1911, Jonathan Clingo of Littleport (then aged 85) told folklore collector Cecil Sharp of the former Plough Monday ceremonies, when the men called morris dancers went around the villages. One was dressed in women's clothes, led by a man with a long feather in his cap and accompanied by a fiddler and a man with a broom. The dancers wore white shirts "with ribbons and scarves all over them and high box hats. . . . No bells, no sticks, no handkerchiefs" (Cecil Sharp's notebook in Clare College, Cambridge, cited by Needham and Peck 1933, 5). However, Sharp had his own ideas of purity that made categorical distinctions between morris dancing, Molly dancing, sword dancing, and mumming, when earlier accounts show that each form overlapped the others in costume, repertoire, and accoutrements. The author has heard the adage "no bells" at Cambridgeshire Plough Monday events, yet an 1846 account in the local press told readers that "the annual invasion of Cambridge by the hard-handed sons of toil took place last Monday and our streets echoed from morn to night with the strains of some vile fiddle, the tinkling of bells, and the oft-repeated cry of 'remember the poor plough-boy'" (*Cambridge Chronicle and Journal,* January 17, 1846, 2).

At Haddenham, the plough was bedecked with ribbons and greenery. It was pulled by young men and driven by a man with a whip. Broom-stem dancing was performed. At Ely, the dancers wore ribbons on their sleeves and all down their trousers. The Ely and Little Downham teams each had a tambourine man who was also the *treasure man* (bagman or boxman) who collected the money. The broom man swept children off the dancing ground, and snow, too, if there was any. The men used to kiss Betty "and one thing and another" (Sharp n.d. [1911] unpublished

Fig. 20.2. Swalwell sword dancers with cross-dressed Bessy, Fool, Ragman, and musician playing a Viceroy one-row melodeon (1911 photograph)

manuscript; Needham and Peck 1933, 5). In 1931, Frederick Shelton of the Little Downham set told Needham and Peck that it is "necessary to keep up the day," which is the motto of Cambridgeshire traditionalists to this day. In 1932, the Little Downham set had six men, one of whom was the Betty and another who played a one-row melodeon. All had their faces darkened and some wore goggles (Needham and Peck 1933, 6). In 1937, the *Ely Standard* reported that "Plough Monday was celebrated according to the old traditions. A party in fancy dress, armed with a broomstick and an accordion, paraded the village" (*Ely Standard,* January 15, 1937, 13).

In 1948, Molly dancer Joseph Kester, who celebrated his hundredth birthday on September 1, 1947 (and died January 1950), described the costume of the Hardwick set. Ribbons were worn over ordinary clothes, except the Lady, who was in female garb, and the Lord, who wore a tall hat. A broad sash about four inches wide—the club color—was worn

Fig. 20.3. Mepal Molly men dance at Wilburton, Cambridgeshire, England, on Plough Monday 2019. (See also color plate 33.)

over the left shoulder to the right hip. One Hardwick set's sash was red with white crimped edges, another was yellow; Madingley's was dark red. There was also a broad waistband that was sometimes the same colors as the sash, but not always, though all members of the set wore the same color. Rosettes were sewn to the front of the sash, on the waistband, and on the arms. A larger rosette was set at the crossing of the sash at the hip. Broad ribbons were worn around the upper arms, again any color, but standardized for a set. The musician generally wore a green sash and a band around his hat, but no other ribbons. The *beggars* (boxmen) wore one or two rosettes pinned to their jackets. The Coton team wore cockades in their hats. The dancers were dressed by the women on Plough Monday morning; it took two to dress a man, one to hold him still while the rosettes were stitched on (Kester, interviewed February 23, 1948, Wortley unpublished manuscript in Cambridgeshire Collection).

In eastern England, blackening or whitening the face is part of the Fenland Molly dancing tradition. Here are three typical accounts of Plough Monday in 1934: The *Ely Standard* noted, "Molly dancers attired in toppers, blackened faces, and gaily-decorated uniforms paraded in many parts of the parish, singing and dancing over the broomstick" (Frampton 1994, 10). "The landlady of The Anchor public house in Little Downham (1927–1940) blacked the Molly Dancers' faces using candle-heated corks" (Frampton 1994, 11). "The Lady, a man in women's dress, had his face whited-up with flour" (Reg Moore, quoted by Frampton 1994, 12). Toward the end of the twentieth century, with the ready availability of all kinds of makeup, face colors tended toward diversity. From Leicestershire, both the Red Leicesters morris side and the Hinckley Bullockers Plough Monday team have red faces when they perform in wintertime. The carnivalesque tendency of Molly dancing also favors multicolor face makeup. In former times, colored makeup was not readily available outside the theater, so now another chapter in the story of coloring-up has begun.

In the late twentieth century, Molly dancing developed into two currents, with distinct forms of costume: the traditional, continuing the pattern described above, and a new form, with a carnivalesque appearance. The former, with faces blackened, included the Old Hunts Molly, the Old Glory Molly Gang, and the Good Easter Molly Gang. The carnivalesque current is best characterized by the black-and-white Pig Dyke Molly and the multicolored Gogmagog Molly. In these latter sets, faces are painted in patterns or in multicolor. A few contemporary Molly sets do not use any face makeup.

As with so many traditional outings by rural fraternities and Fools' guilds, the advent of a police force led to attempts of suppression of the Plough Monday rites. In the reign of William IV and then Queen Victoria, many traditional sports were suppressed. Some were banned on grounds of cruelty, such as bull running, bull baiting, stoning the squirrel, cock fighting, and dog fighting (though the last two continue clandestinely today). Others were part of ancient civic rites and ceremonies that were abolished by the Municipal Reform Act of 1835.

Fig. 20.4. Blowing the May Horns, King's Lynn, Norfolk, May Day 1997

These included suppressing livestock fairs in cities, mass football matches in the streets, vernacular calendar customs, and guising traditions such as parading effigies of giants. For example, in 1836, the Corporation of King's Lynn in Norfolk attempted to prohibit people from celebrating May Day by carrying the May Garland and blowing horns, which was cited as a public nuisance.

Implicit in the suppression of traditional gatherings and customs is the progressives' claim that they are redundant, degenerate remnants of a barbarous past, or at least threats to public order and morals. In either case, they are presented as outmoded in the modern world and thus practices that hinder the progress that modernity demands. The writer of the handbook *Wisbech Hundred* in 1850 expressed this prejudice perfectly: "The utility of marts and fairs is now almost wholly superseded; and those of Lynn and Wisbech have degenerated into a mere gathering of freaks of nature, 'harlotry players,' dirty exhibitions, conjurors, wild beasts, and ragamuffin life in all its gipsyism." But markets and fairs continued, nevertheless. "Ploughmondaying," too, never quite died out, being kept up in many different places by people who wanted to carry on an old English tradition, though not with the vehemence or violence of the previous era before World War I, which saw the beginning of the end of horses working the land and the consequent mechanization of farming tip the practice into serious decline. It was restored sporadically at different places after the end of World War II in 1945, with the plough followers occasionally being themselves followed and watched by the police as their forebears were a century and more earlier.

May Day Garlanding and Guising

May Day, celebrated as the beginning of summer, was a major festival, though not recognized as such by the church. Best known now for its Maypole dancing and also derived from the sweeps' and milkmaids' holiday as a festival of proletarian politics, May Day has many customs and traditions. The May Garland is one of them. In 1854, the Reverend Edward Bradley, writing as Cuthbert Bede, described the

May Garland at Glatton, Huntingdonshire, as "a pyramidal garland—composed of tulips, anemones, cowslips, king-cups, lilacs, laburnums, meadow-orchids, wallflowers, primroses, crown imperials, roses, green boughs." It was a "pyramidal nosegay from the front of which a gaily dressed doll (called 'Madame Flora') stares vacantly. From the base of the nosegay hang ribbons, pieces of silk, handkerchiefs, gay-colored fabric" (Bede 1854, 91–92). The famous 1854 illustration of the Glatton May Garland resembles Jack-in-the-Green and hints at a person inside. The May Garland at Eynesbury always contained hawthorn, the May tree, if it was in blossom (Tebbutt 1984, 61). May bushes of hawthorn were a feature of May Day in many places (e.g., Great Gransden, Cambridgeshire (Anon 1816, 130). These were placed in front of people's houses, especially those where eligible girls lived (Tebbutt 1984, 66). A Norfolk custom recalled by John Glyde Jr. is that if a farmhouse servant brought in a branch of May in full bloom, she received a dish of cream as a reward (Glyde 1872, 113).

In Lynn, Norfolk (now called King's Lynn), the May Garlands were made of two hoops of flowers with a doll set in the middle. The

Fig. 20.5. May Garland, Glatton, Huntingdonshire, 1854

garlands were festooned with birds' eggs and ribbons and were carried around town all day to the accompaniment of children blowing cows' horns (Richards 1812, vol. 1, 262). The Saint James' Workhouse garland was carried annually by pauper children until about 1836, when the town corporation banned the workhouse celebrations as a public nuisance. But other observances could not be banned. At the end of the nineteenth century, Charles Bagge Plowright noted, "On the 1st of May, during the morning, sundry parties of children carry round the town garlands of flowers. The children, girls and boys, are dressed principally in white, with crowns of flowers on their heads, and money-boxes in their hands. They are bare-headed, and their clothing is decorated with brightly colored calico, ribbons, or paper. . . . It is noteworthy, that although there may be ten or a dozen garlands perambulating the town, they all emanate from one particular district, and from it alone, namely the quarter occupied by the fishing population. The local appellation of 'May Ladies' suggests the May Queen" (Plowright 1895, 106–7).

In King's Lynn, as in some other places, there was some prank playing, such as nailing up door latches or the Huntingdonshire joke

Fig. 20.6. May Ladies, King's Lynn, Norfolk (1894 photograph)

of leaning a gatepost against a door so that it fell in when the door was opened (Tebbutt 1984, 66). Despite the ban, people of King's Lynn continued to carry May Garlands, or at least a doll in a box with leaves, sporadically until World War II, avoiding the police wherever possible. The May Garland again appeared on the streets of the town in 1983, when the king's morris dancers restored the custom.

In Cambridge, it was customary for passersby to give the garland bearers coins or sweets in exchange for a view of the dolls ("Madame Flora") that they concealed beneath cloths at the center of their garlands. This continued until 1959, when the police announced that it was forbidden as begging and a threat to public order and that anyone with a garland would be arrested. Of course, after the police diktat, no one dared to go out on the streets that year, so a charming custom was brought to a sudden end. But in 2009, the present author carried the first May Garland that had been seen on the streets of Cambridge for fifty years. He joined the garland parade began at the upper end of Honey Hill in Cambridge, in the oldest part of the city whose street plan dates from the original Roman settlement founded 1,900 years ago. As they processed to the music of fiddle and accordion, they stopped at the Folk Museum, where they were greeted warmly. At key points along the route, they stopped and the May Call was made by the garland bearer.

Today it is the First of May.
Come greet the summer sun.
Cast your clouts,
For May is out,
And summer is begun.

This was followed by summer singing (singing in the summer, as May Day is traditionally the first summer day) of the "May Garland Song," whose traditional words were first written down in 1904 at the Peterborough May Day celebrations. They sang the "May Garland Song" outside the Round Church and the church of Great Saint Mary, which is the official center point of Cambridge, and outside the Eagle Inn and at each end of the street called "Petty Cury," which were the customary dancing places of the Molly dancers on Plough Monday. Toward the end of the route, they entered the Community Café in Jesus Lane, where we played and sang. The parade finished, appropriately, at the Maypole public house.

In former times, it was the custom for milkmaids and chimney sweeps to parade together on May Day. In the early eighteenth century, milkmaids were lent silverware by their customers and carried the pieces, as the *Spectator* reported in 1712, "in a most sprightly style under a pyramid of silver tankards" (Judge 2000, 5). Sometimes men carried the heavy load of silverware, and a similar tradition continues in Austria in the wintertime outings of Perchten in the Pongau. In 1786, the *Hampshire Chronicle,* reporting events in London wrote, "On 1st of May, several curious circumstances took place—the *Sweeps* and *Maids,* with *Jack o' th'Green* danced through the streets" and continued with the political comings and goings of the metropolis (*Hampshire Chronicle,* May 8, 1786, 1).

There are contemporary illustrations of Jack o' the Green that show a man in everyday clothing with foliage on his hat and tied to a staff that he carries (see figure 20.7).

Fig. 20.7. Jack o' the Green

Formerly a pleasant character dressed out with ribands and flowers, figured in village May-games under the name of

JACK-O'-THE-GREEN.

Jack-in-the-Green is an overall bell-shaped green leaf-covered structure worn by a guiser. The 1854 May Garland at Glatton, recorded by Bede, was not a circular garland as carried by the May Ladies or attached to the Maypole. It was a larger structure, which must have been fastened to a frame. The foliage worn as Jack-in-the-Green was similar, being attached to a hooped wickerwork frame that supported it. There was a space left where the guiser could see out. Jack-in-the-Green, his blackened face visible through the foliage, appeared at Ware in Hertfordshire in the 1840s along with a clown, two blackened climbing boys, and a drummer who also played the pan pipes (Jones-Baker 1977, 140).

As the variances between Jack o' the Green and Jack-in-the-Green show, there was no "standard form" of the festivities, for they shared guising features with other folk performances at other times, such as Plough Monday, Guy Fawkes' Night, and Christmas. Sweeps sometimes cross-dressed and whitened their usually sooty faces (Judge

Fig. 20. May Day, Cheltenham, 1892

2000, 12–13). In May 1836, four chimney sweeps were taken to court in London for "creating a mob and disturbance." They were a guiser as Jack-in-the-Green accompanied by two clowns and "My Lord," who was "papered and spangled." The magistrate found them not guilty on the grounds that it was an ancient custom. Then, "the whole of the prisoners were discharged, and, on leaving the court, Jack popped into the Green; and, after regaling themselves at an adjacent public-house, they proceeded opposite the office and struck up a tune, and continued dancing . . . until they got out of the neighbourhood" (*Morning Post,* May 4, 1836). The London guisers danced to a fife and drum.

The Green Man and the Woodwose

In 1939, Lady Raglan published a very influential paper in the journal *Folk-Lore.* Titled "The 'Green Man' in Church Architecture," it gave a new name to the foliated heads or masks that are present in some medieval churches (Raglan 1939, 45–57). Raglan's work on the Green Man and the subsequent documentation of numerous examples of foliated heads by Kathleen Basford focused attention on them in isolation from the mask-and-head tradition of which they are part (Basford 1977, passim).

Fig. 20.9. Foliated head, stone carving, Oxford (See also color plate 34.)

Fig. 20.10. Roman mask stone carving, Stuttgart, Germany

When one studies one thing in great detail, one may not notice something similar next to it, and concentration on the Raglanesque Green Man has burgeoned to the detriment of similar artifacts. Foliated masks are known from Roman times in metalwork and architecture and may have represented Sylvanus, the tutelary god of forests, fields, and farming.

But the foliated representation was never in isolation from closely related masks. A fine example is a large silver plate from a Roman hoard found at Mildenhall in Suffolk in 1942. It has a mask in a circular field at the center, which has a beard of leaves, a mustache that terminates in dolphins, and two further dolphins emerging from his hair. The central circle is surrounded by an outer circle of nerids, seahorses, and a coiling sea serpent. He is closer in form to the Gorgon of the temple at Bath than a Raglanesque face, and so is not a Green Man in terrestrial foliage but represents the watery deity (Painter 1977, 26, plates 1–6). Clearly, this mask of a sea god, perhaps Neptune or Oceanus, and the Gorgo are closely related to the Green Man of Lady Raglan.

Typically, the foliated head is a mask that is surrounded by vegetation and often has leafy branches emerging from its mouth. One with oak leaves and acorns, dating from the mid-1400s, exists in King's College Chapel, Cambridge. The medieval shrine of Saint Frideswide

Fig. 20.11. Orson from the
Masque of Valentine and Orson
(Pieter Breughel de Oude)

in Oxford Cathedral was smashed in the Protestant Reformation but later reconstructed from surviving fragments. Such carved stone faces amid foliage recall the legend of the Christian virgin Frideswide fleeing to the forest to avoid forced marriage. They have been described by some, post-Raglan, as "green men."

Before Lady Raglan redefined the Green Man as a foliated head, the Green Man meant a Woodwose (Anglo-Saxon *Wuduwāsa*), a wild man of the woods.

The Wild Man of the Woods is of human form but garbed all over in leaves and long hair, sometimes a phytomorphic figure clad in leaves, moss, or fabric tatters resembling leaves. A figure in all-over vegetation attached to a frame worn over the body is not Woodwose, but Jack-in-the-Green. Mythically, the wild man may be a child left in the woods and brought up by bears or other animals, as in the story of Valentine and Orson, or a man placed under a spell or otherwise driven to madness, as in the Arthurian story of Sir Tristram. In Eastern Europe, the wild man equivalent is the *leshy* (Polish *leszy* or Czech *leši*), a forest-living trickster

Fig. 20.12. Zapfenmanndl *dressed in fir cones, Saint Johann, Austria*

portrayed either as a man with goat's legs and hoofs or as a gray-bearded man wearing a cone-bearing green cloak (Anglickienė 2013, 137). The *Zapfenmanndl* of German-speaking countries is his counterpart.

In the late 1400s, the Schempartlauf in Nuremberg, Germany, featured wild men. In the Lumeçon festival at Mons in Belgium, the phytomorphic Hommes Sauvages (Wild Men, dressed in green fabric ivy leaves and carrying green clubs) handle the long tail of the dragon while les Hommes Blancs (White Men, dressed all in white) carry le Lumeçon.* A 1759 account of the midsummer Cormass at Dunkirk tells of "machines" with various characters riding on them. The anonymous correspondent to the *Caledonian Mercury,* likening them to familiar images on British inn signs, saw "several fellows dressed so as to resemble our sign of the *Green Man;* a green scaly skin was drawn close over their

---

*Le Lumeçon is the name of the dragon effigy.

own, and their faces were concealed with masks" (*Caledonian Mercury*, July 16, 1759, 1). The Wildmannspiel at Baltscheider in Switzerland is a performance that includes guisers dressed as wild men and a judge.

A notable performance with people dressed as Woodwoses was the Bal des Sauvages, a masquerade ball held at a wedding feast in Paris on January 28, 1393. It is notable for the fatal accident that befell the guisers. King Charles VI and five courtiers were dressed in wild men costumes that unfortunately caught fire on a flaming torch. They were burned to death. The dreadful event is referred to as the Bal des Ardents (the ball of the burning men), and contemporary illustrations survive. Edgar Allan Poe (1809–1849) adapted the event for his story *Hop-Frog* (1849), in which a disabled dwarf, forced to serve a king as his jester, tricks the king and his ministers into performing in flammable orang-utan costumes, which he then sets on fire, burning them alive. "I am simply Hop-Frog, the jester—and this is my last jest." In 1896, the Belgian artist James Ensor (1860–1949), who had a predilection for masks, made an etching of the final scene of Poe's story in *Hop-Frog's Revenge*.

The official coat of arms of the London livery company the Distillers had two Native Americans as supporters of the shield, described as "Indians with bows and arrows." However, the inn-sign painters of public houses such as the Green Man and Still invariably painted their predecessors, European Woodwoses, as armorial bearers. In eighteenth-century Bavaria, mountebanks selling herbal remedies were accompanied by zanies dressed as wild men.

Valentine and Orson was a play performed widely in northern Europe. The play tells how twin brothers were abandoned in the wild wood. Valentine was found by nobles and brought up as a courtly knight, while Orson, called Sansnom (No Name) in early versions, was raised by bears and becomes a Woodwose—a wild man of the woods. The story is based around their encounter and later adventures. A 1559 painting by Pieter Breughel de Oude usually titled *De Strijde tussen Vasten en Vastenavond* (*The Battle between Carnival and Lent*) shows the emaciated fasting of Lent in combat with the rotund and hearty Carnival (the festival called Shrove Tuesday, Mardi Gras, Fastnacht, Fasnet, etc.). Amid the symbols of Lent and Carnival is a vignette of characters from *The Masque of Valentine and Orson*. Orson, the wild man, is shown with long straggly beard and hair and a costume that appears to be covered with regular, round-ended tatters, as can be seen in modern German Fastnacht guising. He carries a club studded with metal spikes. The other characters are masked, with false beards, masks across their lower faces, and darkened, veiled faces. Two boxwomen beg money from people in a house who are watching the performance. Prints based on the painting exist in various forms, some by Breughel himself and others by his son and other copyists. The play *Valentine and Orson* was being performed in Shropshire, England, by traveling players in the nineteenth century (Wakeman 1884, 385). A mural of Valentine and Orson among fairy-tale characters was painted in the Day Nursery of Cardiff Castle when William Burges (1827–1881) rebuilt it for John Patrick Crichton-Stuart, the third Marquess of Bute (1847–1900).

21

Fire, Misrule, and Disorder

$\mathcal{F}$ire plays an important role in traditional festivals, from the purifying Beltane fires of May and the midsummer fires of Saint John to wintertime torchlight processions and bonfires as well as the burning of the Yule Log over the twelve days of Christmas. Like all human activities, bonfires can be used for good or ill purposes. They have been used as a rite of cleansing, incinerating effigies of evil spirits and tyrants as well as banned books and condemned people. In Britain, the major fire festival is Bonfire Night, otherwise called Guy Fawkes' Night. Guido Fawkes (1570–1606) was executed for his part in a sectarian plot to use barrels of gunpowder to blow up the British Parliament and King James I. Guy Fawkes, as he was popularly known, was called "the Devil in the Vault" because he was apprehended on November 5, 1605, with barrels of gunpowder in the vault beneath the Parliament house. After the king's narrow escape, that day was kept up as a remembrance of the Gunpowder Plot, portrayed as a Protestant deliverance from Roman Catholic revolutionaries. In the early years of the celebration, prayers were said in church, and later, effigies of the pope and the devil were carried through the streets in carnivalesque processions and burned on

Fig. 21.1. Fastnacht witches burn their besoms at the end of Carnival.
(See also color plate 35.)

huge bonfires. Fireworks were set off, and general feasting and drinking took place. The celebrations were official; the mayor and members of the corporation of each city and town would attend thanksgiving services in church, an official bonfire would be lit, and official fireworks would be set off. The anti-Catholic sectarian rhyme of the day, of which only the first verse is now repeated, was chanted.

> *Remember, remember, the fifth of November*
> *Gunpowder, treason, and plot.*
> *I see no reason why gunpowder treason*
> *Should ever be forgot.*
>
> *A rope, a rope, to hang the Pope*
> *A piece of cheese to choke him.*
> *A barrel of beer to drink his health,*
> *And a damn good fire to roast him.*

Secret fraternities of young men were formed to keep up the day, in the manner of Carnival societies all over Europe and beyond, and gradually the official element of the bonfire celebrations lapsed. The Bonfire Boys took the day as a time of Carnival misrule when the law could be flouted. Bonfire Night was a great opportunity for drunken reveling and disorder. There are frequent records of masked people tearing down fences and gates to make bonfires, and each parish in any town would vie with others for the biggest fire. Tar barrels would be set alight and kicked along the street or carried on intrepid men's heads. As well as the pope and the devil, it became customary also to burn other effigies. Unpopular local squires, justices, and informers were burned in effigy, and during the eighteenth century, effigies of Guido Fawkes himself began to be made for incineration on the bonfires.

The carnivalesque disorder of Guy Fawkes' Night was deplored even in the eighteenth century. In 1751, the *Gentleman's Magazine* called for action against the revelers who cast fireworks into crowds, broke windows, and tore up fences for their bonfires (Cressy 1992, 78). No action was taken, for this was the norm all over the country. In 1785,

Fig. 21.2. Guy Fawkes effigy paraded on the way to be burned on a bonfire, 1823

there was a bonfire riot in Lewes, Sussex, and in 1788, when an edict from the mayor attempted to ban street bonfires, there was a riot in Southampton. In the early nineteenth century, Bonfire Societies existed in many towns in southern England, including Guildford, Exeter, Horsham, Rye, and Chelmsford. The members of some of these secret fraternities wore distinctive clothing, were masked, and carried weapons for self-defense. Sometimes Bonfire Night turned into brawling between rival Bonfire Societies or a riot against unpopular employers, whose houses would be stoned by mobs of masked men. There are hundreds of accounts of violent November 5 outbursts all over England from the eighteenth to the twentieth centuries.

One of the most vigorous Bonfire Night traditions, which was in Lewes, Sussex, has persisted until the present day. Bonfire Night there seemed for a long time to have had an element of serious misrule with costumed people in uproar. In 1785, there was a riot after magistrates were summoned by householders complaining about bonfires near their houses. Lewes was widely known as a place to avoid on Bonfire Night. The *Morning Advertiser* for November 10, 1847, reported, "For many years past the town of Lewes has been the scene of the grossest riots and excess on the 5th of November, when large mobs disguised with masks and fantastic dresses have held possession of the town." Three of the extant Lewes Bonfire Societies—Cliffe, Lewes Borough, and Commercial Square—were founded in the early 1850s. In 1882, the *Kentish Independent* for November 11, 1882, reported that at Lewes "effigies of Guy Fawkes and the Pope were stuffed with fireworks and blown to pieces."

In 1863 in Guildford, Surrey, where there was a vigorous Bonfire Society, Bonfire Night went off peacefully at first because an army contingent was stationed there to prevent trouble. However, when the military returned to its barracks at Aldershot, "late on Saturday night the 'guys' took advantage of their absence to come out, eighteen or twenty men. Armed with bludgeons, and disguised as 'guys' they went on the rampage" (*Kentish Gazette*, November 24, 1863, 6). They "began their work of revenge . . . appearing in attires of the most fantastic description." Others joined in, and the riot became out of hand as buildings were damaged and money extorted from homeowners. The local militia, the Twenty-Fourth Surrey Rifles, was called out and assisted the police in putting down the riot. The *Aldershot Military Gazette* for November 23 carried the headline "Guy Fawkes' Riots at Guildford: Great Destruction of Property—A Constable Dangerously Wounded."*

In 1865, there was a Guy Fawkes' riot at Bishop's Stortford in Hertfordshire, and in 1866, riots at Braintree in Essex. Chelmsford town center was occupied every year on Guy Fawkes' Night from 1859 to 1888, with a major riot in 1866 that made the national press (Storch 1982, 86–88). The Bonfire Boys at Malton, Yorkshire, rioted in 1867, and in 1875 they rioted at Bournemouth. They repeated the violence there again in 1884. In 1876, a major riot erupted on Bonfire Night in Bourne, Lincolnshire, and in 1879, a Guy Fawkes' riot in Oxford turned into a brawl between "town and gown," the local people against the students and academics. Another broke out in Croydon, south of London, on the same night, repeating a Guy Fawkes' riot there in 1876. In 1880, Peckham in South London was the scene of Bonfire violence, and in 1891, the riot act was read to the rioting revelers at Broadway in Worcestershire. In Cambridge, town versus gown brawls between "townies" (local lads) and "grads" (university undergraduates, identifiable because they were compelled to wear academic gowns) occurred every Bonfire Night for more than a hundred years, until in 1966 a particularly vicious riot led to the permanent suppression of the tradition by the police.

Like Lewes, Exeter in Devon was famous or notorious for its boisterous and violent Bonfire Nights, known locally as the Saturnalia. In the nineteenth century, members of the Young Exeter group kicked burning tar barrels along the streets, and effigies of priests, monks, nuns, and even the local bishop were taken to the bonfire next to the cathedral along with a giant effigy of the pope, carried aloft in a cage. In 1872, there was a major Bonfire Night riot serious enough to get

---

*It is the convention in the British army and writing about them to use the numbers of regiments, divisions, etc.

press coverage, but the trouble there was dwarfed seven years later by the disorder of the 1879 Saturnalia. The city authorities had banned the customary bonfire in the cathedral yard, but after nightfall, people who were determined to keep up the day carried loads of wood to the customary place and lit a bonfire anyhow. As the *Frome Times* reported, "Just as the bonfire had been set alight, one or two policemen ventured among the crowd for the purpose of 'spotting' the ringleaders, but no sooner was their presence discovered, than they were set upon by some scores of men armed with sticks, and driven out of the yard" (*Frome Times*, November 12, 1879, 3). As the fire died down, people began to tear the wooden shutters from shops to feed the flames. Police and military reinforcements arrived as the fire was fed with more and more shutters. The revelers chanted "give us wood" and "give us our rights" as the soldiers fixed their bayonets and the riot act was read out. The army did not open fire, but policemen wielding staves beat their way through the revelers until the crowd fled well after midnight. Several people were arrested and imprisoned, including a man in a monkey costume, described as a "ringleader."

The violent Exeter tradition was the breeding ground for the Skeleton Army, which emerged there in 1881 and was formed to combat the newly formed Salvation Army, which rankled many townspeople with their revivalism (see chapter 22). The Skeleton Army was also associated with Bonfire Night in the Somerset towns of Bridgwater and Weston-super-Mare in the same year. In the latter town, the local newspaper reported that "the 'guy manufactory' was in the neighborhood of Locking Road, and thither might have been seen wending their way at an early hour a number of hobbledehoys attired in quaint and inelegant costumes, with their faces masked and blackened. . . . The procession . . . was headed with a large black flag, on which appeared the Death's head and crossbones, and the words 'Skeleton Army'" (*Weston-super-Mare Gazette*, November 9, 1881, 2).

In the late nineteenth century, local authorities began to take control of Guy Fawkes' Night, and large-scale carnivals with floats were organized in place of the Bonfire Boys' excesses. Effigies of infamous figures were carried on floats through the streets attended by people in disguise and fancy dress—"soldiers, clowns, demons, and other strangely mixed groups." Satire, parody, and mockery were always present among the guisers and the effigies to be burned. In Hampstead, northern London, in 1881, there were five hundred guisers in the parade, including the Fried Fish Fusiliers, the Flask Walk Warriors, and the Starvation Army as well as some on horseback and a "triumphal car" carrying Guy Fawkes guarded by men-at-arms, the Headsman (an executioner), and "a real live ghost" (*Hampstead and Highgate Express,* November 12, 1881). Pirates and celebrated highwaymen like Claude Duval and Dick Turpin featured largely, along with Guy Fawkes himself. "H. H. Down, the King of Clowns," minstrels, brass bands, organ grinders, and dancing men guising as bears were recorded from the Carnival at Chard in 1891 (*Chard and Ilminster News,* November 7, 1891). Gradually, rolling burning tar barrels in the street was discouraged, as was a custom recorded in 1890 in East Yorkshire: "Youths have old besoms dipped in tar, which they kindle on the bonfire, and they rush about swinging the blazing torches above their heads" (Nicholson 1890, 16).

Private observance of Bonfire Night continued, of course, and there was occasional communal disorder on Bonfire Night without a public bonfire. At the time of writing, the last major Bonfire Night riot was on November 5, 2019, in Leeds city center. Local bonfires on waste ground or in gardens where fireworks were set off replaced the enormous collective bonfires that triggered off so much disorder. It became customary for children to make effigies of Guy Fawkes from old clothes stuffed with straw or paper and to show them to passersby with the plea for money for fireworks, "a penny for the Guy." In 1864, Chambers wrote, "The universal mode of observance through all parts of England is the dressing up of a scarecrow figure in such cast-habiliments as can be procured. The head-piece, generally a paper cap, painted and knotted with paper strips in imitation of ribbons, parading in the streets, and at nightfall burning it with great solemnity on a huge bonfire" (Chambers 1864 edition, 549–50). In the late nineteenth century, improvisation of Guy Fawkes masks was supplemented by printed paper, papier mâché, and cardboard versions. They were generally red and had a leering face with mustache and Vandyke beard.

Fig. 21.3. Making a Guy, with typical mask, nineteenth century

In the 1950s, thin plastic Guy Fawkes masks were sold at shops where fireworks were on sale. Occasionally, children's comics gave away free Guy Fawkes masks, such as *Whizzer and Chips* in 1969 and *Whoopee* in 1983. In 1982, David Lloyd designed a stylized white Guy Fawkes mask for Alan Moore's graphic novel *V for Vendetta*. Subsequently, after a movie version of the graphic novel was made, this mask was manufactured under license from Time Warner and worn in large numbers out of the British Guy Fawkes' Night context by anti-capitalist demonstrators, including the Occupy movement and the Anonymous activist group. Their disruptive acts carried on the ancient tradition of disguised mobs running amok, as had happened long before with the masked anti-corn laws demonstrators in Liverpool in 1841 and in many other places (*Liverpool Standard and General Commercial Advertiser*, June 8, 1841, 6–7).

22

Crime, Rebellion, and Ritual Disguise

Hunting and Resistance in Disguise

In southern England in the early 1720s, gangs of local men formed hunting parties to raid the deer parks and forests of aristocrats. They had initiation rituals and essentially were a guild of illegal huntsmen. There were two main gangs of these heavily armed poachers, around Waltham in Hampshire and in the royal forest of Windsor. They wore disguises, blackening their faces, and became known as the Waltham Blacks after a particularly violent raid in October 1721 on the deer park of the bishop of Winchester at Farnham. In 1723, an act of Parliament was passed that made being found disguised or armed in a forest a felony. The penalty for this was death on the gallows. The Waltham Black Act, as it became known, also stipulated the death penalty for setting fire to corn, hay, straw, wood, houses, and barns. The act was in force for a century, being repealed in 1823. However, despite the death penalty if caught, poachers continued to use disguises, most notably the havelock, a black muslim covering for the whole head and shoulders with only two eye holes and a breathing hole (Humphreys 1995, 167). A more widespread version of the havelock is an over-the-head knitted hood with mouth and eye holes, originally known as a balaclava helmet (and also called a ski mask). It got its name from its use in the Crimean War (1853–1856) when British soldiers suffering from the cold received them as presents from knitters back in Britain. It is still in use by poachers, terrorists, Special Forces, and riot police who wish to avoid identification. In eastern England in the mid-twentieth century, local groups of poachers were still carrying out "fairly elaborate" initiation ceremonies, which were serious and "in real earnest" (Newman 1940, 42). The hare- or rabbit-skin cap of rural Fools has a connection with poaching.

Similarly, highwaymen frequently masked themselves. For example, before he was apprehended and hanged, the "Gentleman Highwayman" James Maclaine (1724–1750) wore a similar over-the-head mask during his highway robberies.

From the 1820s to the late 1850s in industrial South Wales, disaffected coal miners and ironworkers formed gangs to attack strike breakers and informers. They wore masks or kerchiefs over their faces and dressed in cowhides. They were led by a masked man with horns guising as Y Tarw Scotch (the Scotch Bull). Others in the gang blackened their faces with coal dust, turned their jackets inside out, or wore women's clothing. They blew horns and rattled chains and

Fig. 22.1. Masked highwaymen rob a traveler.

made cattle-like sounds when they raided and destroyed the houses of those whom they targeted (Wilkins 1903, 178; Jones 1971, 220–49 passim). In southwest Wales, during an economic recession in 1843, the "Rebecca Riots" broke out in the counties of Pembroke, Carmarthen, Glamorgan, Cardigan, and Radnor. Toll gates on the public roads were seen by the trusts that ran them as a ready source of income, and the high tolls charged were resented by poor people who were forced to pay money they could ill afford to use the roads.

Groups of disguised men dressed in women's clothing attacked by night and destroyed the toll gates and the gatekeepers' houses. The gatekeepers were not physically harmed and were allowed to leave with their belongings. Each group was led by a captain called "Rebecca," and the other members of the group were called "her daughters." This imagery came from the biblical story of Rebekah, from Genesis 24:60: "And they blessed Rebekah, and said unto her, Thou art our sister, be thou the mother of thousands of millions, and let thy seed possess the gate of those which hate them." In June 1843, a large band of Rebecca rioters marched into Carmarthen and attacked the workhouse. Cavalry sent from Cardiff dispersed them. After that, the Rebeccaites turned violent and attacked those whom they blamed for the unfair system of landholding and the corrupt administration of justice. The government sent in troops and a contingent of London police to quell the Rebeccaites. But a government commission sent to South Wales late in the year found that the riots had occurred because of genuine grievances. The toll gates were abolished, and relief measures were introduced. Rebecca had succeeded.

The *Tablet* reported on a miners' strike at the Killingworth and West Moor collieries in the Tyne and Wear district of northeastern England. "A number of men, some being dressed in women's clothing, and others in masks, with their coats turned inside out, assembled at West Moor Colliery and proceeded to destroy the works. They drove the men that were there away, threw the corves [baskets for coal —N.P.] and materials on the surface down the shaft, gutted the houses of some who had not joined in with the strike" (*Tablet,* July 14, 1849, 14). As so often in industrial disputes, as with the Scotch Cattle and Rebecca and her daughters in Wales, there was a ritual, almost carnivalesque element to their disguising.

The *Graphic* newspaper for June 14, 1879, reported a trial of a burglar who had been apprehended with stolen property in his house at Mile End, eastern London. At his trial, a police officer noted that a piece of coal had been found on him that was explained as "every burglar who carries in his pocket a piece of charmed coal may defy the authorities" (Jones 1880, 193). Although undoubtedly an amulet, a piece of coal also could be broken up into dust and used to blacken the face as a disguise, like the two famous eighteenth-century instances of the Waltham Blacks poachers and the assailants of Charles Wesley in Worcester (described below). The Imperial War Museum in London has a piece of coal sent during World War I in 1917 to a soldier of the City of London Yeomanry by his sister as a lucky charm (Davies 2018, 143).

Tatterdemalions and the Skeleton Army

During the eighteenth and nineteenth centuries, itinerant preachers often attracted the ire of the local people they attempted to evangelize. Resistance was often carnivalesque and violent. In 1750, there was a riot by Protestants in Cork, Ireland, against the evangelist John Wesley, and in July 1751 in Worcester, England, Charles Wesley was attacked by people who objected to the new Methodist sect and broke up his meetings. In his journal he recounted, "We were hardly met when the sons of Belial poured in upon us, some with their faces blacked, some without shirts, all in rags. They began to 'Stand up for the Church' by swearing and cursing, by singing and talking lewdly, throwing dust and dirt over us; with which they filled their pockets, such as had any to fill. I was soon covered head to foot, and almost blinded. Finding it impossible to be heard, I told them I should apply to the Magistrates for redress, and walked upstairs." At the time, Methodist preachers were attacked in many places, often by people disguised in the traditional manner. Charles Wesley's elder brother, Samuel, condemned them as "tatterdemalions." After initial outbursts, the protests always die down, as they did against the Methodists, but it is always possible that at a later date similar things would happen again.

Exeter in the west of England had a strong and often violent tradition of celebration and protest; in 1739, John Wesley and his followers had to "fight their way everywhere," and in 1745, a Methodist meeting was stormed by a mob who pelted the attendees with potatoes and dung. The *London Morning Post* for May 16, 1745, reported that "many were trampled underfoot; many fled without their hats and wigs; and some without coats, or with half of them in tatters. Some of the women were lamed, and others stripped naked, and rolled most indecently in the kennel, their faces being besmeared with lampblack, flour, and dirt" (quoted in the *Western Times,* March 22, 1882). This antireligious outburst was more than the usual violence of a violent age when one could be whipped, put in the pillory, or publicly hanged for more than two hundred offenses, some of them trivial, or transported to the colonies as a slave.

Satire, comedy, and the carnivalesque were part of the vernacular resistance against the earnestness and authoritarianism of politicians and preachers. In 1750, a burlesque titled *Harlequin Methodist* was staged in London, and in Ipswich in 1758, a spoof *Letter from a Mountebank Doctor to a Methodist Preacher* by Herlothrumbo, supposedly a quack doctor, was published. It likened the business of the quack doctor with that of the Methodist preacher. It began "Dear Brother" and continued, "As we both depend on the publick for our subsistence, give me leave to propose a coalition between us, which, I doubt not, will prove of great advantage to us both." Herlothrumbo showed how the audience of the Methodist preacher was the same as the mountebank and asked, "Are the mob your customers? So they are mine: are you the scorn and jest of men of sense? So am I." He proposed that the quack and the Methodist should share the same platform: "My stage is large enough for us both." Herlothrumbo's zany style was versatile; he could alternate comedy with hymn writing: "My assistant *Merryman* may serve us in a double capacity, when he has displayed his humour to divert the mob, he may afterward assist you in *setting a hymn of your own composing.* I can assure you, he has an admirable talent in this way, can *twang* it through his nose very harmoniously, and put on as fascinated a Face as any of your profession" (*Ipswich Journal,* April 15, 1758, 1).

The Skeleton Army

Many years after the Methodists were resisted, it happened again in Exeter. The largest confrontation with preachers in Britain was elicited in the 1880s by the newly founded Salvation Army. The original Salvation Army, founded in 1878, was a uniformed religious organization modeled on the infantry regiments of the British army with a command structure with officers designated by military ranks such as Captain and Colonel. It was founded by William Booth (1829–1912), who, as commanding officer, styled himself General Booth and wore a general's uniform. Its members, who did not carry arms, lived in barracks in working-class districts, marched in formation to brass bands carrying banners emblazoned with "Blood and Fire." They made forays to picket places where they loudly denounced those there whom they perceived to be sinners. Their meetings were considered intimidating by many residents of the towns where they preached. In some places they employed local toughs and gangsters to protect their street parades against the Skeleton Army. Their military uniforms and revivalist chanting and singing that went on well into the early hours of the morning, disturbing the neighbors, were viewed as an unwanted intrusion into the normal life of the small towns and city districts where they chose to settle. They picketed public houses and liquor stores, preaching at drinkers, and set up barracks where they lived together. In October 1881, when "a detachment of the Salvation Army" arrived in Exeter in Devon, western England, local people were alarmed as uniformed members of the army marched through the city in military formation behind a banner reading "Blood and Fire" and publicly convened what they called a "council of war." They were accompanied by "an outside bodyguard, consisting of well-known roughs and would-be fighting men . . . for the purpose of protecting the 'officers'" (*Exeter and Plymouth Gazette Daily Telegram,* October 3, 1881, 2).

Exeter in 1854 had seen bread riots put down by the local militia, and there was always boisterous disorder on November 5 each year, called locally the Saturnalia. There was serious trouble on Bonfire Night in 1872, but in 1879, the Saturnalia revels disintegrated into a violent conflict with armed soldiers and police sent in to suppress the rioting by "Young Exeter." In 1881, a carnivalesque opposition group styling itself the Skeleton Army was set up in Exeter. There was violent conflict whenever the Skeleton and Salvation Armies came together, and the Salvation Army hired local hard men as bodyguards.

In October 1881, the press reported a "Tumultuous Procession at Exeter." "About seven o'clock a number of men and lads assembled in the West Quarter, many of them wearing round their hats strips of calico which were printed the words 'Skeleton Army,' with a skull-and-cross bones device in the center; while others had tickets stuck in their hats inscribed 'Skeleton Army! Death or glory boys! Admit one to the council of war.'" Cards had been circulated stating that the parade of the "Skeleton Army" would be held and that there would be a presentation of colors by a "Major" Martin [in a later report, his name was spelled Martyn —N.P.]. "Shortly after the hour named, a group of roughs appeared on the scene, carrying a large red flag, with a skull and cross bones in the center. After some burlesque speeches the order was given to march, and the mob then proceeded through the principal streets of the city, walking eight or ten abreast, and rapidly increasing in numbers until, on passing the Guildhall, there were over 3,000 persons in the procession" (*Devon Evening Express,* October 8, 1881, 2). The procession went to the Salvation Army temple, where they held a demonstration and some threw stones and pieces of brick at the building before the police finally arrived and the meeting broke up. Shortly afterward, in Bridgwater, not far from Exeter, riots flared up when the Salvation Army appeared there. A mob attacked their barracks and the Watch Committee pleaded with the Salvationists not to hold meetings after dark (*Devon Evening Express,* October 22, 1881, 1).

A month after the first major disorders in Exeter, on November 5, Guy Fawkes' Night in Bridgwater and Weston-super-Mare featured detachments of the Skeleton Army. At Bridgwater, the Skeleton Army was in a parade along with four marching bands as well as "gangs of masqueraders" called the Fiends and the Pirates of Penzance (*Western Daily Press,* November 8, 1881, 8). The Skeleton Army at Bridgwater carried a black death's-head flag, the old Jolly Roger of the pirates. Masks and blackened faces disguised the participants. Reports of the Skeleton Army's disorder and violence appeared in newspapers across the United Kingdom. In February 1882, a contingent of the Skeleton Army was formed in Bethnal Green in the East End of London and fought the Salvation Army in "a general melée" that was quelled, eventually, by the police (*Hackney and Kingsland Gazette,* February 15, 1882, 3). They carried banners bearing the skull emblem and the letters "BBB" signifying Beef, Beer, and Bacca (tobacco).

By March 1882 in Exeter, the birthplace of the Skeleton Army, disorder was growing, and on the eleventh of that month, Mayor Thomas Andrew issued this proclamation banning both sides from taking to the streets: "Whereas several breaches of the peace and riotous collisions have lately been occasioned by processions of persons calling themselves the 'Salvation Army' and 'Skeleton Army' through the Public Streets of Exeter, causing obstruction therein, and terror and annoyance to the Citizens . . . notice is Hereby Given that such processions cannot be permitted to take place, and the Justices desire to caution all persons

Fig. 22.2. Skeleton emblem of the Skeleton Army, 1882

against taking part in, or in any way aiding and abetting the same." It was ignored by both sides (*Daily News*, March 13, 1882, 3).

The *Skeleton,* a newspaper published in Honiton, Devon, on December 16, 1882, is one of the few surviving documents of the movement. It is an ironic text whose header is a skeleton holding a trident on which is a banner with three death's heads. The *Skeleton* commented on the Skeleton Army's situation in the West Country: "The weather here has been chilly during the past week, but the five officers of the Exeter Division of the Salvation Army are open to prove that it is quite as warm in Honiton, and a little bit warmer, than it is in Exeter." The *Skeleton* notes ironically that an evening service of the Salvationists had been broken up: "There was no evening service on Sunday the 3rd inst., but it must be taken for granted that it wasn't because of the 'Skeletons?'" Seemingly, some Salvationist converts changed their minds and went over to the Skeleton Army: "Out of seven 'saved' since the 'Army' has been here," the anonymous author wrote, "four have joined the 'Skeletons'; and please bear in mind that in saving these seven, at least seventy-seven have been ruined. Big average, eh!" The *Skeleton* also refers to "the General," the anonymous commander of the Skeleton Army. The self-styled general of the Salvation Army, William Booth, applied to the Honiton magistrates to ban "the rival Skeleton Army to assemble," but the application was refused. The police promised to protect the Salvation Army but could do little, "the mob having complete possession of the town" (*Leeds Mercury,* December 23, 1882, 10).

The Skeleton Army spread rapidly across the nation wherever the Salvation Army appeared. By the end of 1881, there were already contingents in Exeter, Bridgwater, Weston-super-Mare, Whitechapel, and Bethnal Green in London. In 1882 and 1883, Skeleton Army contingents were founded in Honiton, Bath, Bridport, and Guildford in the south (which also had a thriving Bonfire Society), eastward along the coast to Worthing, Shoreham, Brighton, and Gravesend, and as far north as Leith in Scotland. The press of the time has sporadic mentions of the Skeleton Army in numerous places. In the industrial town of Stockport, just south of Manchester, "sticks were freely used; windows were broken" (*Scotsman,* August 11, 1882, 6).

Wherever its contingents were formed, the Skeleton Army broke up Salvation Army meetings and attacked their buildings. Some of them wore insignias and uniforms. A correspondent to the *Devon Evening Express* (January 30, 1882) noticed one member "with a metal shield fastened to the front of his hat upon which was engraved a skull and cross bones and the words 'Death or glory!'" The *Southern Reporter* noted, "They somehow procure cast-off military jackets and helmets" (March 1, 1883, 4), and on a march in Kingsland Road in the East End of London, a Skeleton contingent was led by two captains on horseback and accompanied by a drum, whistles, and pots and pans in the tradition of the charivari. "To the Salvationist banners it opposes banners ornamented with drawings of skeletons and cross bones" (*Leeds Times,* February 19, 1883, 4). Whenever they encountered the Salvation Army, the Skeleton Army greeted it with an uproar and pelted members with rotten eggs and flour. Stones were pitched at the Salvationists, and sometimes eggs filled with blue paint were thrown. In 1883, it was claimed that "the Skeleton Army is encouraged and paid by the publicans" (*Graphic,* February 19, 1883, 2). In August 1883, the mayor of Luton received a death threat from the Skeleton Army "decorated with a pistol and a dagger" (*Banbury Advertiser,* August 23, 1883, 3). At the very end of 1883, in the New Year celebrations in Morpeth in the northeast of England, the Skeleton Army appeared: "About 11 o'clock, after the pubs had closed there," reported the *Morpeth Herald,* 'there was quite a crowd of young men assembled in the Market Place. These formed themselves into processional order, and under the pseudonym of the 'Skeleton Army' marched up Newgate Street to Buller's Green Cross, where an open air meeting was held. The dawn of the New Year being proclaimed . . . bottles were uncorked and the 'soldiers' who were 'athirst' were served with that wonderful elixir of local origin known as 'Hot Tom'" (*Morpeth Herald,* January 5, 1884, 5).

Later that year, the seaside town of Worthing was targeted by the Salvation Army. By then, the Skeleton Army was ready for them, composed of members of the local Bonfire Society. When it marched through town, "handkerchiefs and yellow ribbons waved from windows in support of the Skeleton Army" (*East Anglian Daily Times,* October 16, 1884, 4).

On August 17 of that year, the largest contingent yet of the Skeleton Army, numbering about four thousand, gathered near the barracks of the Salvation Army, where an alleyway contained both the doors of the barracks and a popular seller of alcohol. The Salvation Army had harassed the owner, and the Skeleton Army took its revenge. Tar was daubed on the door and the building was stoned and stormed. George Head, landlord of the Salvation Army barracks, opened fire with a revolver on the Skeletons, wounding three. Later, in revenge, the Skeleton Army attacked his house and shop and ransacked them. The police battled with the Skeletons, and more buildings were damaged (Hare 1988, 221–31).

These were the famous Skeleton Army Riots, as newspaper headlines around Britain announced (e.g., *Edinburgh Evening News*, August 12, 1884, 4). In October 1884, the press reported "Salvation Army processions have been proscribed at Worthing, and so have those of the Skeleton Army" (*Grantham Journal*, August 25, 1884, 7). Trouble in Worthing did not end then, however. In December of that year, the

THE SKELETON RIOT AT WORTHING

Fig. 22.3. The Skeleton Army and the Excelsior Bonfire Society attack the Salvation Army barracks at Worthing, Sussex, 1884.

press reported a march of hundreds of women wearing the colors of the Skeleton Army (*Royal Cornwall Gazette,* November 7, 1884, 7).

Across Britain during the eight or so years that the trouble lasted, fifty-six Salvation Army barracks and citadels were stormed and ransacked by the Skeleton Army and about a thousand Salvationists were severely beaten. The movement gradually petered out as arrested members received prison sentences with hard labor. As late as 1887, the drumming and clamor of the Skeletonites in Buckingham was condemned by a Bicester newspaper (*Bicester Herald,* March 11, 1887, 2) after a court case in which Skeleton Army and Salvation Army members had taken legal action against one another and all charges were dismissed (*Buckingham Advertiser and Free Press,* March 5, 1887, 5). The authorities became less and less tolerant of the Skeleton Army, and eventually it was made a criminal offense to be a member or supporter. The rise and fall of the Skeleton Army is an example of how preexisting carnivalesque groups, in this case the Bonfire Society, can form the focus for new forms of protest and celebration when circumstances alter.

23

Pantomime and Futurism

Pantomime Masks and Heads

The pantomime emerged from the harlequinade and became "the greatest theatrical tradition in England." Pantomime is a unique British theatre performance, a comic play in exaggerated colorful costumes with music, song and dance, and often "pantomime animals" such as horses with actors inside. Unlike the United States pantomime, it does not involve mimes who do not speak. Pantomimes are staged around the Christmas season, and in the 2010s, they accounted for more than one-third of the income of British theaters. Taking themes from traditional tales such as "Jack and the Beanstalk," "Cinderella," "Puss in Boots," and "Aladdin and the Wonderful Lamp," pantomime involves cross-dressing, slapstick comedy, dance, and song. Richard Wynn Keene (1809–1887) was a master of masks and theatrical properties. Before he became the mastermind behind the famous Christmas pantomimes at the Royal Drury Lane Theatre in London, he invented the material known as Keene's Cement, which is still in use today. After 1854, he was known as Dykwynkyn. He designed and made ingenious theatrical properties, especially masks, life-size puppets, and monsters. For a pantomime titled *Jack and the Beanstalk; or Harlequin's Leap-Year and the Merry Pranks of the Good Little People,* which started its run on December 26, 1859, he designed the costumes with "big-head" masks.

The design of one of the characters from this pantomime, executed in pencil and watercolor, is preserved in the Victoria and Albert Museum in London (signed *Dykwynkyn,* museum number S.243-2011). The character was called Plough Monday, a "big head" dressed in a rustic smock with a rosette and looped ribbon. He carried a top hat with colored patches or ribbons and a whip with white ribbons tied to it. Plough Monday appeared in the first scene along with Twenty-Ninth of February, billed as "her first appearance for four years" (as 1860 was a leap year). This is another example of the crossover between theatrical performance and rural calendar customs. In 1876, Dykwynkyn devised the mechanical animals that appeared in the staging of Richard Wagner's *Der Ring des Nibelungen* cycle at Bayreuth in Bavaria. Among his masterpieces were the chariot drawn by mechanical rams ridden by Fricka in *Die Walküre* and the fire-breathing dragon Fafner. Other

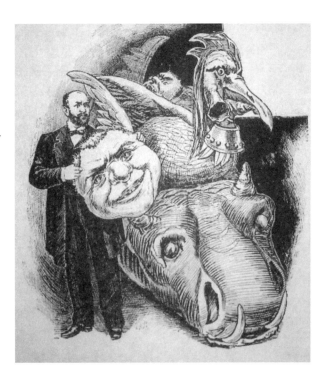

Fig. 23.1. The London impresario Sir Augustus Harris with pantomime masks and properties, 1891

mechanical animals included a bear, a magpie, and an ousel (a bird that resembles a blackbird).

In an interview given to Harry How in London in 1891, the impresario Sir Augustus Harris explained pantomime mask and property making, some of it on a large scale: "We have made in this room a giant's head six feet high; it needed the services of six men to creep inside and work the machinery" (How 1891, 562). For the pantomimes, full-head masks and larger heads were sculpted first in clay. Writing of a giant head, How noted, "The interior of the giant cranium is filled with pots, pans, and odd things to hold the clay together; then a cast will be taken of it in plaster-of-Paris. When it is thoroughly set it will be cleaned and oiled, and then layers of paper will be placed on it, on which the features are painted. A wonderful array of models are being dried in front of the great fires—immense kitchen grates—huge Cavaliers' hats, Crusaders' heads, interspersed with legs, while a fine Punchinello is quietly resting on the ground" (How 1891, 562). In 1894, How revisited mask making for the pantomimes and explained the process in much more detail. Then, W. Clarkson was the master in charge of making pantomime masks and properties for the pantomimes at the Drury Lane Theatre (How 1894, 663–64). "Now—to make a head. Procure a lump of clay, and gradually mold it with the fingers into something resembling the shape required," wrote How. "When this has been done to one's satisfaction, grease it well over, and take a cast in plaster-of-Paris. Let it dry. Grease the interior of the cast. Take layer after layer of papier-maché—first brown, then white, then a layer of linen to strengthen it, and work on it in this way until of a substantial thickness. The papier-maché is now dried in front of a fire, taken out of the mold, the rough edges cut off and joined together—for, of course, there are two sides to this particular head—dried again, and painted 'to order.' Now you have a head!" (How 1894, 663).

Some pantomime heads were operational like the snapping jaws of folk-performance hobby horses, Habergeiss, and the like and the snap jaws and flapping wings of guisers' dragons. Describing the giant's head for the pantomime *Jack and the Beanstalk,* How writes that the "giant's cranium is always the center of the greatest curiosity. Why? He can

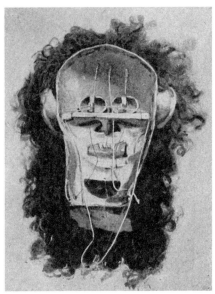

Fig. 23.3. and Fig. 23.4. Drury Lane Theatre pantomime giant's head mask, front and back view, showing operating strings, 1894

open his mouth, move his eyebrows and even wink with his left or right optic at will. Let us examine the interior of our old friend's head. See how simple it is; just a little mechanical arrangement. The wearer of the big head has three strings—one for the mouth, and one for each of his eyes. He has only to pull the right one to produce the desired effect. There are also two loose strings with small weights attached. These govern the eyebrows so that when the giant turns his head to look down on diminutive Jack, the force of the weight lifts up one of the eyebrows" (How 1894, 663–64).

Pantomime animals are closely related to those used in mumming customs. The pantomime horse, operated by two men, is well known, but many other animal costumes graced the lavish Victorian Christmas pantomimes. How wrote in 1894 how "the heartiest laughter, the brightest eyes, the happiest hearts will be found this Christmas when the [boxing] kangaroo enters and gives his owner a terrible thrashing; when the lion wrestles, and Jumbo dances the hornpipe; when the donkey comes on and, seizing hold of the balancing pole, commences

Fig. 23.4. Puss in Boots, Drury Lane Theatre pantomime costume, 1894

to walk the tight-rope . . . and dear old Puss in Boots? Props, nothing but props . . . for there are human beings inside, and so we get our stage animals" (How 1894, 668).

Masks in the Modernist Avant-Garde

Art historians who study only recent art history often miss cultural forerunners of their favored artists, whom they consider to be pioneers of unique genius. But everything has some continuity with past culture, even if the unique genius is not conscious of it. The emergence of abstract art was influenced by many preexisting artifacts. Avant-garde European modernists were influenced by masks from various parts of sub-Saharan Africa, but they were interested in their forms, not their social, magical, or religious meanings, which they either did not know or did not care about. Contrary to this tendency was the Belgian artist James Ensor, whose upbringing in Ostend was among the Carnival masks made and sold by his grandparents and uncle. He is known for his mask paintings *Old Woman with Masks* (1889), *The Intrigue* (1890), *The Strange Masks* (1892), *Death and the Masks* (1897), *Self-Portrait*

Fig. 23.5. Fancy dress competition costume, 1895, titled Our Back Garden, *with watering-can mask*

with Masks (1899), and *The Theatre of Masks* (1908). "Reason and Nature are the enemy of the artist," he said.

In London in the early 1890s, fancy dress contestants competed for valuable prizes (Steelcroft 1895, 694–702). The bizarre costumes that these contestants wore had no forerunners in mumming, masquerade, and carnival costumes, and their comic and ironic forms predated Alfred Jarry, the futurists, the Dadaists, and the surrealists, whose theatrical costumes are considered innovative.

The best-known work of French playwright and provocateur Alfred Jarry is the anarchic *Ubu Roi,* which premiered at the Théâtre de'Oeuvre in Paris in 1896. The title role was played by the masked actor Firmin Gémier, who wore a cardboard horse's head around his neck in the "manner of the Old English theatre," as Jarry put it. Jarry was continuing the ancient tradition of misrule in the contemporary theater. The performance caused uproar, and violence broke out in both the orchestra and audience. The Italian futurists, led by Filippo Tomaso Marinetti, sought a violent overthrow of existing art and society. Claiming that "war is the only hygiene," that traditional art and libraries should be destroyed, and expressing "scorn for women," the movement presaged some of the elements of the later Italian Fascist movement. Following on from Jarry, futurist designers constructed dehumanizing costumes that constrained the performers into making awkward, jerky, machinelike movements. In 1919, Ivo Panaggi designed mechanistic masked costumes for the *Balli Meccanichi.* A photograph exists of one with a cylindrical metal mask with a slot for the actor to see out of (rather like the primitive armor of the Australian outlaw Ned Kelly) (Goldberg 1988, 24–25). *Supermarionettes,* life-size puppets, appeared in performances alongside costumed performers who blurred the borderline between puppet and human.

In 1908 in the *Mask: A Journal of the Art of the Theatre,* John Balance (1872–1966) argued that masks, once so vital to the ancients, in his day had lost their respect, owing to the vanity of actors, being turned into a jest, relegated to the toy shop and fancy dress ball (Balance 1908, 9–10). Balance called for a restoration of the use of masks in the theater, "not revival but creation" (Balance 1908, 11). The limitations imposed by the mask or the animal guise restrain the performer into altering his or her personality in accordance with the meaning of the character and the reaction of the audience to the presented appearance. In so doing, masks take us beyond reality. Jacques Copeau (1879–1949), whose Théâtre de Vieux-Colombier in 1921 founded a school of experimental commedia using masks, understood that masks serve to liberate the body. From his papier mâché mask, he argued, the actor receives the reality of the part, being controlled by it and compelled to obey it unreservedly. Immediately as the actor dons the mask, there is a feeling of a new being flowing inward, a being that was hitherto unknown by the performer. Not only is the outward appearance altered, but also the actor's personality and reactions, and the actor experiences emotions that cannot otherwise be felt or feigned without its aid (Duchartre 1966, 52).

In 1912 in Stuttgart, Germany, Oskar Schlemmer (1888–1943) began work on his *Triadic Ballet,* which used masks and ten years later was performed at the Bauhaus in Dessau. In Russia in 1913, the futurists Vladimir Mayakovsky and Alexei Kruchenykh staged *Victory over the Sun,* an opera whose performers wore cubist cardboard costumes with outsize papier-mâché masks. In 1916 in Zürich, Switzerland, Romanian architect Marcel Janco produced abstract modernist masks for the performers in the Dadaist *Cabaret Voltaire.* He followed the rural tradition of using anything available to make masks. The folk tradition of the straw man appeared in the next year in Oskar Kokoschka's play *Sphynx and Straw Man,* staged in Zürich in 1917. Writing ten years later, the Dadaist Hugo Ball recalled that "the dynamism of the masks was irresistible."

In 1917, as World War I continued to rage, Pablo Picasso designed cubist costumes that covered the entire body and head for the ballet *Parade,* a collaboration between Erik Satie, Jean Cocteau, Léonide Massine, and Picasso. The Swiss and German Dadists sometimes wore outrageous and disturbing costumes on the street. In 1919, during the food shortages, the influenza pandemic, and civil war in defeated Germany, the artist Georg Grosz took on the persona of *Dada Tod* (Dada Death). He donned a full-head mask of a white skull, and while dressed in a long trench coat and carrying a walking stick, he smoked a cigarette in a cigarette holder and walked along the Kurfürstendamm in Berlin as a memento mori to passersby (Goldberg 1988, 68–69). As noted in chapter 16, in a 1922 London production of *Façade* by Edith Sitwell and William Walton, the spoken word was projected through a Senger Megaphone, whose end was the mouth of a painted mask (Sitwell 1949, 182–85).

Through the 1920s, the Bauhaus design school at Dessau in Germany staged a number of avant-garde modernist performances where masks played an important role. Schlemmer was a key figure in teaching stage theory at the Bauhaus. For his 1922 *Triadic Ballet,* he designed costumes made of padded cloth to distort body shapes with whole-head masks made of papier mâché coated with colored and metallic paint (Schlemmer, Moholy-Nagy, and Molnar 1961, 34). For *The Figural Cabinet,* also staged in 1922, Schlemmer made metallic masks of similar form. A drawing labeled "variations on a mask" survives from his teaching of a class on stage theory (Schlemmer, Moholy-Nagy, and Molnar 1961, 40–42, 46). After the Bauhaus was closed, former Bauhaus member Xanti Schawinski's *Danse Macabre* was staged at Black Mountain College, North Carolina, in 1938. It had masked performers but also an audience dressed in cloaks and masks. The masks were of conventional form (Goldberg 1988, 122).

Surrealist artists of the period frequently turned to classical imagery presented in disturbingly new ways. Thomas Esmond Lowinsky (1892–1947) painted the surrealist work *The Mask of Flora* in 1931. It shows a cracked, gray mask with vegetation growing from it, with a dreamlike sea- and mountain-scape behind it. It is owned by the Wolverhampton Art Gallery. Another surrealist mask painting was made in 1934 by Esther Gwendolyn "Stella" Bowen (1893–1947), depicting the hands of poet Dame Edith Sitwell holding a black African mask (of the Dan people from the Ivory Coast). Known for her elegant long fingers and the elaborate baroque rings she wore, Sitwell once said, "My hands are my face." Bowen's painting's surrealist sensibility expresses that the mask, far from concealing identity, can express it. Her mask is not the face of Edith Sitwell but of her *Façade.*

Some musical performers in the late twentieth and early twenty-first centuries chose to wear masks, some to disguise themselves, like the Russian punk band Pussy Riot, who wore ski masks in their notorious intervention in Moscow's Cathedral in 2012 that landed them in jail. Others wore masks as part of performance, like the celebrated fox mask worn by Peter Gabriel in the band Genesis in the 1970s. In 1989, the Insane Clown Posse adopted threatening clownesque costumes and masks. The heavy metal band Slipknot (founded in 1995) wore masks to enhance their transgressive image, and the band Clinic from 1997 wore the clinical masks that later became universal in the COVID-19 pandemic. Masks in the style of the Venetian plague doctors were worn by members of the Knife in 1999. As with the revamped Guy Fawkes masks of the anti-capitalist demonstrators, ancient forms returned in new guises.

24

Authoritarian Suppression of Festivals

I went to the Garden of Love,
And saw what I never had seen:
A Chapel was built in the midst,
Where I used to play on the green.
And the gates of the Chapel were shut.
And Thou shalt not writ o'er the door.

"The Garden of Love," William Blake
(1757–1827)

As William Blake's poem points out, authoritarians always attempt to have complete control over those whom they rule. Festive days, being times of merriment and license, have been attacked frequently by rulers in many lands and under many types of regimes—religious, royal, and revolutionary. These attempts to impose strict forms of order invariably targeted masked and carnivalesque performances, which were banned by edict and enforced often with severe punishments for those who would not or could not desist.

Richard Barnett noted that medieval literature contains copious references to the New Year custom of disguising as animals and that between the fourth and eleventh centuries, clergymen in Gaul, Germany, Spain, Italy, and England attempted to ban the practice (Barnett 1929, 393). The bishop of Barcelona in 370 CE condemned people for guising as a stag (Alford 1978a, 122). A *vetula,* a calf's-head mask from Leichtenstein that dates from about 400 CE, is preserved in the Austrian Folk Museum in Vienna, showing that the practice was widespread. There are numerous penitential books from all over western and central Europe that list things forbidden by the Christian Church and punishments for people who do them. Among forbidden acts was a guising custom of New Year's Day, such as: "If any on the Kalends goes about as a Stag or a Bull, that is making himself into a wild animal . . . penance three years." In the ninth century, Paulinus, the bishop of Nola in Italy, tells us of the mummers and guisers of his locality who were "wont to clothe themselves with skins of cattle and put upon them the heads of beasts" (Strutt 1845, 250). Hincmar of Rheims used the word *Talamasca* in the year 850 in a condemnation, and in the eleventh century (ca. 1020), Burchard of Worms, Germany, condemned demonic larvae (masks) that were commonly called Talamascas. These masks were worn by mummers who performed in rites for the dead.

In the thirteenth century, the Catholic Church in England made a concerted effort to stamp out customs and events that were not part of the ecclesiastical calendar. One of the extremists was Robert Grosseteste, the bishop of Lincoln, who between 1236 and 1244 issued a series of edicts that condemned traditional vernacular customs in his diocese. The list demonstrates the diversity and vitality of the folk traditions observed then. The prohibitions included miracle plays, "the May Game," "mell-suppers," ram raisings, and other contests of athletic prowess, together with ceremonies known respectively as the Festum Stultori (Festival of Fools) and the Inductio Mali sive Autumni (Festival of Misrule). Scot-ales, drinking parties in remote places away from taverns or inns where everyone paid for their own drinks, were held on ancient festival days, so they were among the banned activities. In 1240, Walter de Chanteloup, the bishop of Worcester, issued his Constitutions that also targeted traditional festivities. They specify the *Indus de Rege et Regina*, which is probably a catchall for any folk festivals the bishop wished to ban. Orders of the city of London in 1334, 1393, and 1405 forbade people from "going about the streets at Christmas *ove visere ne faux visage* i.e. wearing masks, and entering the houses of citizens to play at dice therein" (Chambers 1933, 393–94). In 1417, "mummyng" is specifically included in a similar prohibition (Riley 1868, 658). In 1431, the Council of Basel banned the Festival of Fools, and in 1444, the festival was banned by the theologians at Paris University.

One of the most extreme events connected with the Carnival season was a number of so-called Bonfires of the Vanities held in Florence in the 1490s. Girolamo Savonorola (1452–1498) was a fanatical monk whose preaching convinced the city authorities that not only should the Carnival be banned but also that all "vain things" should be publicly destroyed in great bonfires. On Shrove Tuesday 1495, a *felò della vanita* was lit, and fine clothes, tapestries, ancient manuscripts, books by certain nominated authors as well as those on magic, astrology, and divination, paintings, musical instruments, cosmetics, and mirrors, along with Carnival masks and costumes were consigned to the flames. Some artists were forced to burn their own paintings. Art and artistry were destroyed as "vain," and, of course, there was no Carnival. These bonfires continued through to Shrove Tuesday 1497, though by then not much could have been left to burn. The next year, Savonorola and his henchmen were themselves publicly burned, and Carnivals resumed.

In England in the third year of King Henry VIII, the Acte against Disguysed Persons and Wearing of Visours (3 Hen. VIII, c. 9) was put into force. It began: "Lately within this realm diverse persons have disguised and appareled them, and covered their faces with masks and other things in such manner that they should not be known and diverse of them in a company together naming themselves mummers have come in to the dwelling place of diverse men of honor and other substantial persons; and so departed unknown" [English modernized —N.P.]. An edict was issued that to prevent this, "no person should appear abroad like mummers, covering their face with visors and in disguised apparel . . . offenders are to be treated as suspects or vagabonds." The punishment for this was three month's imprisonment, and there was a twenty shillings fine for even possessing a mask without wearing it (Strutt 1845, 252).

The effect of the Protestant Reformation in Britain and Germany was to suppress festivities connected with Catholic belief. Many of the guilds, which were instrumental in staging various performances, were abolished, partly because they were sponsored by the Catholic Church and partly, in England, because royal power was expanded under the Tudor dynasty and all aspects of life were taken under centralized control. King Henry VIII's edict against mummers was part of this expansion of power, and the first act of King Edward VI in 1547 was to appropriate "all fraternities, brotherhoods, and guilds being within the realm of England and Wales . . . and all manors, lands, tenements, and other hereditaments belonging to them or any of them" (Toulmin Smith 1870, xliii).

Across Europe, the authorities sporadically banned masks and public performances—civic, rural, and private. The Protestant Reformation led to the Schembartlauf in Nuremberg being abolished in 1539 as a result of the preaching of Andreas Osiander (1498–1552). In 1542, Bishop Bonner of London "did his utmost to stop acting in churches," William Andrews noted. "He issued a proclamation to the clergy of his diocese, prohibiting all manner of common plays, games, or interludes, to be played, set forth, or declared within their churches or chapels" (Andrews 1890, 21). In 1543, the bishop of Zealand condemned horse guising on the "unholy watchnight"—that is, New Year's Eve—and instructed his parishioners to stop observing the "really evil custom." In 1551, the city authorities of Frankfurt am Main banned public dance-outs, and in 1571 in Münster, Germany, the city authorities issued an edict against guild feasts and Shrovetide celebrations, "all guild feasts and similar gatherings, which have caused many great abuses, shall no longer be held . . . sword dancing and mumming are banned" (Humberg 1976, 355). In Scandinavia, numerous attempts to suppress guising continued, with religious leaders issuing edicts every few years until 1808.

In *The Anatomie of Abuses* (1879) the English Puritan Philip Stubbes attacked almost every aspect of enjoyment as unchristian, insisting that they should be prohibited. Unwittingly, in his detailed condemnations, he recorded details of some customs that otherwise would have been forgotten. He condemned stage plays of all types equally: "All stage-plays, enterludes & comedies are either of divine or prophane matter, If they be of divine matter, then are they most intolerable, or rather sacrilegious." Secular plays were even worse in his eyes: "Of comedies, the matter & ground is love, bawdrie, cozenage, flattery, whoredome, adultery, the Persons or agents, whores, queans, bawds, scullions, Knaves, Curtezans, lecherous old men, amorous young men, with such like of infinite variety." He claimed that "players were first invented by the devill, practised by the heathen gentiles, and dedicate to their false ydols, Goddes & Goddesses, as the howse, stage & apparell to Venus, the musicke to Appollo, the penning to Minerva & the Muses, the actors and pronuntiation to Mercurie and the rest." He called the theater "Venus Pallace, & Sathans Synagogue, to worship devils & betray Christ Jesus" (Stubbes [1584] 1879, 143). Morris dancing, mumming, football, and "the Great Wickednesse at Christmas" came in for his opprobrium. At Christmas, he wrote, "There is nothing else used but cards, dice, tables, masking, mumming, bowling and such like fooleries" (Stubbes [1584] 1879, 173–74, 184). There was no fun in Puritanism. In 1576, Archbishop Grindal of Canterbury warned ministers and churchwardens not to permit "any Lord of Misrule or Summer Lords and Ladies, or any disguised persons, or others, in Christmas, at May Games, or any morris-dancers, or at any other times, come irreverently in the churchyard and there to dance or play any unseemly parts, with scoffs, jests, wanton gestures or ribald talk" (Furnivall, appendix in Stubbes [1584] 1879, 304). In 1591, the Shearmen's Guild of Shrewsbury was banned from putting up a "tree" for May Day. The case went to court, the ban was overturned, and the Maypole was "used as heretofore have be" (Hibbert 1891, 121).

In the next century, Puritans became a major power in British politics. In 1638, along with many other customs, the Scottish Parliament in Edinburgh abolished Christmas. Six years later in England, during the Civil War, Parliament ordered a fast to be observed on the last Wednesday of each month. In December 1644, this was the twenty-fifth, Christmas Day. On December 19, 1644, Parliament took the opportunity to decree that Christmas, a festival of "carnal and sensual delights," was now abolished and that all observances of it were subject to punishment. The next year, *The Directory for Public Worship* was issued, which removed all observances of saints' days and Christmas that had been in the Church of England's *Book of Common Prayer*. The prohibition continued until 1659, the year before the exiled king, Charles II, returned and all legislation enacted by the revolutionary government was overturned.

From the eighteenth century, opinionated publications began to be a source of calls to ban carnivalesque activities. In Britain in 1751, a correspondent to the *Gentleman's Magazine* called for action against the disorder and destruction of Guy Fawkes' Night, citing out-of-control revelers who threw fireworks into crowds, broke windows, and tore up fences for their bonfires (Cressy 1992, 78). In the nineteenth century, there were sporadic attempts to ban the Straw Boys in Ireland from claiming their traditional right to visit weddings uninvited and enjoy the hospitality. Police were sent to intercept bands of Straw Boys on their way to weddings (*Cork Constitution*, February 19, 1886, 3). Attempted suppression of Plough Monday in England continued throughout the nineteenth century. Members of the press, which by now was everywhere, acted with condescension toward their fellow citizens, whom they saw as a threat. There was no awareness that many of the men who paraded on Plough Monday had no work in the winter and so to survive in an era when there was no welfare were forced to rely on the small amount of money they could gain by performing songs, mummers' plays, and morris, Molly, broom, and sword dances. The press repeatedly called on the authorities to persecute the performers and suppress these traditions, neither understanding nor valuing their dances and music as an integral part of local tradition and not seeing the plight of poverty-stricken workers who were out on the streets performing. To the journalists and worthies of their respective localities, they were "the lower grades of our community" who should have known their place. The fact that they were providing entertainment and being paid for it did not cross the minds of those to whom snobbery and condescension were a way of life.

There are numerous press accounts from all over the north, midlands, and east of England, most of them more or less disparaging, although some record valuable details of the costume, disguises, and performances of Plough Monday. "On this day every year," the *Staffordshire Advertiser* wrote in 1818, "there are in various parts of the country, multitudes of idle and disorderly people, who call themselves Plough Bullocks, and who travel from place to place, threatening to commit depredation on the premises of all who discountenance their scandalous proceeding, by refusing to give them money . . . therefore we cannot forbid recommending to our readers, to withhold their sanction from these disorderly ruffians, and to summon them before the Magistrates" (*Staffordshire Advertiser,* January 3, 1818, 3). Three years later, "A. B.," an unnamed letter writer to the *Stamford Mercury,* was virulent: "It gave me great pleasure . . . that the Magistrates have determined to visit with exemplary severity the misconduct of persons who appear as Morris Dancers or Plough Bullocks, or under any other name of a similar character" (*Stamford Mercury,* January 26, 1821, 4).

As mentioned earlier, in chapter 20, in May 1836, a case was brought before the magistrates by Richard Bird, a beadle who was "street keeper" of Bedford-Row, Holborn. The four defendants were chimney sweeps whom he accused of "having created a disturbance" and assaulting him. The account in the *Morning Post* records that "the prisoners were dressed up in eccentric style. Sharpe and Ellis were clowns; Davies was papered and spangled as 'My Lord,' and Vincent as 'Jack-in-the-Green.'" It transpired that Bird had used his staff of office to hit a child on the head and had been set upon, only being saved by the police from a severe beating. Mr. Bennett, one of the magistrates said, "I certainly must say that it is very irregular to go about the streets creating a mob and disturbance, but it is an ancient custom and ought not to be interfered with." The prisoners were discharged (*Morning Post,* May 4, 1836, 4).

In Victorian times, there were numerous calls by influential citizens from all across England for the abolition of ancient customary

Chimney Sweepers on May-Day.

Fig. 24.1. Chimney sweeps on May Day, early nineteenth century

traditions. Police action, as always, went in waves in response to the level of moral outrage by the press and citizens of influence, and gradually, unofficial traditions were driven down. During the second half of the nineteenth century, the British press continued to stir up a moral panic against Plough Monday customs especially, and gradually, in many places, the traditions were forcibly brought to an end. But in the late nineteenth century, after decades of academic "collecting" of folklore (as it was called in the idiom of the day), it was recognized finally that these ancient customs were of true value, both as instances of historical continuity and as important elements of local identity. Many traditions banned for a period were then reinstated and reinvigorated, sometimes as local festivals that attracted more people than ever before. Mr. Bennett, the enlightened magistrate of 1836, would have agreed that such ancient customs ought to be maintained. In the past, as a defense against interference by the authorities in their activities, participants on Plough Monday used to insist that "no law in the world can touch 'em, 'cause it's an old charter" (Chambers 1869, 1, 95). And they were right.

Postscript

In *A Vision,* his spiritual essay on the nature of being human, William Butler Yeats wrote that the mask represents the person we want to become. It can be one of two contradictory images: a true mask, which is an expression of our true self, or a false mask that denotes our wrong choice. But do we ever behold truly the face behind the face, or do we nurse the fear that it may be yet more terrifying than the mask itself? For the everyday world is but a theater of masks, so well depicted in the grotesque paintings of James Ensor.

Glossary

Berserkir (singular, Berserker): Initiated Viking-age warriors dedicated to Odin who used the power of bears or wolves to go into combat in a state of violent frenzy.

blitz: Short for *Blitzkrieg*—"lightning war"—used to describe the mass bombing of British cities by the German air force during World War II.

derilan: Keeper of a Scottish holy well. It has connotations of eccentricity and divine madness.

dewar: Scottish hereditary keeper of a sacred relic.

eigi einhamr: Literally not of one skin (or shape); the ability to transform from one shape to another, the power to take on other bodies.

Furor Normanorum: Norman warriors' battle frenzy (cf., Berserkir, Wood).

genius loci: Spirit of the place.

Green Man: A carving in wood or stone of a foliated head, so-called by Lady Raglan in *Folk-Lore* in 1939. Also (original meaning), a man dressed in foliage such as a Woodwose (cf.) or a forester in traditional clothing.

guild: Cooperative organization of people practicing an art or craft, or devotees of a particular religious cultus.

guisar: Someone who performs in disguise of any form.

hammrammr: Having the ability to change shape, to take on different bodies.

harrowwarden: Guardian of a spiritually significant place (Anglo-Saxon: *heargweard*).

landwisdom: Knowledge of the nature and custom of the country. Anglo-Saxon: *landwîsa*.

legendarium: The overall body of stories, legends, tales, poems, traditions, songs, and writings about any particular thing or place, without a judgment of veracity according to the precepts of historical research.

leshy: A Slavic wild man of the woods.

locus terribilis: Literally, "terrible place" or "place of terror," a place of particular preternatural qualities that are inimical to human well-being.

lomping: Threatening activity carried on by disguised men carrying staves, mainly on Plough Monday.

maukin (also malkin): A scarecrow (straw man). The word also is used for an animal (a hare) and a brush used to clean bakers' ovens.

melodeon: A diatonic button accordion that plays different notes for "push" and "pull" on the same button. This distinguishes it from a button or piano accordion proper, which has the same note on push and pull.

mumming: Appearing in disguise while remaining silent, except in mummers' plays, in which lines must be delivered.

ostentum: Something that appears or is noticed suddenly, with a meaning immediately apparent to the beholder.

pantomime: A British theatrical performance, staged around Christmas, with a story based on a fairy-tale theme, including masks, disguises, cross-dressing, slapstick comedy, dance, and song.

pasteboard: Also known as papier mâché, it is a light but strong material made from layers of paper pasted together, often with a linen backing. It was the traditional material for some masks as well as Carnival, pageant, and pantomime animals.

phytomorphic: In the form of a plant, as wild men clad in green leaves.

sociocide: An event where a whole community and its entire culture is wiped out; however, it is unlike genocide in that the people continue to live, isolated and desolate.

trompe l'oeil: A style of painting that looks like real things when viewed from certain viewpoints.

Úlfheðnar (singular, Úlfheðinn): Viking-age wolf-warriors; Berserkirs (q.v.) who wore wolfskins over their armor.

Woodwose: A wild man of the woods (Old English: *wuduwāsa*).

Bibliography

Ackerman, John Yonge. 1885. *Remains of Pagan Saxondom*. London: John Russell Smith.

Adams, W. H. Davenport. 1895. *Witch, Warlock, and Magician: Historical Sketches of Magic and Witchcraft in England and Scotland*. London: Chatto and Windus.

Addy, Sidney Oldall. 1888. *A Glossary of Words Used in the Neighbourhood of Sheffield*. London: English Dialect Society.

———. 1895. *Household Tales with Other Traditional Remains Collected in the Counties of Yorkshire, Lincolnshire, Derbyshire, and Nottinghamshire*. London: David Nutt; Sheffield: Pawson and Brailsford.

———. 1907. "Guising and Mumming in Derbyshire." *Journal of the Derbyshire Archaeological and Natural History Society* 29: 31–42.

Alford, Violet. 1939. "Some Hobby Horses of Great Britain." *Journal of the English Folk Dance and Song Society* 3, no. 4 (December): 221–40.

———. 1978a. *The Hobby Horse and Other Animal Masks*. London: Merlin Press.

———. 1978b. "The Minehead Town Hobby Horse." *English Dance and Song* 30, no. 4: 137.

And, Metin. 1964. *A History of Theatre and Popular Entertainment in Turkey*. Ankara, Turkey: Dost Yayinlari.

———. 1976. *From Folk Dancing to the Whirling Dervishes—Belly Dancing to Ballet*. Ankara, Turkey: Dost Yayinlari.

———. 1980. *On the Dramatic Fertility Rituals of Anatolian Turkey*. Nagoya, Japan: Asian Folklore.

Andrews, William. 1890. *Curiosities of the Church*. London: William Andrews.
———. 1898. *Bygone Norfolk*. London: William Andrews.
Anglickienė, Laima. 2013. *Slavic Folklore: Didactical Guidelines*. Kaunas, Lithuania: Vytautas Magnus University.
Anonymous. 1807. "Curious Custom in the Isle of Thanet." *European Magazine and London Review* 51: 358.
———. 1816. *Time's Telescope, or A Complete Guide to the Almanack*. London: Sherwood, Neely, Jones.
———. 1852. *Magic and Witchcraft*. London: Chapman & Hall.
———. (1893) 2015. "The Black Dog." In *Irish Fairy and Folk Tales*. Reprint, New York: Barnes & Noble.
———. 1895a. "Twelfth Night on the Moors." *Pall Mall Gazette*, January 8, 1895, 1–2.
———. 1895b. "Bogey." *Strand Magazine* IX: 120.
Anon. 1899. "Straw Bear at Ramsey." *Fenland Notes and Queries*, IV, 228.
———. 1901. "Grateful Fréjus." *Folk-Lore* 12: 307–10.
———. ca. 1949. *Costume for Molly Dancing*. Unpublished manuscript, Cambridgeshire Collection.
———. 1997. *King's Lynn May Garland*. King's Lynn, UK: The King's Morris.
Antliff, W. 1885. "The Leicester Plough-Bullocks." *Nottingham Guardian*, January 7, 6.
Appleton, J. G. 1950. "Hideous and Hellish Occurrence at Bungay." *East Anglian Magazine* 9: 276–79.
Ashton, John. 1893. *A History of English Lotteries: Now for the First Time Written*. London: Leadenhall Press.
Atkinson, Frank. 1968. *The Great Northern Coalfield 1700–1900*. London: University Tutorial Press.
Austin, John C. 1977. *Chelsea Porcelain at Williamsburg*. Williamsburg, Va.: Colonial Williamsburg Foundation.
Aydelotte, Frank. 1967. *Elizabethan Rogues and Vagabonds and Their Representation in Contemporary Literature*. London: Routledge.
Ayres, James. 1977. *British Folk Art*. London: Thames & Hudson.
Bächtold-Stäubli, Hanns, ed. 1927–1942. *Handwörterbuch des Deutschen Aberglaubens*. 9 vols. Berlin: Koehler und Amerlang.
Bärtsch, Albert. 1993. *Holz Masken: Fastnachts- und Maskenbrauchtum in der Schweiz, in Süddeutschland und Österrech*. Aarau, Switzerland: AT Verlag.

Bakhtin, Mikhael. 1968. *Rabelais and His World.* Translated by Hélène Iswolsky. Cambridge, Mass.: MIT Press.

——. 1984. *Problems of Dostoyevsky's Poetics.* Edited and translated by Caryl Emerson. Minneapolis: University of Minnesota Press.

Balance, John. 1908. "A Note on Masks." *Mask: A Journal of the Art of the Theatre* I, no. 1: 9–12.

Bales, E. G. 1939. "Folklore from West Norfolk." *Folklore* 50, no. 1 (March): 66–75.

Banks, M. M. 1938. "The Padstow May Festival." *Folklore* 49, no. 4 (December): 391–94.

Baring-Gould, Sabine. 1865. *The Book of Were-Wolves.* London: Smith, Elder.

Baring-Gould, Sabine, and John Fisher. 1907–1913. *The Lives of the British Saints.* 4 vols. London: Honourable Society of Cymmrodorion.

Barley, L. B., and M. W. Barley. 1957. "Plough Monday Play from Branston near Lincoln." *Lincolnshire Historian* 2, no. 4: 36–43.

Barley, M. W. 1936. "The Alkborough Jags Play." *Local Historian: Lindsey Local History Society* 8: 30–32.

——. 1953. "Plough Plays in the East Midlands." *Journal of the English Folk Dance and Song Society* 7, no. 2 (December): 68–95.

Barnes, William. 1863. *A Grammar and Glossary of the Dorset Dialect with History, Outspreading, and Bearings of South West England.* Berlin: A. Asher.

Barnett, Richard D. 1929. "The Running of the Deer." *Folk-Lore* 40, no. 4: 393–94.

Barratt, William. 1926. *Deathbed Visions.* London: Methuen.

Barretti, Guiseppe. 1786. *Tolondron.* London, R. Faulder.

Bartlome, Vinzenz, and Urs M. Zahnd. 2003. "Grundung und Sage." In *Berns mutiger Zeit,* edited by Rainer Schwinges, 21–24. Bern, Switzerland: Schulverlag.

Basford, Kathleen. 1978. *The Green Man.* Ipswich, UK: D. S. Brewer.

Bate, Seldiy, and Nigel Bourne. 1987. "The Abbot's Bromley Horn Dance." *Exploring the Supernatural* 1, 7, February 1987, 82–85.

Battin, Sébastien. 1829. *Archives Historiques et Littéraires du Nord de France et du Midi de Belgique.* Tome I, *Tradition des dragons volantes dans le nord du France.* Valenciennes, France: Bureaux du Archives, 97–110.

Bearman, C. J. 1997. "Up to a Point, Dr. Hutton: Fact and Myth in the Folk Music Revival." *English Dance and Song* 59, no. 3: (Autumn): 2–4.

Bede, Cuthbert (Rev. Edward Bradley). 1854. "May Garland at Glatton." *Notes and Queries* series 1, no. 10: 91–92.

———. *1861.* "Modern Mumming." *Notes and Queries* series 2, no. XI (April 6): 271–72.

———. 1886. "The Straw Bear of the Plough Witches." *Notes and Queries* series 7 1, no. 5 (January 30): 86.

Begg, Ean. 1985. *The Cult of the Black Virgin.* London: Penguin.

Behrend, Michael. 1978. "The Girton Hobby Horse and Others." *Albion* 1: 4–9.

Bernabò-Brea, Luigi. 2001. *Maschere e personaggi del teatro Greco: Nelle terracotte Liparesi.* Rome: L'Erma di Bretschneider.

Besant, Annie, and C. W. Leadbeater. 1901. *Thought-Forms.* London: Theosophical Publishing House.

Bird, F. W. 1911. *Memorials of Godmanchester: Reminiscences of F. W. Bird.* Edited by W. H. B. Saunders. Peterborough, UK: Peterborough Advertiser.

Blackmore, Susan J. 2017. *Seeing Myself. The New Science of Out-of-the-Body Experiences.* London: Robinson.

Blind, Karl. n.d. "Wodan, the Wild Huntsman." *Gentleman's Magazine* n.s., 25: 32.

Blomefield, Francis. (1736) 1805–1810. *An Essay toward a Topographical History of the County of Norfolk,* 11 vols. London: William Miller.

BLRC 1896. "Harvest Customs." *Notes and Queries* series 8, no 9: 128, 216.

———. 1910. "Christmas Mummers as Mammals or Birds." *Notes and Queries* series 11, no. 2: 507.

Boardman, John. 1989. *Athenian Red-Figure Vases of the Classical Period.* London: Thames & Hudson.

Boreman, Thomas. 1741. *The Gigantick History of the Two Famous Giants in Guildhall.* London: Thomas Boreman.

Bortoft, Henri. 1996. *The Wholeness of Nature—Goethe's Way toward a Science of Conscious Participation in Nature.* Hudson, N.Y.: Lindisfarne Press.

Bottrell, William. 1880. *Stories and Folk-Lore of West Cornwall.* Penzance, UK: F. Rodda.

Boutellier, Marcelle. 1966. "L'œuvre et les collections folkloriques de Lionel Bonnemère (1843–1905)." *Arts et Traditions Populaires* 1–2 (January–June): 17–42.

Bovey, Nigel. 2015. *Blood on the Flag.* London: Shield Books.

Braekman, Willy L. 1997. *Middeleeuwse witte en zwarte magie in het Nederlands taalgebied*. Gent, the Netherlands: Koninklijke Academie voor Nederlandse Taal-en Letterkunde.

Bradtke, Elaine. 1999. *Truculent Rustics: Molly Dancing in East Anglia before 1940*. London: FLS Books.

Brand, John. (1777) 1810. *Observations on Popular Antiquities: Including the Whole of Mr. Bourne's Antiquitates Vulgares*. London: Vernor, Hood & Sharpe.

Breton, André. 1974. *Manifestos of Surrealism*. Translated by Richard Seaver and Helen R. Lane. Ann Arbor: University of Michigan Press.

Briggs, Katharine. 1977. *A Dictionary of Fairies. Hobgoblins, Brownies, Bogies, and Other Supernatural Creatures*. Harmondsworth, UK: Penguin Books.

Brockie, William. 1886. *Legends and Superstitions of the County of Durham*. Sunderland, UK: B. Williams.

Broomhead, D. 1982. "An Eighteenth-Century Play from Cheshire." *Roomer* 2, no. 4–5: 23–29.

Brown, C. 1874. *Notes about Notts*. Nottingham, UK: T. Forman & Sons.

Brown, Theo. 1958. "The Black Dog." *Folklore* 69, no. 3: 175–92.

Bruce, J. Collingwood, and John Stokoe. 1882. *Northumbrian Minstrelsy*. Newcastle-upon-Tyne, UK: Society of Antiquaries of Newcastle-upon-Tyne.

Bunn, Ivan. 1974. "'Old Shuck' at Gt. Yarmouth." *Lantern* 5 (Spring): 2–3.

———. 1977a. "Black Shuck. Part One: Encounters, Legends, and Ambiguities." *Lantern* 18 (Summer): 3–6.

———. 1977b. "Black Shuck. Part Two." *Lantern* 19 (Autumn): 4–8.

Bunn, Ivan, and Michael W. Burgess. 1976. *Local Curiosities: A Miscellany of Ghosts, Legends, and Unusual Facts from the Lowestoft Area*. Lowestoft, UK: East Suffolk and Norfolk Antiquarians.

Burne, Charlotte Sophie. 1886. *Shropshire Folk-Lore: A Sheaf of Gleanings*. London: Trübner.

Burne, Charlotte Sophie, and Georgina F. Jackson. 1883. *Shropshire Folk-Lore*. London: Trübner.

Burton, Robert. (1621) 1926. *The Anatomy of Melancholy*. 3 vols. London: Bell and Sons.

Butterworth, Philip. 2013. "Late Medieval Performing Dragons." In *Early English Drama*, vol. 43, *Yearbook of English Studies*, 318–42.

B.V.M. 1902. "Plough Monday." *Newark Herald*, March 15.

Byrom, Michael. 1983. *Punch in the Italian Puppet Theatre.* Fontwell, UK: Centaur Press.

———. 1988. *Punch and Judy: Its Origin and Evolution.* Norwich, UK: DaSilva Puppet Books.

Calloway, Stephen. 1998. *Aubrey Beardsley.* London: V&A Publishing.

Campbell, John Gregorson. 1900. *Superstitions of the Highlands and Islands.* Glasgow, UK: J. MacLehose.

Campbell, Marie. 1938. "Survivals of Old Folk Drama in the Kentucky Mountains." *Journal of American Folklore* 51, no. 199 (January–March): 10–24.

Carpenter, Kevin, ed. 1995. *Robin Hood. The Many Faces of the Celebrated English Outlaw.* Oldenburg, Germany: Universität Oldenburg.

Cawte, E. C. 1978. *Ritual Animal Disguise.* Cambridge, UK: D. S. Brewer.

Cawte, Edwin Christopher, Alex Helm, and Norman Peacock. 1967. *English Ritual Drama.* London: Folklore Society.

Chadwick, H. M. 1899. *The Cult of Othin.* Cambridge, UK: Cambridge University Press.

Chambers, E. R. 1933. *The English Folk-Play.* Oxford, England: Clarendon Press.

Chambers, Robert. 1841. *Select Writings of Robert Chambers,* vol. 7. Edinburgh: W. & R. Chambers.

———. 1869. *The Book of Days: A Miscellany of Popular Antiquities in Connection with the Calendar.* 2 vols. London and Edinburgh: W. & R. Chambers, (second edition 1869, first 1864).

Chope, R. Pearse. 1938. Devonshire Calendar Customs, Part II. Fixed Festivals." *Transactions of the Devonshire Association* 70: 402–3.

Clark, H. P. (ca. 1820) 1930. "Old Sussex Harvest Customs." *Sussex County Magazine* IV: 796–97.

Cleather, Alice Leighton, and Basil Crump. 1911. *The Ring of the Nibelumg: An Interpretation Embodying Wagner's Own Explanations.* London: Methuen.

Cocchiara, Giuseppe. 1963. *Il mondo alla rovescia.* Turin, Italy: Boringhieri.

Cocks, Reginald. 1902. "Waxworks in Westminster Abbey." *Sunday Strand* (January–June): 431–35.

Cohen, S., and L. Taylor. 1992. *Escape Attempts: The Theory and Practice of Resistance to Everyday Life.* London: Routledge.

Collingwood, W.G., & Stefánsson, Jón, 1902. *The Life and Death of Cormac the Skald.* Viking Club Translation Series 1, Ulverston, Holmes (Cormacs Saga).

Collodi, Carlo. 1883. *Le avventure di Pinoccio: Storia di un burattino.* Florence, Italy: Felice Paggi.

Cooper, Emmanuel. 1994. *People's Art: Working-Class Art from 1750 to the Present Day.* Edinburgh and London: Mainstream Publishing.

Cork, Richard. 1990. *Wadsworth and the Woodcut.* In Lewison, Jeremy (ed.) *A Genius of Industrial England Edward Wadsworth 1889-1949.* Bradford: Arkwright Arts Trust and Bradford Art Galleries and Museums 12–29.

Corrsin, Stephen D. 1997. *Sword Dancing in Europe: A History.* Enfield Lock, UK: Hisarlik Press.

Cott, Hugh. 1940. *Adaptive Coloration in Animals.* Oxford, UK: Oxford University Press.

Cranmer-Byng, Hugh, Lancelott Cranmer-Byng, Herbert Mahon, and Herbert Goldstein. 1910. *Pageant Music and Libretto. The Saffron Walden Pageant 1910.* London: Moore, Smith, & Co.

Cressy, David. 1992. "The Fifth of November Remembered." In *Myths of the English,* edited by Ray Porter, 76–83. Cambridge, UK: Polity Press.

Croker, T. Crofton. 1824. *Researches in the South of Ireland.* London: John Murray.

———. 1826–1828. *Fairy Legends and Traditions of the South of Ireland.* 3 vols. London: John Murray.

Curnow, Trevor. 2004. *The Oracles of the Ancient World.* London: Duckworth.

Dacombe, Marianne R., ed. 1935. *Dorset Up Along and Down Along. A Collection of History, Tradition, Folk Lore, Flower Names, and Herbal Lore.* Dorchester, UK: Longmans.

Dacombe, Ursula. 1950. "This Night We Come A-Souling." *Farmers' Weekly,* December 22, 45–50.

Dalí, Salvador. 1935. *La conquète de l'irrationel.* Paris: Surréalistes.

Dalyell, John Graham. 1834. *The Darker Superstitions of Scotland: Illustrated from History and Practice.* Edinburgh: Waugh and Innes.

Daniel, George. 1842. *Merrie England in the Olden Time.* 2 vols. London: Richard Bentley.

Davidson, H. R. Ellis. 1973. "Hostile Magic in the Icelandic Sagas." In *The Witch Figure,* edited by Venetia Newell, 37–38. London: Routledge.

Davidson, Hilda Ellis. 1988. *Myths and Symbols in Pagan Europe.* Syracuse, N.Y.: Syracuse University Press.

Davies, J. Ceredig. 1911. *Folk-Lore of West and Mid Wales.* Aberystwyth, UK: *Welsh Gazette.*

Davies, Owen. 2018. *A Supernatural War: Magic, Divination, and Faith during the First World War.* Oxford, UK: Oxford University Press.

Dawkins, M. 1906. "The Modern Carnival in Thrace and the Cult of Dionysus." *Journal of Hellenic Studies* 26: 191–206.

Day, George. 1894. "Notes on the Essex Dialect and Folk-Lore, with Some Account of the Divining Rod." *Essex Naturalist* 8: 71–85.

Deacon, George. 2002. *John Clare and the Folk Tradition.* London: Francis Boutle.

Delahaye, Hippolyte. 1912. *Les origines du culte des martyres.* Brussels, Belgium: Bureaux de la Société du Bollandists.

Deneke, Bernward. 1975. *Le carnaval en Allemagne: Le masque dans la tradition européenne.* Binche, Belgium: Exposition 1975 Catalogue.

Denham, Michael Aislabie. 1892 and 1895. *The Denham Tracts.* 2 vols. London: Folk-Lore Society.

Dennis, Victoris Solt. 2005. *Discovering Friendly and Fraternal Societies.* Prince's Risborough, UK: Shire.

Depiny, August. 1933. "Das Linzer Volksfest 1833." *Heimatgaue* 14: 132–33.

Dessaix, Emile. 1898. "A Procession of Giants." *Strand Magazine* XV (January–June): 343–50.

De Tournai, Gautier. 1941. *L'Histoire de Gilles de Chin,* edited by Edwin B. Place. New York: AMS Press.

De Vere, Aubrey. 1879. *Legends of the Saxon Saints.* London: C. Kegan Paul & Co.

Dewar, H., 1962. "The Dorset Ooser." *Proceedings of the Dorset Natural History and Antiquarian Field Club* 84: 170–80.

Disher, Maurice Willson. (1925) 1968. *Clowns and Pantomimes.* New York: Benjamin Blom.

Dorson, Richard M. 1968. *The British Folkorists.* London: Routledge & Kegan Paul.

D'Oudégherst, Pierre. 1571. *Les Chroniques et annales de Flandres.* Antwerp, Belgium: Christophle Plantin.

Dowen, K. 2017. "Seventeenth-Century Buff Coats and Other Military

Equipment." In *Leather in Warfare: Attack, Defence, and the Unexpected,* edited by Q. Mould. Leeds, UK: Archaeological Leather Group/ Royal Armouries.

Duchartre, Pierre Louis. 1966. *The Italian Comedy.* Translated by Randolph T. Weaver. New York: Dover.

Earp, Frank. 1991. *May Day in Nottinghamshire.* Wymeswold, UK: Heart of Albion Press.

Edwards, Gillian. 1968. *Uncumber and Pantaloon.* London: Bles.

———. 1974. *Hobgoblin and Sweet Puck.* London: Bles.

Egidius. 1935. "Magic in Norfolk." *East Anglian Magazine* (August): 93–95.

Ekwall, Eilert. 1980. *English Place-Names.* Oxford, UK: Clarendon Press.

Eliade, Mircea. 1959. *The Sacred and the Profane.* New York: Harcourt, Brace, Jovanovitch.

Elworthy, F. T. 1900. *Horns of Honour.* London: Murray.

Emminson, F. G. 1970. *Elizabethan Life: Disorder.* Chelmsford, UK: Essex Record Office.

Epton, Nina. 1968. *Spanish Fiestas.* London: Cassell.

E.S.T. 1850. "Shusck the Dog-fiend." *Notes and Queries* series 1, no. 29: 468.

Evans. E. C. 1969. "Physiognomies in the Ancient World." *Transactions of the American Philosophical Association* n.s., 59, 5: 1–101.

Evans, E. Estyn. 1957. *Irish Folk Ways.* London: Routledge & Kegan Paul.

Evans, George Ewart. 1971. *The Pattern under the Plough.* London: Faber and Faber.

Evans, J. Gwenogvryn, and Sir John Rhys. 1893. *The Book of Llan Dâv.* Oxford, UK. limited edition of 350 copies, privately published.

Evans-Wentz, W. Y. 1911. *The Fairy Faith in Celtic Countries.* London: Oxford University Press.

Ewing, Juliana Horatia. 1887. *The Peace Egg and a Christmas Mumming Play.* London: SPCC.

Favale, Virginio, and Paolo Alei. 2003. *Venice Carnival.* London: Artmedia Press.

Fairholt, Frederick William. 1859. *Gog and Magog: The Giants in the Guildhall; Their Real and Legendary History. With an Account of Other Civic Giants, at Home and Abroad.* London: J. C. Hotten.

Fano, Nicola. 2001. *Le maschere italiane.* Bologna, Italy: Il Mulino.

Farquaharson-Coe, A. 1975. *Devon's Witchcraft.* Saint Ives (Cornwall), UK: James Pike.

Flaxman, E. J. 1949. "Stories of the Yarmouth Rows." *East Anglian Magazine* 9: 9–12.

Fol, Valeria. 2004. "Mask and Masquerade from Mysterious Initiation to Carnival in Bulgaria." In *Carnival!,* edited by Barbara Mauldin, 45–63. London: Thames & Hudson.

Fontenrose, Joseph. 1971. *The Ritual Theory of Myth.* Berkeley: University of California Press.

Forby, Robert. 1830. *The Vocabulary of East Anglia.* 2 vols. London: J. B. Nichols and Son.

Forsyth, Isla. 2014. "The Practice and Poetics of Fieldwork: Hugh Cott and the Study of Camouflage." *Journal of Historical Geography* 43 (January): 128–37.

Frampton, George. 1989. *Whittlesey Straw Bear.* Peterborough, UK: Cambridgeshire Libraries Publications.

———. 1991. *More Honoured in the Breach than in the Observance: Plough Monday Customs of Cambridgeshire, Past and Present.* Unpublished manuscript.

———. 1993. *Pity the Poor Ploughboy—Balsham's Plough Monday.* Tonbridge, UK: privately published.

———. 1994. *Necessary to Keep Up the Day: Plough Monday and Musical Tradition in Little Downham.* Tonbridge, UK: privately published.

———. 1996: *Vagrants, Rogues, and Vagabonds: Plough Monday Tradition in Old Huntingdonshire and the Soke of Peterborough.* Tonbridge, UK: privately published.

Francis, Hywel. 1976. *The General Strike 1926.* Edited by Geoffrey Skelley. London: Lawrence & Wishart.

Frank, James. 1983. "Straw Bear Country." *Countryman* (Winter): 33–37.

———. 1994: "In the Steps of the Straw Bear." *Cambridgeshire Journal* 9 (December–January): 14–15.

Franklin, Anna. 2002. *The Illustrated Encyclopaedia of Fairies.* London: Vega.

Fraser, Antonia. 2002. *King Charles II.* London: Phoenix.

Fraser, Grace Lovat. 1969. *Claud Lovat Fraser.* London: Victoria and Albert Museum.

Gaignebet, Claude, Jean Sébille, and Dominique Tonneau-Rycknelynck. 2004. *Les triomphes de carnaval: Pour une iconographie de l'art païen festif.* Gravelines, France: Musée de Gravelines.

Gailey, Alan. 1972. "A Missing Belfast Chapbook: The Christmas Rime, or, the Mummers' Own Book." *Irish Book Lover* 2: 54–58.

———. 1974. "The English Mummers and Their Plays." *Folk Life* 10 (1): 136–137.

Gatty, Ivor. 1946. "The Old Tup and Its Ritual." *Journal of the English Folk Dance and Song Society* 5, no. 1: 24–30.

George, M. D. 1967. *Hogarth to Cruikshank*. London: Allen Lane.

Ghiron-Bistagne, Paulette. 1970. "Les demi-masques." *Revue archéologique* fasc. 2: 232–82.

Gill, Walter. 1929. *A Manx Scrapbook*. London: Arrowsmith.

Glyde, John, Jr. 1872. *The Norfolk Garland*. Norwich, UK: Jarrold.

———. (1866) 1976. *Folklore and Customs of Suffolk*. Original title, *A New Suffolk Garland*. Norwich, UK: EDP Publishing.

Goldberg, Rose Lee. 1988. *Performance Art*. London: Thames & Hudson.

Gomme, Alice B. 1930. "Mummers' Plays, Some Incidents In." *Folk-Lore* 41, no. 2: 195–98.

Gordon, Mel. 1983. *Lazzi: The Comic Routines of the Commedia dell'Arte*. New York: Performing Arts Journal Publications.

Grace, M., ed. 1937. *Records of the Guild of St. George in Norwich*. Norwich, UK: Norfolk Record Society.

Graham-Campbell, James. 2013. *Viking Art*. London: Thames & Hudson.

Graves, Robert. 1955. *The Greek Myths*. Harmondsworth, UK: Penguin.

Grimm, Jacob (trans. Stallybrass, James Steven), 1888. *Teutonic Mythology*. London: George Bell and Sons.

Gross, Charles. 1890. *The Gild Merchant: A Contribution to British Municipal History*. Oxford, UK: Clarendon Press.

Guerdon, Gilbert. 1892. "Street Musicians." *Strand Magazine* 3: 65–72.

Gueusquin, Marie-France. 1985. "Le guerrier et l'artisan: Rites et représentation dans la cite au France du Nord." *Ethnologia Français* n.s. T, 15, no 1: 45–62.

Gunnell, Terrey. 1995. *The Origin of Drama in Sweden*. Cambridge, UK: D. S. Brewer.

Gurdon, Lady Camilla. 1892. "Folk-Lore from South-East Suffolk." *Folk-Lore* 3, no. 4: 558–60.

Gutch, Mrs. (Eliza), coll. and ed. 1901. *Folk-Lore of Yorkshire: North Riding*. Vol 2, *Publications of the Folk-Lore Society County Folk-Lore*. London: David Nutt.

Gutch, Mrs. (Eliza), and Peacock, Mabel. 1908. "Festivals." *County Folk-Lore*

Volume 5, Printed Extracts No VII, Examples of Printed Folk-Lore concerning Lincolnshire. London: David Nutt, 83–134.

———, coll. and ed. 1911. *Folk-Lore of Yorkshire: East Riding.* Vol. 6, *Publications of the Folk-Lore Society County Folk-Lore.* London: David Nutt.

Gwen, John. 1921. "The Derbyshire Mumming Play of St. George and the Dragon, or as It Is Sometimes Called, the Pace Egg." *Folk-Lore* 32: 181–93.

Hackett, William. 1853. "Porcine Legends." *Transactions of the Kilkenny Archaeological Society.* Vol. 2, 303–10.

Haddon, Alfred C. 1898. "A Wedding Dance-Mask from County Mayo." *Folk-Lore* 4, no. 1: 123–24.

Hall, S. C., ed. 1847. *The Book of British Ballads.* First series. London: Jeremiah How.

Hallowell, A. Irving. 1926. "Bear Ceremonial in the Northern Hemisphere." *American Anthropologist* n.s. 28, 1: 1–175.

Hand, Wayland. 1980. *Magical Medicine: The Folkloric Component of Medicine in the Folk Belief, Custom, and Rituals of the Peoples of Europe and America.* Berkeley: University of California Press.

Handelman, Don, 1984. "Inside-Out, Outside-In: Concealment and Revelation in Newfoundland Christmas Mumming." In *Play, Text, and Story: The Construction and Reconstruction of Self and Society,* edited by G. Bruner. Washington DC: American Ethnological Society.

Handler, Richard, and Jocelyn Linnekin. 1984. "Tradition, Genuine or Spurious." *Journal of American Folklore* 97, no. 385: 273–90.

Happe, P. 1964. "The Vice and the Folk-Drama." *Folklore* 75: 161–93.

Hare, Chris. 1988. "The Skeleton Army and the Bonfire Boys, Worthing 1884." *Folklore* 99, no. 2: 221–31.

Harland, John, and T. T. Wilkinson. 1867. *Lancashire Folk-Lore.* London: Frederick Warne.

Harper, Clive. 2012. "The Witches' Flying Ointment." *Folklore* 88: 105–6.

Harris, Mary Dormer. 1911. *The Story of Coventry.* London: J. M. Dent & Sons, Ltd.

Harrod, Henry. 1872. "Some Pariculars relation to the Abbey Church of Wymonham in Norfolk." *Archaeologia* 43: 264–72.

Hasenfratz, Hans-Peter. 2011. *Barbarian Rites: The Spiritual World of the Vikings and the Germanic Tribes,* translated by Michael Moynihan. Rochester, Vt.: Inner Traditions.

Hasluck, F. W. 1914. "Dieudonné de Gozon and the Dragon of Rhodes." *Annual of the British School at Athens* 20: 70–79.

Hayward, B. 1992. *Galoshins: The Scottish Folk Play*. Edinburgh: Edinburgh University Press.

Heanley, Rev. R. M. 1902. "The Vikings: Traces of Their Folklore in Marshland." Vol. 3, part 1, *The Saga Book of the Viking Club*. Orkey, Shetland, UK: Society for Northern Research.

Heaton, Phil. 2012. *Rapper: The Miners' Sword Dance of North-East England*. London: English Folk Dance and Song Society.

Helm, Alex, ed. 1965a. *Five Mumming Plays for Schools*. London: English Folk Dance and Song Society and Folk-Lore Society.

———. 1965b. "In Comes I, St. George." *Folklore* 76, no. 2: 118–36.

———. 1981. *The English Mummers' Play*. London: D. S. Brewer and Rowman and Littlefield for the Folklore Society.

Helm, Alex, and E. C. Cawte. 1967. *Six Mummers' Acts*. Leicester, UK: Guizer Press.

Henderson, William. 1866. *Notes on the Folk-lore of the Northern Counties of England and the Borders*. London: Longmans Green.

———. 1879. *Folk-Lore of the Northern Counties*. London: Folk-Lore Society.

Hennels, C. E. 1961. "The Broomstick Dancers of the Fens." *East Anglian Magazine* 21: 188–89.

Herrick, Robert, 1902. *The Poems of Robert Herrick*. London, Grant Richards.

Hervey, Thomas K. 1888. *The Book of Christmas: Descriptive of the Customs, Ceremonies, Traditions, Superstitions, Fun, Feeling, and Festivities of the Christmas Season*. Boston: Roberts Brothers.

Hewett, Sarah. 1900. *Nummits and Crummits: Devonshire Customs*. London: Thomas Burleigh.

Hibbert, Francis Aidan. 1891. *The Influence and Development of English Gilds*. Cambridge, UK: Cambridge University Press.

Hildburgh, W. L. 1944. "Indeterminability and Confusion as Apotropaic Elements in Italy and Spain." *Folk-Lore* 55: 133–49.

Hillen, Henry. 1910. "On Kitty Witch Row, Great Yarmouth." *Antiquary* 46: 188.

H.J.S. 1937. "The Plough Boy's Play: A Version Recorded." *Yorkshire Post*, January 11, 6.

Hole, Christina. 1978. *A Dictionary of British Folk Customs*. London: Paladin Granada.

Holmes, T. V. 1892. "Modern Legends of Supposed 'Wolves' in Epping Forest." *Journal of Proceedings of the Essex Field Club* (February 23, 1884–January 29, 1887): cciv–ccix.

Holt, Robert Burbank. 1890. *Whitby Past and Present*. London: Copas & Co; Whitby: Horn & Son.

Hone, William. 1827. *The Every-Day Book*. 2 vols. London: Hunt and Clarke.

How, Harry. 1891. "Illustrated Interviews VI: Sir Augustus Harris." *Strand Magazine* 2: 553–63.

———. 1894. "Pantomime Masks and Properties." *Strand Magazine* 8: 662–72.

Howard, Michael. 1998. "Margaret Murray and the Dorset Ooser." *Cauldron,* November 16.

Howells, William. 1831. *Cambrian Superstitions: Comprising Ghosts, Omens, Witchcraft, Traditions, etc.; To Which Are Added a Concise View of the Manners and Customs of the Principality.* London: Longman and Co.

Howitt, William. 1838. *The Rural Life of England*. London: Longman.

Howlett, England. 1899. "Sacrificial Foundations." In *Ecclesiastical Curiosities,* edited by William Andrews, 30–45. London: William Andrews.

Howlett, Richard. 1907. "Norwich Artillery in the Fourteenth Century." *Norfolk Archaeology* 16: 46–75.

Howley, Mike. 1962. "The Little Tup." *Folk* 2: 9–10.

Hufford, David J. 1995. "Beings without Bodies: An Experience-Centered Theory of the Belief in Spirits." In *Out of the Ordinary: Folklore and the Supernatural,* edited by Barbara Walker, 11–45. Logan: Utah State University Press.

Hukantaival, Sonja. 2009. "Horse Skulls and 'Alder Horse': The Horse as a Depositional Sacrifice in Building." *Archaeologica Baltica* 11: 350–56.

Humberg, Norbert. 1976. *Städliches Fastnachtsbrauchtum in West- und Ostphalia: Die Entwicklung vom Mittelalter bis ins 19. Jahrhundert.* Münster, Germany: Volkskundliche Kommission für Westfalen.

Humphreys, John. 1995. *More Tales of the Old Poachers*. Newton, UK: Abbot, David, and Charles.

Hunt, Robert. 1865. *Popular Romances of the West of England*. London: John Camden Hotten. Series 1, 147.

Hutton, Ronald. 1994. *The Rise and Fall of Merry England*. Oxford, UK: Oxford University Press.

———. 1996. *The Stations of the Sun*. Oxford, UK: Oxford University Press.

Ignotus. 1867. *The Last Thirty Years in a Mining District*. N.p.

Jacobs, John. 1894. *More English Fairy Tales*. London: Nutt.

Jahn, Ulrich. 1884. *Die deutschen Opfergebräuchen beim Ackerbau und Vierzucht*. Breslau, Germany: Verlag Wilhelm Koebner.

Jekyll, Gertrude. 1904. *Old West Surrey*. London: Longmans, Green & Co.

J.E.P. 1937. "Witches I Have Known." *East Anglian Magazine* July: 450–52; August: 507.

Jevons, Frank Byron. 1916. *Masks and Acting*. Cambridge, UK: Cambridge University Press.

Jobson, Allan. 1966. *A Suffolk Calendar*. London: Robert Hale.

Johnson, Tom, 2013. *The Graveyard Wanderers, the Wise Ones, and the Dead in Sweden*. Hinckley, UK: Society for Esoteric Endeavour.

Jones-Baker, Doris, 1977. *The Folklore of Hertfordshire*. London, Batsf

Jones, D. J. V. 1971. "The Scotch Cattle and Their Black Domain." *Welsh History Review* 5, no. 3: 220–49.

Jones, M. C., J. B. Partridge, Ella M. Leather, and F. S. Potter. 1913. "Scraps of English Folk-Lore VII." *Folk-Lore* 24, no. 2: 254–61.

Jones, Prudence, and Nigel Pennick. 1995. *A History of Pagan Europe*. London: Routledge.

Jones, Rhian E. 2012. "Symbol, Ritual, and Popular Protest in Early Nineteenth-Century Wales: The Scotch Cattle Rebranded." *Welsh History Review* 26: 34–57.

Jones, T. Gwyn. 1930. *Welsh Folk-Lore and Folk-Customs*. London: Methuen.

Jones, William. 1880. *Credulities Past and Present: Including the Sea, Miners, Amulets, and Talismans*. London: Chatto & Windus.

Jonson, Ben. (1616) 1816a. "Part of King James's Entertainment, in Passing to His Coronation." *The Works of Ben Jonson* 6: 428–60: London: W. Bulmer & Co.

———. (1616) 1816b. "The Masque of Christmas." In *The Works of Ben Jonson*, vol. 7, 271–85. London: W. Bulmer & Co.

Joynes, Andrew, comp. and ed. 2001. *Medieval Ghost Stories: An Anthology of Miracles, Marvels, and Prodigies*. Woodbridge, UK: Boydell & Brewer.

Judge, Roy. 1979. *Jack-in-the-Green: A May Day Custom*. Cambridge, UK: D. S. Brewer.

———. 1991. "May Day and Merrie England." *Folklore* 102, no. 2: 131–48.

———. 2000. *The Jack-in-t reen*. London: Folklore Society.

Keightley, Thomas. 1860. *The Fairy Mythology: Illustrative of the Romance and Superstition of Various Countries*. London: Bohn.

Kennard, Joseph Spencer. 1935. *Masks and Marionettes*. New York: Macmillan.

Kennedy, Patrick. (1893) 2015. "The Witches' Excursion." In *Irish Fairy and Folk Tales*, edited by William Butler Yeats, 431–33. New York: Barnes & Noble.

Kenyon, Nicholas, and Hugh Keyte. 1990. *Una stravaganza dei Medici: The Florentine Intermedi of 1589*. London: Channel 4 Television.

Kieckhefer, Richard. 2000. *Magic in the Middle Ages*. Cambridge, UK: Canto.

Kille, Herbert W. 1931. "West Country Hobby-Horses and Cognate Customs." *Proceedings of the Somersetshire Archaeological and Natural History Society* 77: 63–77.

Kirby, Ernest Theodore. 1971. "The Origin of Mummers' Plays." *Journal of American Folklore* 84: 275–80.

———. 1974. "The Shamanistic Origins of Popular Entertainment." *Drama Review* 18, no. 1: 4–15.

Knight, Charles, ed. 1845 and 1846. *Old England*. 2 vols. London: Charles Knight.

Köhler, Johann August Ernst. 1867. *Volksbrauch, Abergalauber, Sagen und andere alter Nieberlieferungen im Voigtlande*. Leipzig, Germany: Verlag von Fr. Fleischer.

Kropotkin, Petr. (1914) 1955. *Mutual Aid: A Factor in Evolution*. Boston: Extending Horizons Books.

Künzig, Johannes. 1950. *Die Alemannisch-Schwäbisch Fasnet*. Freiburg-im-Breisgau, Germany: Landestelle für Volkskunde.

Kutter, Wilhelm. 1973. "Maskenzeiten und Larventypen in Südwestdeutschland." *Schweizerisches Archiv für Volkskunde* 68/69: 348–71.

Lambert, Margaret, and Enid Marx. 1989. *English Popular Art*. London: Merlin Press.

Lanzi, Fernando, and Gioia Lanzi. 2004. *Saints and Their Symbols: Recognizing Saints in Art and Popular Images*. Collegeville, Minn.: Liturgical Press.

Lawner, Lynn. 1998. *Harlequin on the Moon: Commedia dell'Arte and the Visual Arts*. New York: Harry Abrams, Inc.

Leather, Ella Mary. 1912. *The Folk-Lore of Herefordshire*. Hereford, UK: Jakeman and Carver; London: Sidgwick and Jackson.

Lecouteux, Claude. 2015. *Demons and Spirits of the Land*. Rochester, Vt.: Inner Traditions.

Ledbury, John. 1993. "The Historical Evidence for Sword Dancing in Britain." *Rattle Up My Boys* 4, no. 3: 1–8.

Lee, Rev. Frederick George, ed. 1875. *Glimpses of the Supernatural.* 2 vols. London: Henry S. King and Co.

Leland, Charles Godfrey. 1897. "The Straw Goblin." *Folk-Lore* 8, no. 1: 87–88.

MacAldowie, Alex. 1896. "Personal Experiences in Witchcraft." *Folk-Lore* 7, no. 3: 309–14.

MacFarlane, K. 2010. "A Counter-Desecration Phrasebook." In *Towards Pre-enchantment,* edited by G. Evans and D. Robson, 107–29. London: Artevents.

MacPherson, J. M. 1929. *Primitive Beliefs in the North East of Scotland.* Edinburgh: Longman Green and Co.

Maddern, Phillippe. 2004. "Order and Disorder." In *Medieval Norwich,* edited by Carole Rawcliffe and Richard Wilson. London: Hambledon Continuum.

Magnússon, Eiríkr. 1888. *Volsunga Saga: The Story of the Volsungs and Niblungs, with Certain Songs from the Elder Edda,* translated by William Morris; edited, Introduction, and Notes by H. Halliday Sparling. London: Walter Scott.

Malcolmson, Robert W. 1973. *Popular Recreations in English Society 1700–1850.* London: Cambridge University Press.

Malory, Sir Thomas. (1472) 1906. *Le Morte d'Arthur.* 2 vols. London and Toronto: J. M. Dent.

Mann, Ethel. 1934. *Old Bungay.* London: Heath Cranton.

Mannhardt, Wilhelm. 1875 and 1877. *Wald- und Feldkulte.* 2 vols., Berlin: Gebrüder Borntraeger.

Manning-Sanders, Ruth. 1973. *Festivals.* London: E. P. Dutton.

Marshall, Sybil. 1967. *Fenland Chronicle.* Cambridge, UK: Cambridge University Press.

Mason, M. H. 1902. *Nursery Rhymes and Country Songs: Both Tunes and Words from Tradition.* London: Metzler & Co.

Maxwell-Stuart, P. G. 2014. *The British Witch: The Biography.* Stroud, UK: Amberley Publishing.

Mayer, David. 1969. *Harlequin in His Element: The English Pantomime, 1806–36.* Cambridge, Mass.: Harvard University Press.

Maylam, Percy. 1909. "The Wooset." *Notes and Queries* 10th series, 11, no. 263: 27.

———. 1909. *The Hooden Horse, an East Kent Custom*. Canterbury, UK: privately printed.

Mayo, Canon Charles. 1891. "The Dorset Ooser." *Notes and Queries for Somerset and Dorset* 2, no. 16 (December): 289.

McConnell Stott, Andrew. 2009. *The Pantomime Life of Joseph Grimaldi, 1802–1832*. Edinburgh: Canongate Books.

Mic, Constant. 1927. *La Commedia dell'Arte*. Paris: Editions de la Pléiade.

Miles, Clement Arthur. 1912. *Christmas in Ritual and Tradition*. London: T. Fisher Unwin.

Mill, Anna Jean. 1927. *Medieval Plays in Scotland*. London: William Blackwood.

———. 1970. "The Perth Hammermen's Play." *Scottish Historical Review* 49, no. 148, part 2: 146–53.

Millington, Peter. 2005. "Plough Bullocks and Related Plough Monday Customs in the Nottingham Area, 1800–1930." *Transactions of the Thoroton Society of Nottinghamshire* 109: 127–37.

Mitchell, Stephen. 2011. *Witchcraft and Magic in the Nordic Middle Ages*. Philadelphia: University of Pennsylvania Press.

M.M.D. 1900. "The Straw Bear." *Fenland Notes and Queries* 4: 228.

Molloy, Pat. 1983. *And They Blessed Rebecca: An Account of the Welsh Toll-Gate Riots 1839–1844*. Llandysul, UK: Gomer Press.

Napier, A. David. 1986. *Masks, Transformation, and Paradox*. Berkeley: University of California Press.

Neat, Timothy. 2002. *The Horseman's Word*. Edinburgh: Birlinn.

Needham, Joseph. 1936. "Geographical Distribution of English Ceremonial Dance Traditions." *Journal of the English Folk Dance and Song Society* 3, no. 1: 1–45.

Needham, Joseph, and Arthur L. Peck. 1933. "Molly Dancing in East Anglia." *Journal of the English Folk Dance and Song Society* 1: 1–7.

Newman, Leslie F. 1930. "Mummers' Play from Middlesex." *Folk-Lore* 41, no. 1: 95–98.

———. 1940. "Notes on Some Rural and Trade Initiations in the Eastern Counties." *Folk-Lore* 51, no. 1: 32–42.

Newman, Leslie F., and E. M. Wilson. 1952. "Folklore Survivals in the Southern 'Lake Counties' and in Essex: A Comparison and Contrast." *Folklore* 63: 91–104.

Nicholls, Robert Wyndham. 2012. *Masquerade Prototypes in Western Europe.* Jackson: University of Mississippi Press.

Nicholson, John. 1890. *Folk Lore of East Yorkshire.* London: Simpkin, Marshall, Hamilton, Kent, & Co; Hull, UK: A. Browne & Sons; Driffield, UK: T. Holderness.

Nicoll, J. R. Allardyce. (1931) 1963. *Masks, Mimes, and Miracles.* New York: Cooper Square.

———. 1963. *The World of Harlequin.* London: Cambridge University Press.

O'Donnell, Elliott. 1912. *Werwolves.* London: Methuen.

Old Timer. 1925. "Nottinghamshire and Derbyshire Guisers." Local Notes and Queries, *Nottinghamshire Guardian,* February 7.

Olsen, Ole. N.d. *Asgaardsreien.* Leipzig, Germany: August Cranz.

O'Neill, John. 1895. "Straw." *Journal of American Folk-Lore* 8, no. 31: 291–98.

Ord, John. 1920. "The Most Secret of Secret Societies: Ancient Scottish Horsemen." *Glasgow Weekly Herald,* November 13.

Ordish, Thomas Fairman. 1891. "Folk Drama." *Folk-Lore* 2: 314–35.

Otto, Rudolf. (1917) 1936. *The Idea of the Holy: An Enquiry into the Non-rational Factor in the Idea of the Divine and Its Relation to the Rational.* London: Oxford University Press.

Owen, Elias. 1887. *Welsh Folk-Lore.* Oswestry, UK: Woodall, Minshall, & Co.

Owen, Trefor M. 1987. *Welsh Folk Customs.* Llandysul, UK: Gomer.

Painter, K. S. 1977. *The Mildenhall Treasure.* London: British Museum Publications.

Page, Michael, and Robert Ingpen. 1985. *The Encyclopedia of Things That Never Were: Creatures, Places, and People.* London: Guild Publishing.

Palmer, Roy. 1976. *The Folklore of Warwickshire.* London: B. T. Batsford.

———. 2004. *The Folklore of Shropshire.* Woonton, Almeley, UK: Logaston Press.

Palmer, William. 1974. "Plough Monday 1933 at Little Downham." *English Folk Dance* (Spring): 24–25.

Pappenheim, Max. 1885. *Die Altdänischen Schutzgilden.* Breslau, Germany: W. Koebner.

Papworth, Cyril. 1984. *Polka Round: The Cambridgeshire Feast Dances.* Comberton, UK: Privately published.

———. N.d. *The Comberton Broom Dance.* Unpublished manuscript.

Parsons, Ben, and Bas Jongenelen. 2010. "The Sermon of St. Nobody: A Verse

Translation of a Middle Dutch Parodic Sermon." *Journal of American Folklore* 122, no 487: 92–107.

Parsons, Catherine E. (1915) 1985. *Notes on Cambridgeshire Witchcraft.* Reprinted from the *Cambridgeshire Antiquarian Society's Communications* 19: 1915. Cambridge: Cambridge Folk Museum.

———. 1952. *Horseheath: Some Recollections of a Cambridgeshire Parish.* Unpublished manuscript.

Patten, R. W. 1974. *Exmoor Custom and Song.* Dulverton, UK: Exmoor Press.

Patterson, W. H. 1872. "The Christmas Rhymers in the North of Ireland." *Notes and Queries* series 4, 10: 487–88.

Peacock, Mabel Geraldine W. 1897. "Omens of Death." *Folk-Lore* 8: 377–78.

———. 1898. "Christmas Tup." *Notes and Queries,* 9th series, 2, no. 44: 348.

———. 1901. "Plough Monday Mummeries." *Notes and Queries,* 9th series, 7: 323–24.

———. 1907. "The Fifth of November and Guy Fawkes." *Folk-Lore* 18, no. 4: 449–50.

Peate, Iorweth. 1963. "Mari Lwyd—Láir Bhán." *Folk-Life* 1, no. 1: 95–96.

Pegg, Bob. 1981. *Rites and Riots: Folk Customs of Britain and Europe.* Poole, UK: Blandford Press.

Pennick, Nigel. 1985. *Einst War Uns die Erde Heilig.* Waldeck-Dehringhausen, Germany: Felicitas-Hübner-Verlag.

———. 1986. *Skulls, Cats, and Witch Bottles.* Cambridge, UK: Nigel Pennick Editions.

———. 1997. *The Celtic Saints: An Illustrated and Authoritative Guide to These Extraordinary Men and Women.* London: Thorsons.

———. 1998. *Crossing the Borderlines.* Chieveley, UK: Capall Bann.

———. 1999. "Regarding the Ooser." *3rd Stone* 35 (July–September): 39–40.

———. 2002. "The Goddess Zisa." *Tyr* 1: 107–9.

———. 2005. "Vom Fortbestehen alter Grenzen." *Hagia Chora* 20: 103.

———. 2011. *The Toadman.* Hinckley, UK: Society of Esoteric Endeavour.

———. 2013. "The Ensouled World." *Silver Wheel* 4: 138–44.

———. 2019a. *Runic Lore and Legend: Wyrdstaves of Old Northumbria.* Rochester, Vt.: Destiny Books.

———. 2019b. *Witchcraft and Secret Societies of Rural England: The Magic of Toadmen, Plough Witches, Mummers, and Bonesmen.* Rochester, Vt.: Destiny Books.

Pennick, Nigel, and Helen Field. 2003. *A Book of Beasts*. Milverton, UK: Capall Bann Publishing.

Pennick, Nigel, Rupert Pennick, and John Nicholson. 1974. *The Primer of English Violence: Being a Chronological Survey of Uprisings, Invasions, Riots, and Disaffection in the British Isles (1484 to the Present Day)*. Cambridge, UK: Cokaygne Publishing.

Penry, Tylluan. 2014. *An Introduction to Anglo-Saxon Magic and Witchcraft*. Tonypandy, UK: Wolfenhowle Press.

Pentikäinen, Juha. 2007. *Golden King of the Forest: The Lore of the Northern Bear*. Helsinki: Etnika Og.

Percy, Thomas. 1891. *Reliques of Ancient English Poetry: Consisting of Old Heroic Ballads, Songs, and Other Pieces of Our Earlier Poets*. 3 vols. London: Swan Sonnenschein.

Peter, Thurstan. 1913. "The Hobby Horse." *Journal of the Royal Institution of Cornwall* 19, no. 2: 248–54.

———. 1916. "St. George Mumming Play." *Notes and Queries* 1: 390–93.

Piatti, Barbara, and Yvonne Rogenmoser. 2019. *Feste und Bräuche in der Schwyz*. Zürich, Switzerland: NordSüd Verlag.

Piesse, G. W. Septimus. 1860. "The Mummers." *Notes and Queries* 2nd series (December 15): 466–67.

Piggott, Stuart. 1929. "The Character of Beelzebub in the Mummers' Play." *Folk-Lore* 40, no. 2: 193–95.

Pleij, Herman. 1992. "Van vastenavond tot carnival." In *Vastenavond— Carnaval: Festen van de omgekeerde wereld*, edited by M. Mooij, 10–44, 177–79. Hertogenboschs, Noordbrabants Museum: Zwolle, Waanders.

———. 2001. *Dreaming of Cockaigne*. Translated by Diane Webb. New York: Columbia University Press.

Plowright, Charles Bagge. 1895. "May Day Customs at Lynn—A Survival." *Transactions of the Norfolk and Norwich Naturalists Society* vi: 106–7.

Pluskowski, Aleksander, ed. 2007. *Breaking and Shaping Beastly Bodies: Animals as Material Culture in the Middle Ages*. London: Oxbow Books.

Porta, Giovanni Baptista, 1560. *Magica Natura, sive De Miraculis Rerum Naturalium*. Antwerp, Christopher Plantin.

Porter, Enid, 1974. *The Folklore of East Anglia*. London, Batsford.

Porter, Enid. 1969. *Cambridgeshire Customs and Folklore*. Fenland material provided by W. H. Barrett. London: Routledge & Kegan Paul.

Porter, Ray, ed. 1992. *Myths of the English*. Cambridge, UK: Polity Press.

Poulton, Sir Edward Bagnall. 1890. *The Colour of Animals: Their Meaning and Use Especially Considered in the Case of Insects*. London: Kegan Paul, Trench, and Trübner.

Prestige, G. L. (1936) 1964. *God in Patristic Thought*. London: SPCK.

Putterill, John [the Reverend Jack]. 1950. "The Folk Dances of Thaxted." *East Anglian Magazine* 9: 340–42.

Radzinowicz, L. 1945. "The Waltham Black Act: A Study of the Legislative Attitude towards Crime in the 18th Century." *Cambridge Law Journal* 9, no. 1: 56–87.

Raglan, Lady. 1939. "The 'Green Man' in Church Architecture." *Folk-Lore* 50: 45–57.

Raistrick, Arthur. 1947. "The Mummers' Play." *Dalesman,* April, 24–29.

Randall, Arthur. 1966. *Sixty Years a Fenman*. Edited by Enid Porter. London: Routledge & Kegan Paul.

Ranke, K. 1969. "Orale und literale Kontinuität." In *Kontinuität? Geschichtlichkeit und Dauer als volkskundliches Problem. Festschrift Hans Moser,* edited by H. Bausinger and W. Brückner. Berlin: E. Schmidt.

Rattenbury, Arnold. 1979. *The Dragon, the Monster, the Fool, and Other Creatures*. Exhibition catalogue. Salisbury, UK: Salisbury Festivities.

———. 1981. "Methodism and the Tatterdemalions." In *Popular Culture and Class Conflict 1550–1914,* edited by Eileen Yeo and Stephen Yeo, 28–61. Brighton, UK: Harvester Press.

Rawe, Donald R. 1972. *Padstow's Obby Oss and May Day Festival: A Study in Tradition and Folklore*. Wadebridge, UK: Lodenek Press.

Read, D. H. Moutray. 1911. "Hampshire Folklore." *Folk-Lore: A Quarterly Review* 22: 292–329.

Rees, William Jenkins, and Thomas Wakeman. 1853. *Lives of the Cambro-British Saints*. Llandovery, UK: W. Rees; London: Longmans.

Renier-Michiel, Giustina. 1994. *Origine delle feste veneziane*. Venice, Italy: Filippi.

Rennie, William, and Fernee, Ben. 2009. *The Society of the Horseman's Word*. Hinckley, UK: Society of Esoteric Endeavour.

Richards, William. 1812. *The History of Lynn*. 2 vols. Lynn, UK: C. Whittingham.

Richter, Hans. 1965. *Dada Art and Anti-Art*. London: Thames & Hudson.

Rider Haggard, Lilias, ed. (1935) 1974. *I Walked by Night: Being the Life & History of the King of the Norfolk Poachers, Written by Himself.* Woodbridge, England: Boydell Press.

Riley, H. T. 1868. *Memorials of London and London Life in the 13th, 14th, and 15th Centuries.* London: Longmans Green.

Robertson, Margaret R. 1984. *The Newfoundland Mummers' Christmas House-Visit.* Ottawa: National Museum of Canada.

Robinson, David N. 1990. "Poachings: Plough Plays in Lincolnshire." *Lincolnshire Life* 30, no. 7: 3.

Roper, Charles. 1893. "On Witchcraft Superstition in Norfolk." *Harper's New Monthly Magazine* 87, no. 521 (October): 792–97.

Rosenfeld, S. 1939. *Strolling Players and Drama in the Provinces 1660–1765.* Cambridge, UK: Cambridge University Press.

Roud, Steve. 2003. *The Penguin Guide to the Superstitions of Britain and Ireland.* London: Penguin Books.

Rowling, Marjorie. 1976. *The Folklore of the Lake District.* London: B. T. Batsford.

Rudkin, Ethel H. 1933. "Lincolnshire Folk-Lore." *Folk-Lore* 44, no. 3: 279–95.

———. 1934. "Lincolnshire Folk-Lore: Witches and Devils." *Folk-Lore* 45, no. 3: 249–67.

———. 1938. "The Black Dog." *Folk-Lore* 49: 111–13.

Russell, Ian. 1979. "Here Comes Me and Our Old Lass, Short of Money and Short of Brass: A Survey of Traditional Drama in North-East Derbyshire 1970–78." *Folk Music Journal* 3, no. 5: 399–478.

Samuel, Raphael, and Paul Thompson, eds. 1990. *The Myths We Live By.* London: Routledge.

Sand, Maurice. 1915. *The History of the Harlequinade.* London: Martin Secker.

Sapir, David. 1977. "The Anatomy of Metaphor." In *The Social Use of Metaphor: Essays on the Anthropology of Rhetoric,* edited by J. D. Sapir and C. Crocker. Philadelphia: University of Pennsylvania Press.

Saunders, W. H. Bernard. 1888. *Legends and Traditions of Huntingdonshire.* Huntingdon, UK: Geo. C. Caster.

Saxo Grammaticus. 1905. *The Nine Books of the Danish History of Saxo Grammaticus,* translated by Oliver Elton. London, Copenhagen, Stockholm, Berlin and New York: Norroena Society.

Scarcella, Alessandro. 1998. *Le maschere veneziane.* Rome: Newton Compton.

Scheerer, Erika. 1953. "Beim Maskenschnitzer von Rottweil." *Württembereger Land* 1: 25–27.

Schlemmer, Oskar, Laslo Moholy-Nagy, and Farkas Molnar. 1961. *The Theater of the Bauhaus.* Middleton, Conn.: Wesleyan University Press.

Schwedt, H., E. Schwedt, and Blümcke. M. ,1984. *Masken und Maskenschnitzer der schwäbisch-alemannischen Fasnacht.* Stuttgart, Germany: Konrad Theiss Verlag. Scott, Sir Walter. 1828. *The Fair Maid of Perth.* Edinburgh: Cadell & Co.

Scotus. 1911. "Christmas Mummers as Mammals or Birds." *Notes and Queries,* 11th series, 3, no. 54: 14.

Scuden, Antonio. 2000. "Arleccino Revisited: Tracing the Demon from the Carnival to Kramer to Mr. Bean." *Theatre History Studies* 20: 143–55.

SeJason. 2005. "Guising, Ritual, and Revival: The Hobby Horse in Cornwall." *Old Cornwall* 13, no. 6: 39–46.

Sennett, R. 1998. *The Corrosion of Character.* New York: W. W. Norton.

Sharp, Cecil. 1911. *The Sword Dances of Northern England Together with the Horn Dance of Abbots Bromley: Part I.* London: Novello & Co.

Shepard, Ernest H. 1957. *Drawn from Memory.* London: Methuen.

Shuttleworth, Ron. 1994. *Constructing a Hobby Animal—Mainly for Morris Dancers.* Coventry, UK: privately published.

Sikes, Wirt. 1880. *British Goblins.* London: Sampson Low.

Singer, William. 1881. *An Exposition of the Miller and Horseman's Word, or the True System of Raising the Devil.* Aberdeen, UK: James Daniel.

Sitwell, Edith. 1922. *Façade.* London: Favil Press.

Sitwell, Osbert. 1949. *Laughter in the Next Room: Being the Fourth Volume of Left Hand, Right Hand!* London: Macmillan & Co., Ltd.

Skeat, W. W. 1876. *A List of English Words, the Etymology of Which Is Illustrated by Comparison with Icelandic.* Oxford, UK: Clarendon Press.

Slight, H. 1842. "Christmas: His Pageant Play, or Mysterie, of 'St. George,' as Played by the Itinerant Actors and Mummers in the Courts of the Nobility and Gentry, the Colleges, in the Halls of the Ancient Corporations and Guild Merchants, and in the Public Hostelries and Taverns." *Archaeologist and Journal of Antiquarian Science:* 1–10, 176–83.

Sly, Rex. 2003. *From Punt to Plough: A History of the Fens.* Slough, UK: Sutton Publishing.

Smith, G. C. Moore. 1909. "Straw Bear Tuesday." *Folk-Lore* 20, no. 2: 202–3.

Smith, Georgina. 1981. "Chapbooks and Traditional Plays: Communication and Performance." *Folklore* 92, no. 2: 196–202.

Smith, P., and G. Smith. 1966. "T'Owd Tup." *Folk Music Ballads and Songs* n.s., 2: 8–13.

Smith, Winifred. (1912) 1964. *The Commedia dell'Arte.* New York: Benjamin Blom.

Spufford, Margaret. 1994. "The Pedlar, the Historian, and the Folklorist: Seventeenth-Century Communication." *Folklore* 105: 13–24.

Steelcroft, Framley. 1895. "Some Curious Fancy Dresses." *Strand Magazine* 9 (January–June): 694–702.

Sternberg, Thomas. 1851. *The Dialect and Folk-Lore of Northamptonshire.* London: John Russell Smith.

Stewart, Jude. 2015. *Patternalia: An Unconventional History of Polka Dots, Stripes, Plaid, Camouflage, and Other Graphic Patterns.* New York: Bloomsbury U.S.A.

Stone, Trevor. 1992. "Seventy Years of the Goathland Plough Stots." *Rattle Up My Boys* 3, no. 5 (Autumn): 1–8.

Storch, Robert D. 1982. "Please to Remember the Fifth of November." In *Popular Custom in Nineteenth-Century England,* edited by Robert D. Storch. London: Croom Helm; New York: St Martin's Press.

Strutt, J. 1845. *Sports and Pastimes of the People of England.* London: Thomas Tegg.

Stubbes, Philip. (1584) 1879. *The Anatomie of Abuses,* edited by Frederick J. Furnivall. London: N. Trubner & Co.

Sturluson, Snorri (ca. 1235). 1967. *Heimskringla. From the Sagas of the Norse Kings,* translated by Erling Momsen. Oslo, Dreyers Forlag.

Summers, Montague. 1926. *The History of Witchcraft and Demonology.* London: Routledge, Trench, Trubner.

———. 1933. *The Werewolf.* London: Kegan Paul.

Surtees, R. 1823. *The History and Antiquities of the County Palatine of Durham.* Vol 3, *Stockton and Darlington Wards.* London: Nichols & Son.

Sykes, Homer. 1977. *Once a Year.* London: Gordon Fraser Gallery.

Sykes, Wirt. 1880. *British Goblins: Welsh Folk-Lore, Fairy Mythology, Legends, and Traditions.* London: Sampson Low, Marston, Searle, and Rivington.

Taussig, Michael. 1993. *Mimesis and Alterity: A Particular History of the Senses.* London: Routledge.

Taxidou, Olga. 1998. *The Mask: A Periodical Performance by Edward Gordon Craig.* Amsterdam: Harwood Academic Press.

Taylor, E. S., *Notes and Queries,* 1st series, 1, no. 468.

Tebbutt, C. F. 1941. *History of Bluntisham cum Earith.* Bluntisham, UK: Privately published.

———. 1942. "Huntingdonshire Folk and their Folklore." *Transactions of the Cambridgeshire and Huntingdonshire Archaeological Society* 6: 119–54.

———. 1950. "Huntingdonshire Folk and their Folklore." *Transactions of the Cambridgeshire and Huntingdonshire Archaeological Society* 7: 54–64.

———. 1978. *St. Neots: The History of a Huntingdonshire Town.* Chichester, UK: Phillmore.

———. 1984. *Huntingdonshire Folklore.* Saint Ives, Huntingdonshire, UK: Friends of the Norris Museum.

Thayer, Gerald Handerson, and Abbot Handerson Thayer. 1909. *Concealing-Coloration in the Animal Kingdom: An Exposition of the Laws of Disguise through Color and Pattern; Being a Summary of Abbot H. Thayer's Discoveries.* New York: Macmillan Company.

Thiele, Verena, and Andrew McCarthy. 2016. *Staging the Superstition of Early Modern Europe.* London: Routledge.

Thompson, C. J. S. 1928. *The Quacks of Old London.* London: Brentano's Ltd.

Thompson, R. Low. 1929. *The History of the Devil—The Horned God of the West.* London: Kegan Paul.

Thorndyke, Lynn. 1964. "Imagination and Magic: Force of Imagination on the Human Body and of Magic on the Human Mind." *Mélanges Eugène Tisserot* 7: 353–58. Vatican City: Biblioteca Vaticana.

Tiddy, R. J. E. 1923. *The Mummers' Play.* Oxford, UK: Clarendon Press.

Tooke, Colin. 1987. *The Rows of Great Yarmouth.* Norwich, UK: Poppyland Publishing.

Toschi, Paolo. 1955. *Le origini del teatro Italiano.* Turin, Italy: Edizioni Scientifiche Einaudi.

Toulmin Smith, Joshua. 1870. *English Guilds.* London: N. Trubner & Co.

Trubshaw, Bob. 1994. "Black Dogs in Folklore." *Mercian Mysteries* 20: 8–10.

———. 1995. "The Metaphors and Rituals of Place and Time: An Introduction to Liminality." *Mercian Mysteries* 22: 1–8.

Turney, H. W. 1950. "The Pageant of St. George and the Dragon." *East Anglian Magazine* 9: 502–4.

Udal, J. S. 1880. "Christmas Mummers in Dorsetshire." *Folk-Lore Record* 3, no. 1: 87–116.

Valiente, Doreem, 1984. *An ABC of Witchcraft Past and Present*. London, Robert Hale.

Van Hamel, A. G. 1933. "Oðinn Hanging on the Tree." *Acta Philologica Scandinavica* 7: 260–68.

Vanneufville, Eric. 2019. *Légendes de Flandre*. Fouesnant, France: Yoran Embanner.

Verdone, Mario. 1984. *Le maschere italiane*. Rome: Newton Compton.

Very, Francis George. 1962. *The Spanish Corpus Christi Procession*. Valencia, Spain: Tipografia Moderna.

Vince, Ronald W. 1984. *Ancient and Medieval Theatre: A Historiographical Handbook*. Westport, Conn.: Greenwood Press.

Vovelle, Michel. 1989. *Histoires figurales: Des monsters médiévaux à Wonderwoman*. Paris: Editions Usher.

Von Zaborsky, Oskar. 1936. *Urväter-Erbe in deutscher Volkskunst*. Leipzig, Germany: Koehler & Amerlang.

Wakeman, Offley. 1884. "Rustic Stage Plays in Shropshire." *Transactions of the Shropshire Archaeological Society* 1st series, 7: 383–88.

Wallis, John. 1769. *The Natural History and Antiquities of Northumberland and So Much of the County of Durham as Lies between the River Tyne and Tweed, Commonly Called, North Bishoprick*. London: W. & W. Strahan.

Walton, Susana. 1988. *William Walton: Behind the Façade*. Oxford, UK: Oxford University Press.

W.C.B. 1908. "St. John Baptist's Eve: Midsummer: Corpus Christi." *Notes and Queries* 10, no. 9: 481.

Wentworth-Day, James. 1973. *Essex Ghosts*. Bourne End, UK: Spurbooks.

Wentz, W. Y. Evans. 1911. *The Fairy Faith in Celtic Countries*. Oxford, UK: Oxford University Press.

Werbner, R. 1989. *Ritual Passage, Sacred Journey*. Manchester, UK: Manchester University Press.

Whistler, Laurence. 1947. *The Masque of Christmas: Dramatic Joys of the Festival*. London: Curtain Press.

Wiegand, Wilhelm. 1889. "Richgard." In *Allgemeine Deutsche Biographie* 28: 420–21. Leipzig: Duncker & Humblot.

Weinhold, Karl Gotthelf Jakob. 1855. *Weihnacht-Spiele und Lieder aus Süddeutschland und Schliesien*. Graz, Austria: Damien und Sorge.

Wilde, Lady Jane Francesca [Speranza]. 1887. *Ancient Legends, Mystic Charms, and Superstitions of Ireland.* Boston: Ticknor and Co.

Wilde, Oscar. 1913. "The Truth of Masks: A Note on Illusion." In *Intentions.* London: Methuen & Co.

Wildhaber, Robert. 1950. "Form und Verbreitung der Maske." *Schweizer Volkskunde* 50: 4–20.

Wiles, David, 1991. *The Masks of Menander: Sign and meaning in Greek and Roman performance.* Cambridge: Cambridge University Press.

Wilken, Hermann. 1597. *Christliche Bedencken und Erinnerung von Zauberei.* Speier, Germany: Albin.

Wilkins, Charles. 1903. *The History of the Iron, Steel, Tinplate, and Other Trades of Wales.* Merthyr Tydfil, UK: Joseph Williams.

Williams, F. Kemble. 1936. "The Sign of the Stallion's Tail." *East Anglian Magazine* 1, no. 11: 587–88.

Williamson, George C. 1925. *Curious Survivals: Habits and Customs that Still Live in the Present.* London: Herbert Jenkins.

Wittstock, Otto. 1896. "Über den Schwerttanz der Siebenbürger Sachsen." *Philologische Studien: Festgabe für Edward Sievers*: XXX: 352–55.

Wolfram, Richard. 1934. "Sword Dances and Secret Societies." *Journal of the English Folk Dance and Song Society* 1, no. 1: 34.

Wood, E. 1890. "Bentley Plough Jags." *Lincolnshire Notes and Queries* 2 no. 3: 88–89.

Woodward, Ian. 1979. *The Werewolf Delusion.* London and New York: Paddington Press.

Wortley, Russell. *Notes Made by Russell Wortley 1938–1975.* Unpublished manuscript, in the Cambridgeshire Collection, Cambridge Central Library.

Wormwood, Eldred. 2020. "Ecstacies of Darkness." *Folkwitch* 2: 18–29.

Wortley, Russell, and Cyril Papworth. 1980: "Molly Dancing in South-West Cambridgeshire." In *Articles and Notes,* edited by Russell Wortley et al., 35–36. Cambridge, UK: Cambridge Morris Men.

Wright, A. R., and T. E. Lones. 1936. *British Calendar Customs I: Movable Festivals.* London: William Glaisher, Ltd.

———. 1938. *British Calendar Customs II: Fixed Festivals, January–May, Inclusive.* London: William Glaisher, Ltd.

———. 1940. *British Calendar Customs III: Fixed Festivals, June–December, Inclusive.* London: William Glaisher, Ltd.

Wright, T., ed. 1855. *The History of Fulke Fitz-Warine, an Outlawed Baron in the Reign of King John.* London: Warton Club.

Yeats, William Butler, ed. (1893) 2015. *Irish Fairy and Folk Tales.* New York: Barnes & Noble.

Yeo, Eileen, and Stephen Yeo. 1981. *Popular Culture and Class Conflict 1550–1914.* Brighton, UK: Harvester Press.

Young, George. 1817. *A History of Whitby, and Streoneshalh Abbey, with a Statistical Survey of the Vicinity to the Distance of Twenty-Five Miles.* 2 vols. Whitby, UK: Clark & Medd.

Zeitlyn, Froma. 1980. "The Closet of Masks—Role-Playing and Myth Making in the *Orestes* of Euripedes." *Ramus* 9: 62–73.

My thanks to Ben Fernee for bringing to my notice some obscure archival newspaper references to the Skeleton Army.

Index

Page numbers in *italics* refer to illustrations.
Numbers in *italics* preceded by *pl.* refer to color insert plate numbers.